MANAGING
EXPECTATIONS

**Driving Profitable Option Trading
Outcomes through Knowledge,
Discipline, and Risk Management**

Anthony J. Saliba

MartinKronicle

ISBN 978-0-9975778-0-8 (Hardcover)
ISBN 978-0-9975778-1-5 (ebook)
ISBN 978-0-9975778-2-2 (audiobook)

Printed in the United States of America

First Printing 2016

MartinKronicle
149 S. Barrington Ave #123
Los Angeles, CA 90049

www.ManagingExpectationsBook.com

10 9 8 7 6 5 4 3 2 1

RISK DISCLAIMER

Trading is risky. Please consult with your financial adviser before making any trading or investment decisions.

The information contained within this book and related web site, including e-mail transmissions, faxes, recorded voice messages, and any other associated content (hereinafter collectively referred to as "Information") is provided for informational and educational purposes only. The Information should not be construed as investment/trading advice and is not meant to be a solicitation or recommendation to buy, sell, or hold any securities mentioned.

MartinKronicle is not licensed by or registered with any regulating body that allows us to give financial and investment advice.

MartinKronicle and Option Technology Solutions, Inc. make no claim regarding past or future performance. While there is always a risk a loss when considering potential for profits. Losses connected with trading options contracts or other leveraged instruments such as commodity futures can be significant. Hence, you should consider if such trading is suitable for you in light of you financial circumstances bearing in mind that all speculative trading is risky and you should only speculate if you have sufficient risk capital.

MartinKronicle is an educational company, not an advisory or stock recommendation service. All examples are provided for educational purposes.

MartinKronicle, subsidiaries, affiliates, officers and employees, shall not be liable for any direct, indirect, incidental, special or consequential damages. All trades and investment decisions in your account are at your own risk. There is no guaranteed trading performance.

www.MartinKronicle.com

RESOURCES

For more information about the books educational videos, other book formats, and the app that goes with this book, please visit:

www.ManagingExpectationsBook.com

TABLE OF CONTENTS

ix

FOREWORD

BY JACK SCHWAGER

I first met Tony Saliba when I chose him as one of the interview subjects for the original *Market Wizards*, a book that included such legendary traders as Bruce Kovner, Paul Tudor Jones, Marty Schwartz, and Michael Steinhardt. Although he was a very successful option trader when I met him, Tony certainly didn't start that way. Quite the contrary!

Although many of the Market Wizards started off with some degree of failure, perhaps none reached the depth of despondency over their losses as did Tony Saliba. At the start of his career when he was a clerk on the exchange floor, one of the traders staked him with $50,000. Saliba went long volatility spreads (option positions that gain if the market volatility increases). In the first two weeks, Saliba ran the account up to $75,000. He thought he was a genius. What he didn't realize was that he was buying these options at very high premiums because his purchases followed a highly volatile period. The market then went sideways and the market volatility and option premiums collapsed. In six weeks Saliba had run the account down to only $15,000.

Recounting this episode, Saliba said, "I was feeling suicidal. Do you remember the big DC-10 crash at O'Hare in May 1979, when all those people died...? That was when I hit bottom."

"Was that a metaphor for your mood?" I asked.

"Yes," answered Saliba. "I would have exchanged places with one of those people in that plane on that day. I felt that bad. I thought, 'This is it; I've ruined my life' . . .I felt like a failure."

Notwithstanding this dismal start, Saliba had one important thing going for him: persistence. After his disastrous beginning, he came close to quitting the world of trading, but ultimately decided to keep trying. He sought the advice of more experienced brokers. They taught Saliba the importance of discipline, doing homework, and a goal of consistent, moderate profitability, rather than trying to get rich quick.

Saliba took these lessons to heart and switched from trading options in Teledyne, which was extremely volatile, to trading options in Boeing, which was a narrow range market. When he did go back to trading Teledyne, his standard conservative order size led to ridicule by the other brokers and the sobriquet "One-Lot." Once again, Saliba persisted, this time putting up with all the ribbing and not being goaded into departing from his cautious approach. Ultimately, the persistence and attention to risk control paid off. At one point, Saliba put together a streak of 70 consecutive months, each with profits in excess of $100,000.

Saliba ultimately succeeded for two reasons:

1. He didn't give up.
2. He learned what to do and what not to do in trading and had the discipline to apply that knowledge rigorously. For example, he had the discipline to put up with the ridicule of trading minimal size because he knew that was what was necessary to adhere to risk management.

Saliba's *Managing Expectations: Driving Profitable Option Trading Outcomes through Knowledge, Discipline, and Risk Management* offers a very comprehensive survey of option topics and option trades. And while this thorough treatment offers the reader a solid education in options, completeness is not the book's main value. What really sets *Managing Expectations* apart is that it is a book written by a trader who learned option theory through trading. Yes, the book offers plenty of option theory, *but it does so from the perspective of a trader.*

Let me take just one example: the covered call (also called a buy-write). It is amazing how semantics can distort perceptions. The "covered call" is often recommended to clients as a "conservative" strategy—one that "hedges" a long stock position with the premium earned from selling a call. In contrast, the sale of a put (often referred to as a "naked put") is, as implied by its very name, typically considered a very risky position. Yet, anyone who truly understands options will know that the "conservative" covered call and the "risky" short put are, in fact, exactly equivalent positions! So how does Saliba describe the covered call (or buy-write)? Here is one paragraph from that chapter:

The diagram both above and below reveal that the buy-write is in fact synthetically equal to a short put position! Therefore, the quick and easy way to "lock in" a buy-write is to purchase the put at the same strike, and in the same month as the written call. The only difference in risk profiles between a covered call and a naked short put is that the stock (in the covered call example) will not expire. So as the share price begins to nosedive, it will prolong your agony and increase your losses.

Saliba absolutely nails it! He not only makes it clear to the reader that a covered call is nothing more than a short put, but he goes one better, pointing out that the covered call can be even more risky because once the put expires, the covered call goes on able to cause even more losses. It is this type of practical, no-nonsense treatment of options that should make Saliba's book a valuable resource and learning tool for any serious option trader.

Jack Schwager
Chief Research Officer, FundSeeder
Author of *Market Wizards* book series

PART I

The Basic Properties of Options and Option Traders

CHAPTER I

The Journey into Optionality

Options are financial derivatives whose value and payoffs are resultant from the value of something else, commonly called the underlying. This underlying is often a singular company, an index, or a government's interest rate, or even the 30-day implied volatility of the market.

An option is a contract to buy or sell a specified quantity of an asset at a fixed price at or before a prearranged date in the future. An option can be bought or sold at the asset's current price (at the money), well below the current price (in the money), or far above the prevailing traded price (out of the money). In addition, options contracts can be traded with expiration dates ranging from one day to several years in the future.

Exchange-traded options can be bought or sold at any time, although there is a specific difference in expiration style. An American style option can be exercised at any time on or before its expiration date. A European style option can be exercised only on its expiration date.

One of the many possible advantages of using options is the ability to build a custom strategy to fit a particular market view or situation. One does not need to be restricted to "bullish" or "bearish" in order to profitably participate in the marketplace. Views encompassing direction (or lack thereof), magnitude, velocity, timing, and volatility can all be traded using option combinations or spreads that fit a specific market situation.

The Making of a Successful Trader

Until you've traded, managed a position, or risked your own money, its hard to understand the importance of discipline, mental awareness, along with handling the various emotional facets that will – no doubt – come your way. The discipline to have a pre-determined and iron-clad risk management plan in place ahead of time, possessing the willingness to allow your winners to run, and most importantly – acquiring the humility to lose money without making situations worse – are all part and parcel of what makes a good trader.

Decades of experience have taught me that a pre-trade risk management plan has helped to remove me from the situation – perhaps keeping me from making less than optimal trading decisions. A good trader simply cannot be afraid to lose money - for it happens to everyone. The chief problem with losing money in a trade is not merely the money – it's the enticement to make irrational decisions – no doubt making things exponentially more risky.

We are trained to equate losing with shame. We are prone to avoid it at all costs. Sometimes losing stimulates a reaction to fight back. But for most of us, we permit losing trades to cause us to deny responsibility, avoid situations, and think irrationally. The result may well be a foolish decision to remove a stop in an options trade. Making blunders and losing trades no doubt have varying effects on individuals.

4

But if you can value and appreciate that traders will lose money, and sometimes lose money on a consistent basis, you will be well on the road to successful trade management. Guaranteed.

Your job as a professional options trader

You are – or, will be – a professional options trader. The bottom line is you are compensated to profitably trade with as little risk as possible. Your trading may involve complex mathematical calculations, software applications, and a lot of patience to identify the right opportunities. On the other hand, your trading may be nothing more than using intuition or "guess work" to be profitable. Either way, the road to accomplishment is not easy nor is the road straight. It takes a lot of hard work and discipline.

Tony (AJS) was an incredible options teacher to me without him even knowing so - Tony educated me while I was a clerk (freshly out of University) in the mid 1980's for a broker in the CBOE's S&P 100 option pit who executed Tony's many different types of complex option strategies. I learned first-hand all about Butterflies, Straddles, Strangles, Ratio Spreads, Calendar Spreads, Iron Condor Spreads...such a gift to a aspiring options trader"

\- Michael McGuire

Below are some key points to help you along the road to successful options trading. Some are intuitive and others not. No matter what, I think you'll someday be thankful for the very valuable advice I'm about to give you!

- **Cost vs. Value:** most professionals are told to buy under "theoretical value" while selling over "theoretical value". This is a good concept for classroom discussion but, its far more complex than that! Theoretical value is just that – theoretical. I would suggest that you look to buy under "theoretical value" and sell over "theoretical value" if you can simultaneously:

1. Remain as "skew neutral" as possible. Perhaps your "theoretical edge" is masked by the fact that skew levels have changed, sticky strike, etc.

2. Buy or sell strategies (for "theoretical edge") that are reducing your current options inventory – not adding to it.

3. Resisting to trade something that can potentially and exponentially hurt you badly in the future (e.g. selling far out of the money options).

4. Explain what this new trade does to your overall greek and volatility exposure. Additionally, one always needs to quantify this in terms of a range.

- **Buy cheap spreads** – good RoR in terms of volatility, path dependency, and skew. For example, buying an undervalued 3-strike butterfly (with little theoretical edge) is far better (over the long run) than buying or selling a 25-delta risk-reversal (i.e. buying (selling) 25-delta put and simultaneously selling (buying) a 25-delta call) – even if that risk-reversal contains more "theoretical edge." Keep your spreads extremely tight!

- **Always trade with discipline:** this is a phrase often heard however so in a reticent way as discipline means different things to different people.

  1. Be pre-determined with your entry point and pre-determined with your exit point. Examples of this include:

     a. I will buy this vertical spread at "such-and-such" level with the intention of "such-and-such" profit target. I will allow myself to lose "such-and-such" and will exit the trade immediately if this loss is realized.

b. I am determined to never be net long or net short more than a pre-determined amount of net delta, gamma, vega, and theta. I have a pre-determined exit plan if this level is breached.

c. I will always know what my net greek position is one day, one week, and one month in the future. I will also always know what my net greek position is with the market both up and down within a 1,2, and 3-standard deviation move.

d. With a profitable trade I will have a pre-determined spread or spreads to assist in parlaying into a potentially bigger RoR trade.

e. With an unprofitable trade I will have a pre-determined spot where I will exit the trade and move on.

- **Implement habits to recognize relative pricing, relative risk, and relative profit and loss.**

  1. <u>Relative pricing:</u> an option is underpriced – i.e. "cheap" – only if something else around it is overpriced or fair-valued and can be immediately used as a hedge.

  2. <u>Relative risk:</u> risk is relative to both the present moment and present place in time. Risk must be quantified within a quantifiable range at all times.

  3. <u>Relatively flat:</u> your position could be flat or relatively flat and there's a big difference between the two. Flat means

a matched position whereas there is no path or greek risk. Relatively flat is an options position vis-à-vis a partial derivative. A trader could be flat delta but short gamma – that is relatively flat.

4. <u>Relative profit and loss:</u> never ever mark or otherwise distort an open options position in your favor.

- **Continuously apply value management to your trading decisions and trading position.**

    1. Is the trade you are considering making your position better?

    2. Know and apply the strategies available for safe positioning. Can I neutralize my risk through:

        a. Conversion/reversal
        b. Box spreads
        c. Vertical spreads
        d. Butterflies and wingspreads
        e. Calendar spreads and jelly roll spreads

    3. Engrain into your heart and mind the often ignored yet crucial risk management points. Do whatever it takes to proactively reduce your risk of:

        a. Skew risk
        b. Pin risk.
        c. Early exercise risk (American style).
        d. Net options units.
        e. Derivative (greeks).

Dealing with Market Outliers

The hardest part about successfully trading options is being willing to put in the days and weeks and months and years of discipline required. Many trade options attempting to chase the dream of "quick riches" and for some that does happen. However, for the most part, good traders spend most of their waking hours dreaming of the big "pay-day" yet knowing the realities of what could happen if they don't do the hard mental work of remaining disciplined.

Baseball has a saying that, "the ball will always find you." It's uncanny but it seems the minute a player is out of position or not physically 100%, the ball seems to be hit to him! This parallel can and does apply to options trading as well. The biggest – sometimes catastrophic – losses occur when the trader lets his guard down with regards to position and trading discipline. You may get away with being overly "short options units" for months – perhaps years. However, one day you will experience a market event that could very well wipe away all the meager gains you achieved with your undisciplined approach.

Think back on some of the bigger market events we've had in the last three decades:

- The U.S. stock market collapse in October, 1987
- 1994 U.S. bond market crash
- Asian Financial crisis in 1997
- Russian debt default and LTCM in 1998
- Tech bubble of 2000
- Great Recession of 2008

I was personally able to make large sums of money as the result of these major events. I didn't make money due to luck nor due to skill. I was profitable because of my daily position, trade, and risk management routine. That self-scrutiny kept my options risk well defined. Additionally, my thorough, in-depth knowledge of options strategy and more importantly, how they perform during crisis, allowed me to make markets aggressively when everyone else was hiding.

Market outliers are sometimes very daunting to live through. Yet, I challenge you to always remember the following:

- Always know what strategies will do during extreme periods. Example: during very high periods of volatility, wingspreads will naturally become very cheap.

- Always know exactly what happens to your current position during both a "melt-down" or "melt-up".

- Be aware of skew shifts and shadow deltas when hedging your position.

- Economic events seem to come in episodic waves and the next one is sure to be different from the last one.

- Volatility is typically persistent and it seems to persistently overshoot and undershoot what conventional wisdom otherwise believes.

- The vast percentage of your profitability is made in very small slices of time. Opportunity knocks very briefly.

The Challenge of Optionality

Trading in the options markets can by summarized by the saying, "You just don't know what you don't know!" On one hand, a trader can spend weeks with high-level research and statistical models only to end up frustrated with a long-line of losses due to the randomness that surrounds us. On the other hand, another options trader can do no more than have the right position on at the right time and basically make a fortune on nothing other than good old fashioned intuition.

A lot has changed in the near four decades since I entered the floor of the CBOE. Today, the stream of information and the speed of its distribution are simply astonishing. In this age of electronic financial derivatives, one can review material from a countless of up-to-the-second sources and subsequently amass a large trading position via a few clicks on the computer. Equally surprising is the sheer depth and liquidity of the exchange markets, where options are often quoted pennies wide and in multiple thousands on both the bid and offer. The markets have evolved from a fragmentation of phone calls and hand signals, to a symphony of speed and harmonization.

Through four decades and one quarter million trades later I've learned that in options trading just as in life, probabilities don't matter. In fact, I would strongly argue that the whole notion of probability just doesn't make sense. At the end of the day, it matters little whether an event has a 1 percent chance or a 99 percent chance of happening. Whether or not the incident actually happens, and the ultimate payoff or loss, is what counts. That potential payoff or loss is what should motivate options traders, clearinghouses, and investors alike. Options trading isn't necessarily efficient and can never be explained away with rational analysis.

CHAPTER 2

Options Equivalency

"The value in knowing synthetic relationships is profound. It can help any trader or asset manager see though the weeds and make better decisions with clarity.

Knowledge of synthetic relationships is a dying art of the new-world trader. Tony always emphasized the power of studying option synthetics as a way to separate yourself from the crowd."

- Chris Hausman

Many consider the study of put-call parity or option synthetics a general waste of time, useful only for market makers and perhaps relevant for classroom study. However, nothing could be further from the truth! The study, understanding, and the strategic application of put-call parity and synthetically equivalent positions can save the end-user a great deal of money over time. Mastering the concept of synthetics allows the option trader to take advantage of temporary mispricing in the market place, and to minimize execution risk and slippage when entering or exiting a position. Additionally and perhaps most importantly, it will help provide the trader with the confidence required to make markets properly and efficiently.

Why Synthetics Matter

Position Exit

- Traders can often find themselves a victim of their own success, as long call or long put positions move in-the-money. Exiting a trade with a synthetic may be easier and more profitable in this instance.

- Market makers widen the bid-ask spread of high priced, high delta options to compensate for hedging risk.

- Funds and other professionals attempting to liquidate a position will sometimes give away a lot of extra profit.

- Better to use the low delta, out of the money side of the strike with a narrow bid-ask spread for exit.

Position Entry

- Using synthetic relationships the smart options trader has two ways to approach a directional trade.

- "Jumping" the underlying side of trade first and adding the option side of the trade second enables the end-user to avoid slippage on signals.

- Volatility around support and resistance levels can create temporary mispricing.

- Use of the low delta, out of the money side of the strike reduces directional risk and slippage.

Hedging Existing Positions

- Change the nature of the position as market view changes.

- Change long positions to long calls or short puts.

- Change short positions to short calls or long puts.

- Fully hedge using combos.

- Change long or short positions into tactical spreads using level II synthetics (later in the book).

Drawbacks

- Closing trades with a synthetic position will leave a residual arbitrage position (conversion, reversal).

- This position will remain until expiration.

- Could tie up capital.

- Could result in pin risk.

Definition of Put-Call Parity

Put-call parity refers to the concept that put options and call options of the same strike and same expiry date are essentially the same instrument. The only difference between a put option on an underlying product, say with a strike of 90 and expiring in June, and a call option on the same underlying product with the same strike and expiration date, is that the put allows its owner to sell the underlying whereas the call allows its owner to buy the underlying.

The difference is actually fairly inconsequential. With a simple hedge using the underlying, a call option can be transformed into a synthetic put option. And the opposite is also true; a put option can be hedged with the underlying product to be transformed into a synthetic call option. This is the essence of put-call parity. The bottom line is puts and calls can be created to be the same thing.

Synthetics

To understand put-call parity, it's important to first explore the arithmetic concept of synthetics. Option combinations can be used to create equivalent risk-return parameters as single futures or options. These are called "synthetic positions". We will start with the most basic relationship which we call "synthetic stock" or "synthetic future."

If you are long a call and short a put of the same strike in the same expiration, you have the exact same profit and loss graph shape as if you are long underlying. We call this (long call/short put) a "combo."

Long Call + Short Put = Long Underlying

Short Call + Long Put = Short Underlying

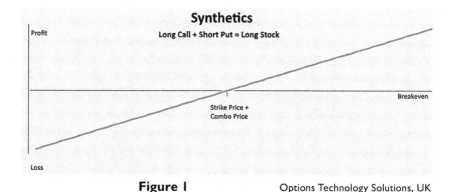

Figure 1   Options Technology Solutions, UK

If you think of the combo equation as a mathematical equation, you can rearrange the pieces to create other synthetic positions. So, the combo equation of:

> **Long Stock/Future = Long Call + Short Put, can become:**
>
> **Long put + long stock/future = long call**
>
> **Long call + short stock/future = long put**
>
> **Short put + short stock/future = short call**
>
> **Short call + long stock/future = short put**

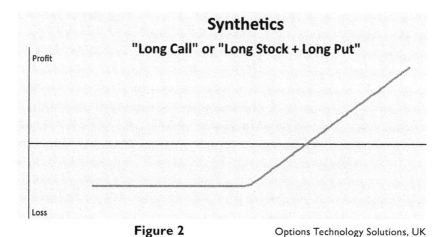

Figure 2   Options Technology Solutions, UK

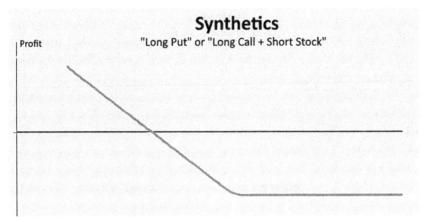

Figure 3   Options Technology Solutions, UK

These synthetic relationships are key building blocks to understanding options. Through the synthetic relationship, you can equate calls and puts. That is, you can think of calls as puts and puts as calls in terms of their risk profiles. Figures 4 through 9 below illustrate various synthetic relationships.

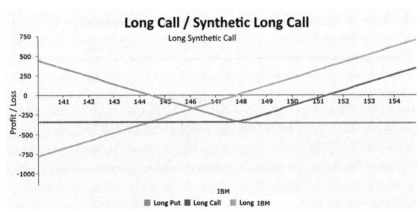

Figure 4   Options Technology Solutions, UK

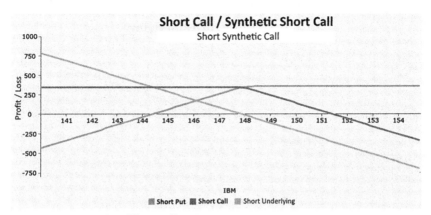

Figure 5   Options Technology Solutions, UK

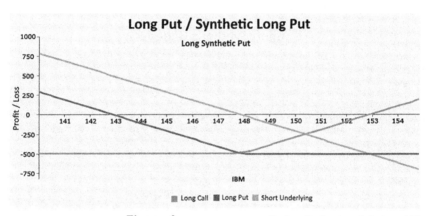

Figure 6   Options Technology Solutions, UK

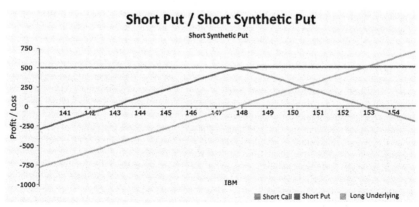

Figure 7   Options Technology Solutions, UK

19

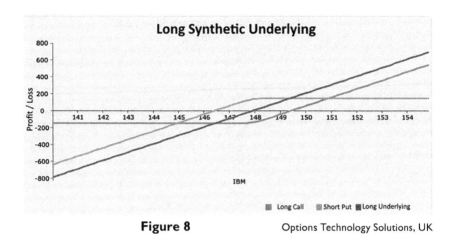

Figure 8   Options Technology Solutions, UK

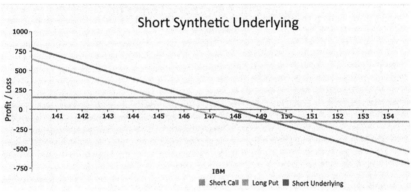

Figure 9   Options Technology Solutions, UK

Basis

The next building block in understanding put-call parity is called "basis." First, what is the difference between buying stock and buying synthetic stock (buy call and short put)?

- If you buy stock, you must put up the full amount (price x shares purchased) immediately.
- If you buy synthetic stock, you pay $0 now. A rational person would rather pay later.

    The cost differential is known as the "carry" and is computed as:

    Stock Price * interest rate (long rate) * time (in years)

The carry is a benefit to owning synthetic stock and a detriment to owning stock. Then, are there any benefits to owning stock over synthetic stock?

Yes. If you own stock, you are entitled to any dividends the company pays out. If you own synthetic stock, you are not entitled to the dividends. The combination of the benefits and detriments to owning stock is called the "basis." The basis is defined as:

Basis = Carry – Dividends

This can be used to calculate the future value of the stock.

So, there are two equations to remember:

Stock Future Value = Stock Price + Basis

Basis = Carry – Dividends

Thus:

Stock Future Value = Stock Price + Carry - Dividends

Example:

A stock is trading for $100. There are 4 dividends this year of $0.75 each. The rate charged for long stock by your brokerage firm is 4%. What is the future value of the shares in one year?

Remembering the formula for future stock: **Stock Future Value = Stock Price + Carry – Dividends**

Carry = $100 * .04 * 1 year = $4

Dividend = $0.75 * 4 = $3

Stock future value = $100 + $4 - $3 = $101

Put-Call Parity

Put-call parity quantifies the proper relationship between European-style puts and calls to prevent arbitrage between synthetic and "natural" positions (as in stock vs. synthetic stock.) The formula is:

Call Price – Put Price = Stock Price – Strike

Price + Basis

Where: Basis = carry – dividends

Shorthand: C – P = S – X + Basis

Although the concept of put-call parity exists in American-style options, it is complicated by early exercise opportunities that will modify the relationship.

Example: The November $65 Call is trading for $3.45 and the November $65 put is trading for $2.10. Its cost of carry is $0.23 with a $0.10 dividend before expiration. Where should the stock be trading if put-call parity is achieved?

Using the formula: C – P = S – X + Basis, we solve for "S",

which is the stock price.

So, S = C – P + X – Basis.

In our example, S = $3.45 - $2.10 + $65 – ($0.23-$0.10);

this would make the proper stock price = $66.22

This is the single most important factor in understanding options as understanding put-call parity allows you to price options without using theoretical value models. When put-call parity is out of line arbitrage opportunities exist.

European vs. American and Put-Call Parity

Put call parity is easier to understand when using European Style Options. Early Exercise possibility in American Style options makes it harder to define.

- **Long call + short put = long future**

  <u>Example:</u> Buy 100 call at 4 sell 100 put at 3 = long future at 101

- **Short call + long put = short future**

  <u>Example:</u> Buy 80 put at 2.50 sell 80 call at 1.50 = short future at 79.

Synthetics Simplified

This simplified equation lets you derive the six basic synthetics relationships very quickly. If you remember basic algebra, moving a variable from one side of the equation to the other side, changes its sign.

Long Call	=	Long Stock + Long Put	+C	= + U + P
Short Call	=	Short Stock + Short Put	-C	= -U – P
Long Put	=	Long Call + Short Stock	+P	= +C – U
Short Put	=	Short Call + Long Stock	-P	= -C + U
Long Stock	=	Long Call + Short Put	+U	= C – P
Short Stock	=	Short Call + Long Put	-U	= -C + P

Synthetic Trading Examples

Example 1:

You are long the AAPL January 100 calls and wish to sell them. The stock is trading 111.00 and the calls are quoted 12.25-12.50 while the January 100 puts are .40 - .60. Banking is 1.00.

Is it better to sell the actual calls or the synthetic calls?

$$C = S - K + P + B$$
$$C = 11.00 + .40 + 1.00$$
$$C = 12.40$$

Answer: better to sell the synthetic calls

Example 2:

You have just received a buy signal and volatility is screaming higher. You wish to short the January 110 puts. The stock is trading at $103 and the January 110 puts are quoted 8.25-8.50 while the January 110 calls are 2.45 - 2.55. Financing is 1.10.

Should you sell the actual or the synthetic puts?

> **P = C + K - S - B**
>
> **P = 2.45 + 110.00 − 103.00 - 1.10**
>
> **P = 8.35**
>
> **Answer: better to sell the synthetic puts**

Example 3:

You have been long another stock from 95.00 and it has rallied into resistance. In addition, implied volatility has gotten smashed to very low historical levels. You are still bullish on the stock but feel there might be a short-term setback coming. You decide to convert the position into a synthetic long call. The stock is now 99.50; the July 100 calls are trading 5.00, the July 100 puts 4.50. Financing is 1.00.

What trade do you make and what is the effective price of your new synthetic position?

> **Buy 100 puts**
>
> **C = 95.00 -100 +4.50 + 1.00**
>
> **C = .50**
>
> **You are synthetically long the 100 calls at .50**

The Synthetic Drill – P.U.C.
(Put, Underlying, Call)

The concept of synthetics is so important that I have designed a drill to help increase the speed at which you recognize the synthetic equivalent of positions involving options. There are four basic properties:

The synthetic of a single item in PUC <u>always contains the two missing items in the equivalent. Conversely if there are two items in PUC, then the synthetic equivalent contains one.</u>

1. **What is the premium consideration?** The premium position will remain the same. If the position has long (short) premium then the synthetic must also have long (short) premium.

> **#1: If the actual position has long (short) premium then the synthetic position MUST also have long (short) premium.**

2. **If the position has zero premium,** i.e. long an option and short an option then the synthetic position has zero premium.

> **#2:**
> - **Simply use the sign of C to determine the sign of U.**
> - **i.e., -C + P = -U and +C – P = +U**

3. **What about the sign of the underlying?** When the call is with the underlying, on the same side of the (=), the sign of the Underlying position will always be the opposite sign of the CALL.

4. **The put and underlying are always the same sign;** both long (+) (+) and short (-) (-), when on the same side of the (=).

#4:

i.e., +P +U = +C and –P – U = -C

The Box Spread – the starting point for option equivalency

Four Ways to View a Box Spread:

1. Vertical Spread

Long box: Long call vertical and long put vertical
Short box: Short call vertical and short put vertical

Example 1:

Long the ABC Aug 55/65 call spread at 9.10 and

Long the ABC Aug 55/65 put spread at .60

= Long the ABC Aug 55/65 Box at 9.70

Example 2:

Short the ABC Aug 60/70 call spread at 8.40 and

Short the ABC Aug 60/70 put spread at 1.75

= Short the ABC 60/70 box at 10.15

2. Combinations

Long Box: Long lower strike (K1) combo and short higher strike (K2) combo
Short Box: Short lower strike (K1) combo and long higher strike (K2) combo

---

Example 1:

Long the XYZ Aug 135 Combo at 7.40 and

Short the XYZ Aug 140 Combo at 2.50

= Long the XYZ Aug 135/140 Box at 4.90

Example 2:

Short the XYZ Aug 120 Combo at 22.60 and

Long the XYZ Aug 140 Combo at 2.50

= Short the XYZ Aug 120/140 Box at 20.10

---

3. Long synthetic underlying at one strike and short synthetic underlying at a higher or lower strike

---

Example 1:

Long the MTG Jan 75 Call at 22.60

Short the MTG Jan 75 Put at 1.40 (Long Jan 75 combo at 21.20);

Short the MTG Jan 85 Call at 14.90

Long the MTG Jan 85 Put at 3.50 (Short Jan 85 Combo at 11.40)

= Long the MTG Jan 75/85 Box at 9.80 (21.20 − 11.40)

---

4. A conversion at one strike and a reversal at a higher or lower strike

> **Example I:**
>
> DEF Aug 60 reversal and DEF Aug 70 conversion = Long DEF Aug 60/70
>
> Box (underlying cancel out)

Synthetics: doorway to reduce risk

Take a simple example where the trader has two open positions:

- Long 1 XYZ 45 call
- Short 1 XYZ 50 call

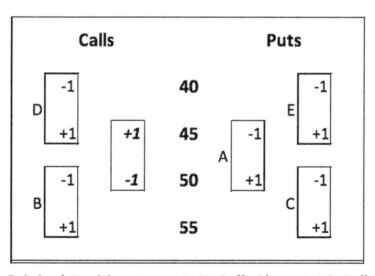

*Original Position: Long 1 **45 Call**; Short 1 **50 Call***

Figure 10

Spread:	Result:
Sell Original Position	Flat
a. Buy 45/50 Put Vertical	Long 45/50 Box
b. Sell 50/55 Call Vertical	Long 45/50/55 Butterfly
c. Buy 50/55 Put Vertical	Long 45/50/55 Iron Butterfly
d. Sell 40/45 Call Vertical	Short 40/45/50 Butterfly
e. Buy 40/45 Put Vertical	Short 40/45/50 Iron Butterfly

Long the strangle, short th straddle. It refers to any butterfly that is long the wings and short the body as long the butterfly.

Short the strangle, long th straddle. It refers to any butterfly that is short the wings and long the body as short the butterfly.

Figure 11

Conversion consists of the purchase of the underlying and shorting a synthetic stock position (buy put, short call, and same strike).

- A Conversion is a combination of long stock and synthetic short stock.
- Long stock, short call, long put.
- Add the dividend (if any) subtract the cost of carry.
- Add the call premium received; subtract the put premium paid.

Example:
Buy 100 IVT @ 45
Buy 1 IVT April 45 Put @ 2.40
Sell 1 IVT April 45 Call @ 3

_OR_

Example:
Buy 1 Mar DM Future @ 60.42
Buy 1 DM Mar 6050 Put @ .22
Sell 1 DM Mar 6050 Call @ .14

- **Risk/Reward:** Known immediately. The conversion is an arbitrage strategy. Profits and/or losses are determined at the time the position is established.

- **Market View:** Neutral.

- **Delta:** The delta of the conversion is equal to the delta of IVT underlying, which is 100, minus the delta of the synthetic short position, which is also 100.

It is incorrect to assume that the conversion and reversal have no risk. By establishing the conversion position, you are long the actual underlying and synthetically short the underlying. If the price of the underlying remains unchanged, then, in practice, the entire position can be offset at parity near expiration.

Other Risks in the Conversion and Reversal:

Be aware of "Pin Risk" at expiration. This position is sensitive to interest rate risk, dividend changes and early exercise. Normally, if the price of the underlying declines, the long put can be exercised in order to lock in the higher selling price. If the price of the underlying rises, the long position offsets the loss on the short call.

The relationship between put and call premiums will be clarified. An arbitrage strategy exists if the price of the put becomes inexpensive relative to the call and the underlying. In this situation, you will buy puts until the price is forced back into line. If the put becomes too expensive, you will do the opposite position, called the reversal, until the put is pushed back in line.

Conversion Pricing Considerations

In order to properly calculate the relationship between the put and call for the conversion, you must first know:

1. **Cost to carry** (or rebate in equities) in order to finance the position until the option expiration. In a futures conversion and reversal the cost to carry is based on the cash flow of the initial options combination. In an equity conversion and reversal the cost to carry is based on the strike price, not the stock price, to reflect the cash flow. Notice that the interest rates for the conversion and reversal are different, because one position uses a borrowing rate and the other a lending rate.

Example: The April options expire in 71 calendar days. The interest rate to finance the underlying is 2.5%. (Remember: in equities, calculate the carry on the strike price (45), not the stock price).

COST TO CARRY =

(Strike x Interest Rate) x (# of days until expiration / days in year)

= 45 x .025 x 71 / 360

= .22

---

2. In equities there is a **dividend consideration:**

Assume there is a dividend between now and the April expiration. The dividend must be factored into the conversion equation. Let's suppose that IVT goes ex-dividend on April 4, for a dividend of $ .25 (or 1/4). Expiration is April 17.

Note: *When you calculate the conversion, the stock and its carry minus the dividend should equal the put and call combination (combo) at the strike (the synthetic stock).*

Reversal consists of shorting the underlying and purchasing of a synthetic long position (buy call, short put, same strike).

- Short stock vs. synthetic long stock.

- Short stock, long call short put.

- Subtract dividend.

- Add credit interest.

- Add put price.

- Subtract call price.

Example:
Sell 100 IVT @ 45
Sell 1 IVT April 45 Put @ 2.40
Buy 1 IVT April 45 Call @ 3

<u>OR</u>

Example:
Sell 1 Mar DM Future @ 60.42
Sell 1 DM Mar 6050 Put @ .22
Buy 1 DM Mar 6050 Call @ .14

- **Risk/Reward:** Known immediately. The reversal is an arbitrage strategy. Profits and/or losses are determined at the time the position is established. *

- **Market View:** Neutral.

- **Delta:** The delta of the reversal is equal to the delta of the synthetic long position, which is 100, minus the delta of IVT underlying, which is also 100. *

33

In order to properly calculate the reversal, you must do the factoring as follows:

- In equities, the cost until expiration is known as a rebate that is <u>received</u> by the trader. Calculate this rebate at an interest rate of 7 % (A lesser percentage than carry on the conversion). Use the strike price (45), **not** the stock price, for the rebate calculation.

> Rebate on 45 Strike Price
> 45 x .07 x 71 / 360 = .62125

- In equities, the dividend in a reversal is <u>owed</u> by the trader, which is $ .25. Take the net of the dividend minus rebate. If the rebate is greater than the dividend, add it to the <u>stock</u> price for the actual. If less than the dividend, then deduct from the <u>stock</u> price to get the actual.

Note: The combined stock price including the rebate less the dividend should equal the synthetic stock (combo).

Synthetic Options and Synthetic Options Positions

With a fundamental understanding of synthetics, you can now start to see where you can neutralize or eliminate risk with other pieces of the equation. Once again, review the four bullet points below:

> - **Long put + long stock/future = long call**
> - **Long call + short stock/future = long put**
> - **Short put + short stock/future = short call**
> - **Short call + long stock/future = short put**

Equivalent Option Strategies

I will now name an options strategy and will list the synthetic equivalent position.

Straddle Position

- Long call synthetic straddle = Long 2 at-the-money calls, short 1 future or 100 shares of stock.
- Long put synthetic straddle = Long 2 at-the-money puts, long 1 future or 100 shares of stock.
- Short call synthetic straddle = short 2 at-the-money calls, long 1 future or 100 shares of stock.
- Short put synthetic straddle = short 2 at-the-money puts, short 1 future or 100 shares of stock.

Vertical Spread – a long call vertical can be synthetically replicated by selling the same strike put vertical. Conversely, a short call vertical can by synthetically replicated by purchasing the same strike put vertical. Due to the rules of options equivalency:

GLD (Reference: $120.75)

- Purchasing the June 120 / 121 call vertical at .55 is the synthetic equivalent of selling the June 120 / 121 put vertical at a price of .45. Remember the two verticals added together must equal 1.00. Thus, if you sold the 120/121 call vertical at a price of .50, that would be the same as purchasing the 120/121 put spread at .50.

- If you could purchase the June 120/121 call spread at .45 along with purchasing the June 120/121 put spread at .45, you would automatically guarantee yourself a profit of .10. No matter what happens, the combination of those spreads will equal 1.00 at expiry.

Butterfly – a long call butterfly can be synthetically replicated by buying the put butterfly with the same strike prices. The risk of a long (short) call (or put) butterfly can be eliminated by selling (buying) the opposite butterfly with the same strike prices.

PART II

Options Moments and Measures – the Greeks

CHAPTER 3

Option Delta

"When I was 25 I was sent from Sweden to Chicago to learn option trading for one of the largest banks in Sweden. I did not know that meeting Tony and his crew at ITI would change my life forever. Tony did not just open my eyes to the world of trading options he also became a friend for life.

Tony's way of trading follows a very smart and much tested way of doing things. He is the real thing. I feel that I use relative value, position discipline and keep your inventory fresh (not counting my family) concepts in all ways of my businesses. His teachings give value far beyond daily options trading. I feel that I have a better life from many of the things I learned from him. I feel that he has been a big part of my success. I hope and believe you can have the same experience."

- Par Sanda

Introduction

The risks related to options are many and include path dependency, implied volatility, and the passage of time. These risks can be calculated with figures produced by simple mathematical formulas known as greeks, as most use greek letters as designations. Each greek estimates the risk for one particular variable.

Delta is the sensitivity of an options price with regards to the movement of the related underlying future or security. It is expressed both as a percentage and a total. A call option with an estimated 25 delta suggests that the call option is one-quarter as sensitive as compared to the corresponding underlying. It implies that you would need 4 25 delta options to replicate the performance of a one-point move in the underlying.

- Professional traders think of an option's delta as a hedge ratio; to what extent the option offsets or emulates the underlying. Professional traders learn very quickly that an options delta is only useful for a fractional move within that precise snapshot of time which it is calculated. An option's delta can and does lose its relevance when there are changes in time, movement, and implied volatility.

- From a pedestrian viewpoint, it appears logical to envision an option's delta using a simple equi-probable/decision tree (i.e. a 50% chance of either an up or down move in the underlying) to price a call option. Yet this mind thought is dangerously flawed due to the conceptual problem of linking the resultant delta value with a probability.

- Probabilities are beneficial when assessing risk with defined and limited outcomes. Applying probability or overemphasizing them in a financial world chock-full of infinite combinations can be dangerous indeed. Delta is a best-guess estimate at a given point of time and place – it's nothing more and nothing less.

> **Textbook definition:** The sensitivity of an options price to the underlying future or security
>
> **Options trader definition:** a hedge ratio. The amount (percentage) needed to be hedged (given current parameters of time, implied volatility, and location) with the underlying to be considered "dollar neutral."
>
> **Urban legends and fallacies:** no matter what you have heard or read, the delta is NOT in any way the probability of an option expiring in-the-money. An option delta is merely a mathematical measure; it would require perfect and uninterrupted hedging to be reliable.

Delta Details – Positive & Negative

To reiterate, an option's delta is a mathematical expression that estimates how much the theoretical value of an option will change with a 1-point move in the corresponding underlying. It is the amount whereby an options trader would consider himself "dollar-neutral" compared to the underlying.

The delta of a call option spans from 0.00 to 1.00; the delta of a put option spans from 0 to (-1.00). Positive delta means that the option is estimated to rise in value if the asset price rises and is estimated to drop in value if the asset price falls. Negative delta means that the option position will theoretically rise in value if the asset price falls and theoretically drop in value if the asset price rises.

- Long (purchased) calls always have a positive delta; short (sold) calls always have negative delta.

- Long (purchased) puts always have a negative delta; short (sold) puts always have a positive delta.

- Long (purchased) underlying always have a positive delta; short (sold) underlying always have a negative delta.

- The nearer an option's delta is to 1.00 or (-1.00), the more the price of the option responds like the actual long or short underlying when the underlying price moves.

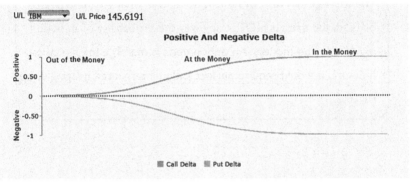

Figure 1   Options Technology Solutions, UK

Consider the ABC January 100 call with a current value of $2.00 and a delta of +.40 with ABC currently trading at $96.00. If ABC should rally one dollar to $97.00, the value of the January 100 call will theoretically rise to $2.40. If ABC falls to $95.00, the theoretical value of the ABC January 100 call is estimated to drop to $1.60. See Figure 2 below:

Stock Price	Delta	Theoretical Value January $100 Call
$97.00	0.4	$2.40
$96.00	0.4	$2.00
$95.00	0.4	$1.60

ABC January 100 call; ABC underlying price = $96.00, delta = .40

Figure 2

Currently the ABC January 100 put is worth $3.00 and has a delta of (-.60) with ABC trading at $96.00. If ABC should rally to $97.00, the theoretical value of the ABC January 100 put will drop to $2.40. If ABC drops to $95.00, the estimated value of the ABC January 100 put will rise to $3.60. See Figure 3 below:

Stock Price	Delta	Theoretical Value January $100 Call
$97.00	-0.6	$2.40
$96.00	-0.6	$3.00
$95.00	-0.6	$3.60

ABC January 100 put; ABC underlying price = $96.00, delta = -.60

Figure 3

The previous tables (Figures 2 and 3) assume that nothing else changes, such as a rise or fall in volatility or interest rates or the passage of time. Alterations in any one of these parameters can change delta, even if the price of the underlying asset doesn't move.

Delta Details – Changes in Volatility & Time

Delta is a best-guess estimate - susceptible to changes in volatility and time to expiration. The delta of at the money options (i.e. .50 delta call or put) is relatively invulnerable to changes in time and volatility. This means that at the money options with six months remaining to expiration compared to at the money options with one-month to expiration both have deltas very similar to .50.

However, the further divergence away from the money an option is, the more susceptible its delta will be to alterations in volatility or time to expiration. Fewer days to expiration or a decrease in volatility push the deltas of in the money calls closer to 1.00 (-1.00 for puts) and the deltas of out of the money options closer to 0.00.

Consequently an in the money option with 10 days to expiration and a delta of .80 could see its delta grow to .90 (or more) with only a couple days to expiration without any movement in the underlying. Similarly, an out-of-the-money option with 10 days to expiration and a delta of .15 could see its delta drop to a .10 delta without any movement in the underlying. Lastly, an at the money option with 10 days to expiration and a delta of .50 will see its delta remain at .50 up through and including expiration day.

Delta & Synthetic Relationships

Notice in Figures 2 and 3 above that each strike price has a combined delta with an absolute value of 1.00. This echoes chapter two, "Principles of Option Equivalency" and holds true for every call and put of the same month and strike price, since the underlying contains a delta of 1.00.

Synthetic long underlying is constructed with a long call and short a put at the same strike price in the same month. Therefore, the delta of a long call plus the delta of a short put (at the same strike in the same month) must equal the delta of long underlying. Conversely, synthetic short underlying is short a call and long a put at the same strike in the same month.

It must be recognized that options delta can be calculated with various input formulas. Using the Black-Scholes model for European style options, the total of the absolute values of the call and put is equal to 1.00. Using varied input models for American style options and other exclusive circumstances, the sum of the absolute values of the call and put (at the same strike in the same month) can be marginally more or slightly less than 1.00.

Options Portfolio/Position Delta

Realistically speaking an option's delta becomes more complex – less reliable - with the complexity of a position. A successful trader will view their delta holistically – balancing it with the risks of time and volatility.

That said, a trader can add, subtract, and multiply deltas to determine the "net delta" of a position and underlying. The position delta is a way to estimate the risk/reward character of your position in terms of sensitivity to the underlying. The calculation is very straightforward:

Position Delta = Option's Theoretical Delta x Amount of Options Contracts

A trader owns five of the ABC June 60 calls, each with an estimated delta of +.40, and short (sold) one hundred shares of ABC stock. The traders position delta would be +100 or (short 100 shares of ABC or -100 deltas, long 5 +.40 delta = +.40 delta x 5 – 100 = +100).

What does +100 mean? The mathematics estimates that if ABC stock should increase by $1.00, the trader will earn $100. On the other hand, if ABC drops $1.00, the trader will lose $100. Once again, it is imperative to realize that these numbers are mere approximations. Remember that delta is relevant for insignificant moves and for brief time periods. Beyond that it gets fuzzy fairly quickly.

The Relationship between Volatility and Delta

As mentioned earlier in this chapter, delta is an estimate and that estimate is partially produced on the trader's assumption about implied volatility levels.

At its core, options implied volatility embodies the degree of uncertainty in the market and the extent to which the prices of the underlying asset are expected to change over time. When there is relatively more uncertainty, people will pay more for options – thus raising the level of implied volatility. In August 2015, for example, as the markets reflected on China and its currency devaluation, participants became fearful and bid up the prices of options or the implied volatility. But when people feel more secure, they tend to collect option premium through the sale of options. This would cause implied volatility levels to drop.

The Change in Delta with Changes in Implied Volatility

All other factors (movement, time to expiry) being constant, an increase in implied volatility causes all option deltas to converge towards .50. In fact, during the unprecedented volatility spike of "Black Monday" (1987) option models did produce .50 deltas for every strike available for trading!

During a rising implied volatility environment, in-the-money call option deltas will decrease towards .50 while out-of-the-money call options will increase towards .50. Reiterating our Chapter 2 discussion on synthetics would imply the opposite would hold true for put deltas. Other words, in a rising volatility environment, in the money put option deltas will decrease towards -.50 while out of the money put options delta would increase towards -.50.

This should begin to make sense, for when ambiguity increases (the reason for higher implied volatility levels) it becomes less clear where the underlying will wind up at expiration. Thus, the absolute value of an in the money option delta will decrease, the absolute value of an out of the money option delta will increase, while an at the money option delta will always remain near a .50 delta.

A somewhat drastic yet helpful approach to understanding this is to look at expiration. At expiry, volatility is 0; all deltas are either 0 or 1, finishing either out of the money or in the money. Any increase in volatility – like an increase in time - causes probabilities to move away from 0 and 1, reflecting a higher level of uncertainty.

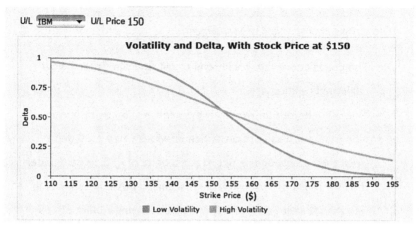

Figure 4   Options Technology Solutions, UK

Higher Implied Volatility and its Inference on an Options Delta

Imagine you were trading the SPX weekly cash options during the spring and summer of 2015 when the SPX cash remained tightly confined within a 50-point range. Given that scenario, it would make sense that the implied volatility levels on this index would be relatively low and thus causing option deltas to be well defined and widely distributed between 0 and 1.00.

However, if you traded SPX weekly cash options during the summer and fall of 2015 when the SPX cratered, it would be safe to suggest that the implied volatility levels would be meaningfully higher than that in the previous scenario, and you would notice a marked convergence of option deltas towards .50.

> *In a rising implied volatility environment:*
>
> - The deltas above .50 would tend to fall, and the deltas below .50 would tend to rise.
> - The .50 delta option would always remain a .50 delta option.
> - For example, a call option, which previously had a .30 delta (with the corresponding put having a delta of -.70), would under the new (higher implied volatility) scenario possibly estimate a delta of .35 (with the corresponding put having a delta of -.65).

Think of it this way. Assume you are watching an underlying that has experienced an average of 1 percent moves per day. Furthermore, presume that the underlying is now undergoing moves of 10 percent or more per day. Given the new market reality, in which the underlying is moving at least 10 times greater per day than before, an options model would logically estimate deltas that converge toward .50 to the various strike prices. Greater uncertainty begets options with deltas closer to .50.

Lower Volatility and Delta

Lower volatility has the exact opposite effect on an options delta, and it is often easier to comprehend.

Consider a hypothetical example that due to civil unrest a certain commodity has experienced unprecedented intra-day gyrations of 10 percent or more per day for weeks unabated. Further, assume that the government steps in with aggressive intervention by halting this commodities movement at one percent per day.

With this new government policy we can be certain that implied volatilities would drop a great deal. Recall, a sharp drop in implied volatility suggests a smaller or tighter band of movement in the underlying going forward, suggesting the following results:

- A .50 delta call or put would remain unchanged at .50 delta.
- A call with a delta greater than .50 would rise towards 1.00.
- A put with a delta greater than -.50 would go more negative towards -1.00.
- A call with a delta less than .50 would fall towards 0.
- A put with a delta less than -.50 would decrease towards 0.

The Change in Delta with Changes in Time

If you comprehend the reality that all options will expire with an options delta of either 0 or 1.00, then it should be intuitive - by extension - to understand that the further out you go in an options term, the more profoundly difficult it becomes to approximate the direction or pathway of the underlying.

Liken to a high implied volatility environment, time to expiry has the exact same nuances whereby the further out your option is along the term structure, the more your option's delta will compare similarly to an upward spike in implied volatility. On the other hand, the closer you are to expiration, the easier it becomes to quantify the expiring strike price, which sounds vaguely familiar to the principle behind options delta in a lower-volatility situation.

As you go out in time and because it becomes more challenging to determine where an underlying will be months in the future (compared to tomorrow), an option delta will change in the following ways:

- In the money call and put options deltas decrease (slightly) as you go out in time.
- At the money call and put options remain essentially constant the further you go out in time.
- Out of the money call and put options increase (slightly) as you go out in time.

Notice below in **Figure 5** and the illustration of term structure and delta and how that looks very similar to delta and changes in volatility in **Figure 4**.

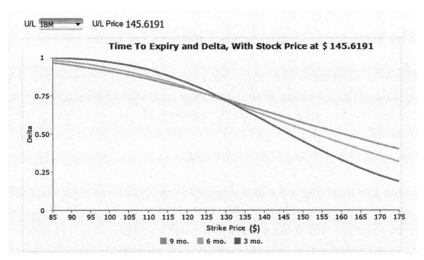

U/L IBM ▾   U/L Price 145.6191

Time To Expiry and Delta, With Stock Price at $ 145.6191

■ 9 mo. ■ 6 mo. ■ 3 mo.

Figure 5   Options Technology Solutions, UK

Delta and the Options Position Trader

Experienced options traders eventually wind up having a love-hate relationship with options delta. Anyone with overreliance on the manual definition - that delta is somehow construed to mean an equal underlying position – has undoubtedly uncovered the stark realization that this is a textbook truism and not reality. Delta is one measure of risk and when used discriminately it can help forecast your risk profile and replication. Overreliance on delta – especially with complex positions – can prove fatal.

Imagine an options market maker who, through the course of each day, accumulates random options positions and hedges them according to the current published delta. If the trader's resultant position miraculously nets out all strike risk, term risk, volatility risk, and path risk than one could over rely on the net position delta. Yet, when complexities are added (i.e. strike price risk, skew risk, time risk, volatility risk) to this position, delta loses its potency and becomes more of a tool and less of a toolbox.

Examples of Simplicity & Complexity

Example One: After your first day of trading your net position consists of at-the-money call and put options (perfectly hedged with underlying) strewn between the 30-day expiry to a 3-year expiry. At this point in time you can relax as your net position is composed of .50-delta options – your position will be unaffected by any change in volatility, time decay, term structure convexity, or skew. Remember an at-the-money option will always remain near .50 delta.

Example Two: Your net position is now long .25 delta puts perfectly hedged with long underlying – providing you with a zero net position delta.

If implied volatility should rise significantly, the delta of that put will rise as well (everything else being unaffected). Your net delta position will become more negative, alerting you to buy more underlying (to remain hedged) against your position. Some questions/issues an options trader will need to answer/face:

- What happens if implied volatility reverses or decreases? You are now naked long underlying against your put position as the delta will decrease.

- What happens if volatility remains stable yet time marches on? Your increased delta will quickly deflate (due to time). You are now naked long underlying against your put position as the delta will decrease. Your increasing betting for continued up moves as your position is more closely linked to the underlying position than the options position.

- What happens if implied volatility continues to spike and/or skew increases? Your put delta will continually become bigger (more negative). Should you keep buying per your new net options delta?

Example Three: Your net position is now long .35 delta calls perfectly hedged with short underlying – providing you with a zero net position delta.

If the underlying should make small positive moves each day and at the same time implied volatility levels drip lower, your net delta will slowly decay lower as the positives of the up-move are slowly and surely being overtaken by time decay and lower implied volatility levels. Some questions/issues an options trader will need to answer/face:

- As the days wear on (small up-moves and lower implied volatility) a trader will need to recognize that the net options delta is becoming the risk relative to the options position. Other words, this position is becoming increasingly more of a bearish statement than a bullish one.

- What happens if there is a decent up-move in the underlying and the net delta becomes more positive? If underlying isn't moving enough compared to the effects of time and lower volatility those perceived long deltas will quickly evaporate.

- What happens if one day implied volatility spikes and the net options delta becomes more positive as well? If you hedge the new delta you could wind up making a decision on buying them back when volatility levels return lower.

Measuring a net delta options position is simple; assessing how to interpret and subsequently hedge is the ultimate challenge. Options are multi-dimensional and require human conviction on movement, implied volatility, and time. Understanding each dimension separately helps to simplify the assessment, but actual market dynamics occur simultaneously. The discussion in Chapter 7 "<u>Minor Options Greeks & Greeks of the Second Order</u>," will help shed light on how first order options Greeks (Delta, Vega, Theta, Rho) can change with respect to price fluctuations, implied volatility, interest rate changes, and the passage of time.

CHAPTER 4

Option Gamma

Introduction

Mathematically, gamma is the first derivative of delta and is used when trying to judge the price movement of an option, relative to the amount the option is in or out of the money. Professionals sometimes refer to gamma as the "delta's delta" as it expresses the curvature or rapidity at which the delta of an option will change relative to movement in the underlying.

The gamma is usually expressed as deltas gained or lost per one point change in the future or security, with the option delta increasing the amount of gamma when the underlying increases, and dropping by the same amount of gamma when the underlying decreases.

Gamma is also expressed as convexity – the chief characteristic of options and their non-linear pay-out is described by gamma itself. In options, if the price of an underlying variable changes, the price of an output does not change linearly, but depends on the second derivative (gamma) of the modeling function. Geometrically, the model is no longer flat but curved, and the degree of curvature is called the convexity or gamma.

Gamma is a mathematical estimate on the stability of your options delta. A large gamma indicates an unstable delta. When gamma is high, delta can begin changing dramatically from even a small move in the underlying.

- Long calls and long puts always have positive gamma.
- Short calls and short puts always have negative gamma.
- Due to their linearity, stocks, or any underlying asset, possess 0.00 gamma - their delta is always 1.00—it never changes.

Positive Gamma

- Positive gamma means that the option delta of a long call will become more positive and move toward 1.00 when the underlying rises and less positive and move toward 0.00 when the underlying price falls.

- Similarly, the delta of a long put will become more negative and move toward 1.00 when the underlying price drops and will become less negative and move toward 0.00 when the underlying price increases.

Position	Delta	Gamma
Long Underlying	Long	0
Short Underlying	Short	0
Long Call	Long	Long
Short Call	Short	Short
Long Put	Short	Long
Short Put	Long	Short

Delta and Gamma Composition

Figure 1

Negative Gamma

The opposite holds true for negative gamma.

- Negative gamma means that the delta of a short call will become more negative and move toward 1.00 when the underlying rises and will become less negative and move toward 0.00 when the underlying price falls.

- The delta of a short put will become less negative and progress toward 0.00 when the underlying rises and will become more negative and move toward 1.00 when the underlying falls.

Assume the SPY June 200 call has a delta of +.45, the June 200 put has a delta of (-.55) and the SPY underlying (ETF) is trading at $196.00. Currently both the June 200 call and put have an estimated gamma of .08

- If SPY trades $1.00 <u>higher</u> to $197.00, the delta of the SPY June 200 call becomes +.53 or (+.45 + ($1.00 x .08)) while the delta of the SPY June 200 put is reduced to (-.47) or (-.55 + ($1.00 x .08)).

- If SPY trades $1.00 <u>lower</u> from $196.00 to $195.00, the delta of the SPY June 200 call becomes +. 37 or (+.45 + (-$1.00 x .08)) while the delta of the June 200 put increases to (-.63) or (-.55 +(-$1.00 x .08)).

Gamma – like delta – is a mathematical expression, an evolving estimate of sorts to assist options traders in trade selection and risk management. Option gamma is fluid, subject to change and sometimes intuitively understood by imagining underlying option strike prices – with their estimated gamma – drawn-out as resembling a large mountain, with the apex of this mountain being the at-the-money call and put strikes.

Given your at the money call and put strikes contain the most gamma – the highpoint of the mountain – it should make sense that option gamma is reduced the further one goes down and away from the tip. Gamma becomes increasingly less (per strike price), flattening out to zero gamma at the mountain's base.

The Nature of Gamma: Gamma versus Underlying

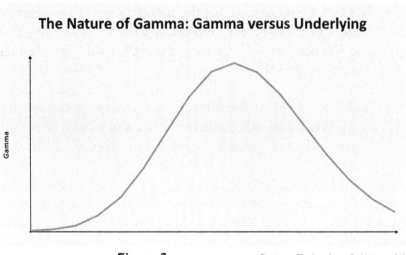

Figure 2   Options Technology Solutions, UK

Intuitive Look at Gamma

Compare three strike prices of the same underlying index and the same expiration date:

- A very deep in the money (1.00 delta) call or put.
- An at the money (.50 delta) call or put.
- A far out of the money (.20 delta) call or put.

In-the-money (1.00 delta) call or put. In the above case, if the underlying moves one-point (remember direction does not matter) it should makes sense that the <u>absolute value</u> of the 1.00 delta option will change (up or down) the most, given it's a very deep in the money option and will replicate 1:1 with the underlying. However at this point the, delta is very stable at 1.00 and thus the gamma for this strike price is almost nonexistent.

At-the-money (.50 delta) call or put. In the above example, whether the one-point index move is up or down is inconsequential as the at the money option contains the most gamma and thus is most vulnerable to its delta changing. Recall, an options gamma estimates the delta's sensitivity and as noted the most sensitive spot will always be the at the money strike.

Out-of-the-money (.20 delta) call or put. In the above illustration, a one-point index move (up or down does not matter) will have less gamma impact on a .20-delta option compared to a .50-delta option and more impact on a .20-delta option as compared to a 1.00 delta option. Other words the stability of a .20-delta option is more so than a .50-delta option and less so than a 1.00 delta option.

Exercise Price	Call			Put		
	Option Price	Delta	Gamma	Option Price	Delta	Gamma
190	10.40	0.90	1.80	0.35	-0.10	1.80
195	6.10	0.75	4.10	1.19	-0.25	4.10
200	3.00	0.50	5.00	3.00	-0.50	5.00
205	1.25	0.25	4.30	6.20	-0.75	4.30
210	0.41	0.11	2.50	10.32	-0.89	2.50

Underlying = $200.00 ; Time till expiry = 34 days ; Implied volatility = 32%

Figure 3

Figure 3 demonstrates a couple points worthy of reiteration. First, notice the absolute value of each strike price delta equals 1.00. Recall from chapter two, "Rules of Options Equivalency," that calls and puts with the same strike price and month will have deltas equal to 1.00. Building upon that foundation, it should be clear that each strike price should have a gamma and the call gamma will always equal the put gamma of the same strike and month.

Gamma strike equivalency may not seem logical as you've learned that calls and puts provide the participant with strikingly different rights and/or obligations. It isn't intuitive that a .20-delta call shares the same gamma as its corresponding same strike .80-delta put. However, it must be engrained inside of a new trader that the mathematic formulas within option greeks do not discriminate between a call and a put of the same month and strike price. The logic relies solely on the relationship of a strike price (whether it be call or put) and that strike prices distance from the underlying.

Changes in Implied Volatility and Gamma

Gamma is a mere snapshot of delta stability; a measure rendered fairly useless when changes in implied volatility are introduced into the equation. However for the purposes of this book, ascertaining how gamma changes with changes in implied volatility (isolating underlying movement, time to expiration) solely depends on whether the option is in the money, at the money, or out of the money.

Increased Implied Volatility and Gamma

From a common sense perspective, higher implied volatility levels implies a skittish market; a market where participants are willing to pay additional premium for options as they expect a larger than average move. And, the larger the implied volatility spike, the greater the expectancy of a large move in the underlying. If it is so that rising implied volatility levels cause option deltas to converge towards .50 (Chapter 3 "Option Delta") then, by extension, it should make sense that your gamma curve (see Figure 2 "Mount Gamma") will flatten out at its summit and making the slope from the peak less steep.

> **During Increased Implied Volatility Environments:**
> - At the money option gamma decreases.
> - In the money option gamma increases.
> - Out of the money option gamma increases.

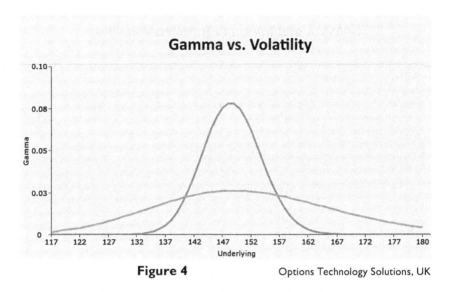

Figure 4   Options Technology Solutions, UK

Decreased Implied Volatility and Gamma

A decrease in implied volatility suggests the market is either complacent or confident of the underlying's imminent direction. And, the lower the implied volatility goes, the more confident the market becomes on any divergence from the current mean. If it is true that falling implied volatility levels cause option deltas to become distinct and diverge away from .50 (Chapter 3 "Option Delta") then, by extension, it should make sense that your gamma curve (see Figure 2 "Mount Gamma") will steepen at its summit and making the slope from the peak more steep. This steepening effect is indicating that the at the money gamma is increasing while the in the money and out of the money gamma is decreasing.

> **During Increased Implied Volatility Environments:**
> - At the money option gamma decreases.
> - In the money option gamma increases.
> - Out of the money option gamma increases.

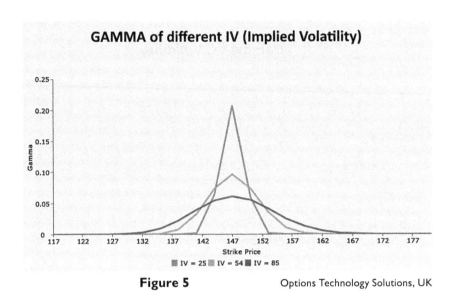

Figure 5 Options Technology Solutions, UK

Changes in Time (Term Structure) and Gamma

Traders know that there lies an unyielding amount of disparity between gamma and time to expiration. As the old floor trading saying goes, "front-month options have "gamma" while back-month options have "volatility," is worth memorizing as your curvature only measures a precise space at a precise time. A complex options position may at one moment appear flat gamma while another severely long or short gamma. Gamma must be viewed together with other greeks within time and space. Singularly, gamma is an extremely weak measure of risk.

We know that the impact of options gamma (i.e. delta stability) depends on whether the option is at the money versus in the money or out of the money. We know that changes in implied volatility will change the distribution of gamma along a strike series.

The passage of time and its impact on gamma has a direct correlation to gamma in a lower implied volatility environment. More time to expiration can be likened to gamma in an increase volatility environment. With less time to expiry (think lower implied volatility) gamma becomes more

62

heavily concentrated with the at the money strike prices, or strikes that are closer to the current price of the underlying. With more time to expiry (think higher implied volatility) gamma becomes more widely distributed amongst a variety of strike prices.

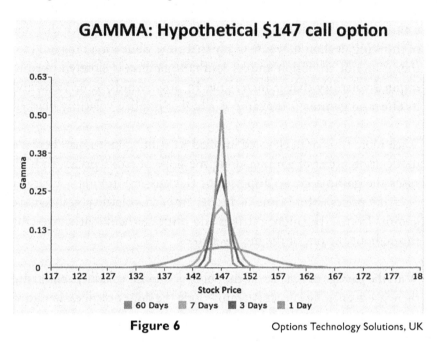

GAMMA: Hypothetical $147 call option

Figure 6   Options Technology Solutions, UK

- More time to expiration and its relationship to gamma equates to an increase in volatility. In this scenario, your option's gamma becomes more widely distributed among strike prices.
- Less time to expiration and its relationship to gamma is comparable to a decrease in volatility. In this scenario, your gamma becomes heavily condensed with your at the money strike prices.
- For an at the money call or put option, the gamma is greatest when the option draws closer to expiry.
- For an in the money or out of the money call or put option, the gamma is greatest the further the option is from its expiration.

Gamma Timeline

For most of us its challenging enough to guess where an index or security will expire next week let alone correctly guessing where it will land 2, 4, or even 12 months in the future. There are simply too many unknowns with an infinite amount of inputs involved. With that line of thinking, it should be safe to say that time value (or, going out into the future) of an option and its resultant gamma is closely linked to implied volatility that is increasing. In other words, time value and its effect on gamma is the same as a higher implied volatility market.

With more time or in elevated implied volatility conditions, there is a moderation effect of gamma along the slope of strike prices. In both cases the gamma curve disperses or flattens out amongst a variety of strike prices. More time or higher implied volatility will remove gamma from at the money strikes and disperse them mathematically throughout the out of the money strikes.

With the passage of time or the dropping of implied volatility conditions, there is a steepening effect of gamma along the slope of strikes. Less time or low volatility implies a narrower range of movement – placing the vast majority of gamma at/around the in the money strikes. Less time or lower implied volatility will take gamma from the out of the money strikes and bunch them up closer to the relevant at the money strikes.

Difference in Gamma for Thirty, Sixty, and Ninety-Day Options

			ABC 121	ABC 123	ABC 125
30 Day	121 Strike	Gamma	26	10	3
60 Day	121 Strike	Gamma	13	12	4
90 Day	121 Strike	Gamma	6	5	4

Figure 7   Options Technology Solutions, UK

Re-cap on Gamma:

- A falling implied volatility situation will raise your at the money gamma while lowering your in the money and out of the money gamma.

- A rising implied volatility situation will reduce your at the money gamma while raising your in the money and out of the money gamma.

- Gamma rises (for at the money and near at the money strikes) as the option approaches its expiration date.

- Gamma is severely time dependent and has some meaningful consequences for option positions across various expiration dates.

- Gamma can only be hedged with other options as underlying has no gamma. Even hedging options with options can be risky as gamma between strike prices does not always provide long-term stability.

- At the money options will always contain the most gamma. Mathematically, equidistant strike calls and puts should have equal gamma although options skew (Chapter 11) can and does put this relationship out of kilter.

- Gamma is the second derivative of the option with regard to the underlying price.

- Gamma does not take into consideration changes in options skew, jumps in the market, or jumps in implied volatility levels.

Gamma Position and Risk Management Conundrum

Experienced options traders know that gamma can be a futile calculation - it does not take into account changes in implied volatility, skew, or market moves. Additionally, sleepless nights will be had with both excessive amounts of negative OR positive gamma as decisions on hedging are mere guesses in the dark and can have a mighty impact on your profit and loss profile.

Trading Scenario #1: Managing long gamma in a rising volatility environment.

Your trading position nets out to be very simple. You are long an equal number of out of the-money .30 delta calls and .30 delta out of the money puts. Since your long call and put strikes are equidistant from the at the money strike (assuming no implied volatility skew) your position carries a net zero delta and a long gamma of +.10 (+5.0 gamma for the .30-delta call and +5.0 gamma for the .30-delta put). Recall that options equidistant from the at the money strike (assuming NO skew) should have the same absolute delta and same gamma.

As luck would have it implied volatility spikes higher on a small down move in the underlying. With the down move and spike in implied volatility, your net delta has become negative and your gamma is increasingly positive (causing you to be even shorter deltas as the implied volatility has risen).

This all appears good as you are accumulating negative deltas in a falling market. And, due to the volatility spike, you are accumulating negative deltas at a brisk pace as the convexity of the options slope is "flattening" with the volatility spike, assigning your more positive gamma than in a normal volatility environment.

Question: Due to the recent pace of events, you now find yourself negative delta and positive gamma. Your position has gone from 0 delta to -.10 delta. You have a decision to make. Should you hedge your deltas by buying them? How should a professional trader think about this?

How to think successfully:

Forget about the negative deltas and positive gamma and come to terms with the fact that you are buying deltas against a long put that is still considered out of the money. Do you think the market is going back up?

What transpires if you buy your negative deltas (according to what the model says), and the implied volatility, after a few days, returns to where it began? Even if volatility is sustained at these higher levels, if the market begins to creep lower, you have long deltas (if you purchased them) that now become part of your portfolio. The deltas you bought will lose money as the underlying drifts lower.

If you buy-in your negative deltas and the market rebounds, you're a hero. If you bought your negative deltas and the market idles, those negative deltas that you bought will quickly become long deltas unless the underlying drops below your long put strike. Recall from **Chapter 3 "Delta"** that options, at expiry, will have either a 0 or 1.00 delta. If, after the original down move and subsequent volatility spike, the underlying asset experiences a "sideways drift," your net delta will quickly turn from negative to zero to long.

It's worth noting that if you buy-in your negative deltas you are – in effect – stating a personal opinion on both implied volatility and future path of the underlying. Your net delta position became short deltas in a dropping market due to both path and a spike in implied volatility. You need to look at the big picture before blindly initiating hedging decisions. Some advice all of which have worked on occasion:

• Lower the implied volatility/move the date forward of your trading model. Both of these actions will reduce the negative deltas that you are tempted to buy-in.

- Reduce or liquidate your options position.

- Partially hedge your negative deltas.

- Sell a further out-of-the-money put option (unhedged) naked to the delta amount you are currently short. Basically, this will create a long put spread as opposed to be simply long a put.

Trading Scenario #2: Classic negative gamma trading scenario

They say that the best traders can trade long and short gamma with equal ease. I disagree as successful short gamma trading requires creativity, iron-clad discipline, and untold loads of nerve.

The market has been sitting idle for weeks and you decide to sell a 30-day at the money straddle which will give you a large short gamma profile however offset by the options decay (Chapter 6: "Theta") that you will receive if the market continues to drift.

After you sold the at the money straddle, the underlying begins to rally every day, although never by very much, and implied volatility remains steady. As the days go by, you find your net position delta becoming more and more negative, because the underlying continues to rise and volatility is sustained. Typically this type of portfolio predicament undergoes a typical series of periods.

First Period: the underlying move upwards isn't overly concerning however it is causing your net delta to become shorter and shorter every day. The passage of time does help reduce your negative delta a bit but not enough.

Second Period: After several days of this irritation (i.e. short gamma in a continuously rising market), you finally give up and purchase some (not all) of the underlying against your ever-increasing negative deltas. You are defeated, but all is not lost. You feel you did the right thing by neutralizing your delta.

<u>Third Period:</u> After several more days the market continues its climb. Your net delta position continues to be more and more negative as your short gamma remains. You cannot take the painful losses any longer and decide to purchase your full amount of futures required by your model to be flat.

<u>Fourth Period:</u> No sooner do you purchase your negative delta position, the underlying makes a sharp turnaround to the downside.

<u>Fifth Period:</u> You are now caught in a classic whipsaw predicament. The down move has certainly helped reduce the price of your short straddle (i.e. the underlying is moving back towards the original at the money) however you must now face the reality of the long underlying position you bought at higher levels. You will now become long underlying as the underlying moves lower.

CHAPTER 5

Option Vega

"I have known Tony Saliba for over 30 years and he comes from a wonderful Italian family. But, believe it or not, he understands the "GREEKS" better than the Italians."

Jeff Kaufmann

Lakeshore Securities

Compared to a stock or bond, options are contracts with a shelf-life and are exposed to a range of unique risks – greeks (i.e. delta, gamma, theta, vega, rho) - each of which measures the sensitivity to some variable including time, volatility, and movement.

Experienced derivative traders know that option prices actually boil down to the market's expectancy of future volatility of the underlying asset, since all the other determinants of an option's price—the underlying price, time to maturity, interest rate, and strike price—are objective. Volatility is the subjective unknown, and seldom does an option's actual, realized volatility replicate the implied volatility reflected in its current traded valuation.

Vega Defined

Interestingly enough options vega is the one option greeks not represented by a formal Greek letter - it represents the sensitivity of an option to the changes in implied volatility for a term equivalent to its expiration date. Vega is an estimate of much the theoretical value of an option changes when implied volatility changes one percent.

- Vega is a number that expresses in what direction and to what extent the option price will move if there is a 1% change in the options implied volatility.

- Vega is the first mathematical derivative of an option price with respect to the underlying asset volatility.

- Option vega is equal for both call and put options with the same month and strike price (e.g., if the SPY August 190 call has a vega of .35, the August 190 put will also have a vega of .35).

- Options with less time to expiration have a lower option vega comparatively to options with a long time to expiration.

- Options are most sensitive to changes in the options implied volatility of the underlying asset when they are at-the-money calls or puts.

- Out of the money and in the money options are not nearly as affected by volatility (relative to at-the-money options).

- Option vega can be hedged with another option only. The best vega hedge is a nearby strike of the same expiration month. This relationship is reduced the further the hedged long month is from the hedged short month.

Typically, options professionals express vega as a distinct measure. For the sake of simplicity, professionals multiply vega by the current level of volatility in an effort to make it correspond to a standard percentage move in asset volatility level. If S&P 500 (SPX) volatility is 28% and the option vega is .2, the option will theoretically gain or lose 20 cents when the volatility rises (falls) by one percentage point to 27%.

Long (purchased) calls and puts always have positive vega. Short (sold) calls and puts always have negative vega. A call and put with the same strike price and month will have the same vega. Underlying futures and securities have zero vega as their values are linear and thus not affected by changes in implied volatility.

Vega risk is the risk due to changes in volatility, or the "volatility of volatility". A strict understanding of vega risk is important in any options strategy or position, as it can generate unforeseen risk, even if all the other greeks are hedged perfectly.

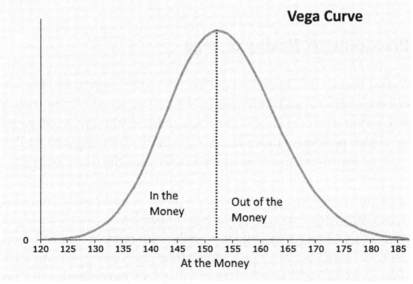

Figure I   Options Technology Solutions, UK

Options vega is similar in shape (see Figure 01 above) to both options gamma and theta as an options vega reaches its plateau when it's at the money. An option's vega differs from both gamma and theta whereas

73

vega generally increases with time while it generally decreases (with time) for both gamma and theta. That being said, the vega of an at the money option is fairly dependable to volatility changes. However, options further away from the money are not as stable given the complexity of changes in the volatility structure.

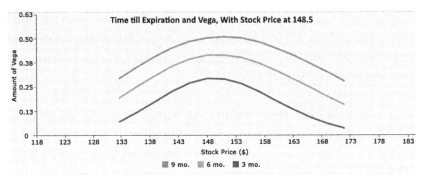

Figure 2　　　　　　　　　　　Options Technology Solutions, UK

Practicality & Reality of Vega

A good trader needs to understand his risk and be ready to address that risk when personal and prearranged risk limits are breached. The trader's ability to interpret vega is of utmost importance as its purpose is to gauge the traders position sensitivity to changes in the assets implied volatility – one of the largest and most unpredictable risks the trader will face.

Vega can be used to evaluate risk across products, strike prices, and time frames although greater caution needs to be taken here as complexity begets complexity. Consider an options portfolio with random long and short positions spread out amongst various strike prices along with different times to expiration. A seasoned trader will quickly recognize that the "net vega" published by a trading model is at-best "raw vega". Like the other greeks mentioned, vega is an estimate and subject to wise discernment. Variables including options skew (see Chapter 11) and term structure (see Chapter 12) can and do alter the true value of an option's vega.

Additionally, the majority of an option price "fair-value" is derived by either a Black-Scholes model or iteration thereof. The options model produces a "fair-value" of an option based on five variables including – the underlying price, the strike price, the term of the option, the interest rate, and the current volatility. A skilled trader will realize (usually through a bad experience) that an options model is using a static volatility input and thus, the "fair-value" option price produced will then assume a static volatility environment. Consequently, option traders realize that options vega is both an estimate and subject to interpretation. It's difficult – if not impossible – to measure the real vega sensitivity of an options portfolio with a static, human recorded asset volatility.

Under the conventions of the Black-Scholes model, underlying asset return volatility is constant, which is rarely supported by research nor is it realistic! Realized as well, option implied volatility fluctuates over any given period of time – thus the importance of vega.

Options Vega and Options Strike Price

In theory it's easy to conceptualize. An option vega – it's sensitivity to changes in implied volatility – is at its greatest point with an at-the-money option. An option's vega becomes less and less the further your option is from the at the money strike. What that means is a 1.00-delta call will have almost no vega, a .70-delta call will have more vega compared to a 1.00-delta call and less than a .50-delta call. Similar would hold true for puts.

In a perfect world – one that uses a static volatility – equidistant strike prices would have the same vega. Other words, mathematically speaking a 5% out of the money call should have the same exact vega as an equidistant 5% out of the money put. Yet, due to options implied skew, it could be precisely true that an equidistant 5% out of the money call could have more/less vega than a 5% out of the money put. This realistic phenomenon will be covered at length in Chapter

"Option Volatility Skew", Chapter 12 "Volatility Surface," and Chapter 20 "Ratio Spreading."

Below is an example of SPY option vega with regards to distance from the at the money strike. Pay special attention to the difference in vega in the equidistant in the money vs. out of the money strike prices.

Call								Expiry	Strike	Put						Theo
Spread	Theo	Ex	Size	Bid	Ask	Size	Ex	Expiry	Strike	Ex	Size	Bid	Ask	Size	Ex	Theo
6.30	37.6..	NBBO	78	34.37	38.41	55	NBBO	Oct. 21, 2016	115	NBBO	26	1.01	1.23	89	NBBO	0
10.14	32.6..	NBBO	75	28.24	31.68	84	NBBO	Oct. 21, 2016	120	NBBO	82	1.37	1.58	34	NBBO	0
5.22	27.6..	NBBO	11	24.57	28.21	37	NBBO	Oct. 21, 2016	125	NBBO	59	1.93	2.04	32	NBBO	0
9.12	22.6..	NBBO	63	19.10	22.68	86	NBBO	Oct. 21, 2016	130	NBBO	49	2.61	2.84	64	NBBO	0.0003
5.91	17.6..	NBBO	85	15.43	19.11	54	NBBO	Oct. 21, 2016	135	NBBO	99	3.68	3.79	97	NBBO	0.006
2.50	12.7..	NBBO	18	13.48	14.09	73	NBBO	Oct. 21, 2016	140	NBBO	68	5.07	5.20	33	NBBO	0.0676
1.41	8.06..	NBBO	84	10.10	10.35	73	NBBO	Oct. 21, 2016	145	NBBO	34	6.86	7.01	11	NBBO	0.4187
1.15	4.23..	NBBO	44	7.27	7.52	82	NBBO	Oct. 21, 2016	150	NBBO	70	9.03	9.23	95	NBBO	1.5981
0.79	1.73..	NBBO	61	5.03	5.34	98	NBBO	Oct. 21, 2016	155	NBBO	93	11.81	12.02	50	NBBO	4.0892
1.21	0.53..	NBBO	43	3.18	3.33	22	NBBO	Oct. 21, 2016	160	NBBO	91	15.11	15.36	17	NBBO	7.8857
0.60	0.11..	NBBO	73	2.04	2.23	53	NBBO	Oct. 21, 2016	165	NBBO	15	17.67	21.10	85	NBBO	12.47
0.61	0.01..	NBBO	15	1.22	1.35	40	NBBO	Oct. 21, 2016	170	NBBO	12	21.84	25.45	79	NBBO	17.37
0.44	0.00..	NBBO	23	0.72	0.82	65	NBBO	Oct. 21, 2016	175	NBBO	45	26.17	29.51	16	NBBO	22.352

Figure 2

Underlying	Expiry	Type	Strike	Quantity	Cost	Theo	Delta	Gamma	Vega	Theta
IBM	161021	C	165	1	1.83	8.6772	0.3928	0.0108	0.3911	-0.0426
IBM	161021	C	160	1	2.95	10.3019	0.4431	0.0111	0.4017	-0.0640
IBM	161021	C	155	1	4.49	12.1671	0.4959	0.0112	0.4058	-0.0447
IBM	161021	C	150	1	6.53	14.2911	0.5505	0.0111	0.4026	-0.0447
IBM	161021	C	145	1	9.27	16.689	0.606	0.0108	0.3914	-0.0438
IBM	161021	C	140	1	12.59	19.3721	0.6612	0.0103	0.3722	-0.0421
IBM	161021	C	135	1	17.47	22.3459	0.715	0.0095	0.3453	-0.0396
IBM	161021	C	130	1	20.54	25.6096	0.7661	0.0086	0.3118	-0.0363
IBM	161021	C	125	1	26.07	29.1557	0.8133	0.0075	0.273	-0.0325

Figure 3

A successful trader will have a solid understanding of both the textbook and realistic definition of options vega. Most products have some sort of implied volatility skew and that skew is not static – it changes with sentiment, time, and supply versus demand. As options trades evolve to a strategy and then a position, it's essential that a trader understand vega on an intuitive level.

Options Vega and Time

- Vega increases with longer time to expiration and decreases with less time to expiration.

- The term structure of implied volatility describes, for a given exercise strike price at a given date in time, the relationship between implied volatility and option maturity.

It should be of little surprise that the less time to expiration the more reasonably accurate "the market" can be in assessing where the underlying will land at expiry. Similarly, more time to expiration equals less precision – more unknowns – on where the underlying will land. Thus, the more time to an option's expiration – the more vega an option will have. This makes sense as time value makes up a larger percentage of the premium for longer-term options and it is the time value that is sensitive to changes in volatility. This results in a higher vega for options with longer time to expiration in order to compensate for the additional risk assumed by the seller.

A consistent options trader will not compare, net, add, or subtract the vegas of an options position resultant of various maturities. They will first know precisely where the long and short vega is BEFORE netting vega.

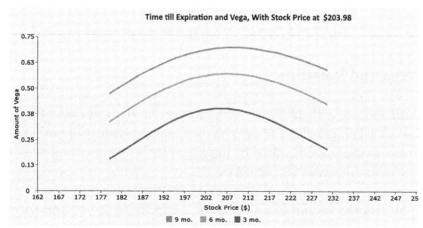

Figure 4   Options Technology Solutions, UK

For example, **SPDR Trust Series (SPY)** (reference: $193. The vega of the January '16 193 strike is currently $0.20, while the June '15 193 strike has a vega of $0.54, compared to the December '16 193 call which has a vega of $0.75. See Figure 5 for greater detail.

Call								Put						
Spread	Theo	Ex	Size	Bid	Ask	Size	Ex	Expiry	Strike	Ex	Size	Bid	Ask	Size	Ex	Theo
0.08	14.8..	NBBO	86	5.01	5.07	34	NBBO	Jul. 15, 2016	209	NBBO	53	5.93	5.99	15	NBBO	11.32..
0.21	14.3..	NBBO	81	4.31	4.36	92	NBBO	Jul. 15, 2017	210	NBBO	93	6.27	6.31	99	NBBO	11.82..
0.15	13.8..	NBBO	87	3.73	3.76	37	NBBO	Jul. 15, 2018	211	NBBO	96	6.71	6.76	48	NBBO	12.32..
0.07	13.3..	NBBO	70	3.22	3.25	61	NBBO	Jul. 15, 2019	212	NBBO	29	7.23	7.25	47	NBBO	12.84..
0.17	12.9..	NBBO	27	2.72	2.75	18	NBBO	Jul. 15, 2020	213	NBBO	78	7.78	7.82	27	NBBO	13.37..
-0.06	12.4..	NBBO	33	2.36	2.36	62	NBBO	Jul. 15, 2021	214	NBBO	26	8.12	7.14	81	NBBO	13.91..
0.13	12.0..	NBBO	10	1.92	1.91	22	NBBO	Jul. 15, 2022	215	NBBO	54	9.04	9.08	13	NBBO	14.46..
-0.04	11.5..	NBBO	45	1.61	1.61	12	NBBO	Jul. 15, 2023	216	NBBO	93	9.54	9.53	89	NBBO	15.02..
0.05	11.1..	NBBO	58	1.29	1.27	42	NBBO	Jul. 15, 2024	217	NBBO	10	10.26	10.26	89	NBBO	15.60..
-0.01	10.07.	NBBO	39	1.04	1.02	36	NBBO	Jul. 15, 2025	218	NBBO	96	10.83	10.82	73	NBBO	16.19..
0.01	10.3..	NBBO	87	0.82	0.80	21	NBBO	Jul. 15, 2026	219	NBBO	37	11.65	11.66	40	NBBO	16.79..
-0.30	9.95..	NBBO	68	0.65	0.63	13	NBBO	Jul. 15, 2027	220	NBBO	70	12.77	12.77	82	NBBO	17.40..
0.00	8.19..	NBBO	58	0.21	0.20	71	NBBO	Jul. 15, 2028	225	NBBO	69	17.19	17.22	62	NBBO	20.61..

Underlying	Expiry	Type	Strike	Quantity	Cost	Theo	Delta	Gamma	Vega	Theta
SPY	160715	C	220	1	0.63	10.7098	0.4625	0.012	0.3765	-0.0957
SPY	160715	C	219	1	0.82	11.1155	0.4741	0.012	0.3774	-0.0961
SPY	160715	C	218	1	0.99	11.5326	0.4859	0.012	0.378	-0.0963
SPY	160715	C	217	1	1.3	11.9612	0.4977	0.012	0.3782	-0.0964
SPY	160715	C	216	1	1.6	12.4015	0.5095	0.012	0.3781	-0.0965
SPY	160715	C	215	1	1.93	12.8535	0.5214	0.012	0.3777	-0.0965
SPY	160715	C	214	1	2.37	13.3173	0.5333	0.012	0.3769	-0.0964
SPY	160715	C	213	1	2.82	13.9731	0.5453	0.0119	0.3758	-0.0963
SPY	160715	C	212	1	3.29	14.2808	0.5573	0.0119	0.3743	-0.0960
SPY	160716	C	211	1	3.89	14.7806	0.5693	0.0118	0.3725	-0.0957
SPY	160717	C	210	1	4.3	15.2925	0.5812	0.0118	0.3704	-0.0952

Figure 5

Vega and Volatility

Vega and implied volatility are certainly not the same thing but they are correlated. Vega tells us an option's (or an option strategy or positions) sensitivity to implied volatility. Implied volatility is the premium – or extrinsic value paid for the option.

Theoretically speaking, if you isolate - underlying movement, time, and options skew - changes in volatility will affect option prices but change thcm differently. Option vega is greatest for options at-the-money options, and it is smaller for options completely out of the money or very deep in the money.

Said differently, if an option you're long (purchased) is far out of the money and near worthless, it matters little how much the underlying's implied volatility shifts, because the odds the option will suddenly become at the money or in the money are still considered relatively small.

If the option is deeply in the money, the chance that the option will suddenly become worthless with increased volatility is also relatively small. But if the option is at the money, which is on the edge of being worthless or valued, then even a relatively fractional change in the implied volatility in the price of the underlying asset can change the position. Thus, the reason why vega is at its highest point for at the money options.

Vega, Implied Volatility, and Risk-Awareness

A professional options trader must comprehend not only vega, but also the relationship of underlying change and its effects on implied volatility and vega.

Keep in mind, vega is merely an expression of an unknown. History has given us many who have shown us how to define what your option will be (theoretically) worth given a 1 percent move in the underlying. Great for textbooks and classrooms! The reality is there are among us forces nearly impossible to predict or quantify; all of these could influence the vega of an option.

- Where on the strike-price curve are your long and short options concentrated?

- If there's a dramatic shift-up in implied volatility how is your net vega going to change?

- If there's a profound shift-down in implied volatility how is your net vega going to change?

- Are you net long or short implied options skew? How will a skew change affect your net vega?

- Are you dissecting your vega position per month? Never should you net, add, or subtract vegas of two different options with various expiries without first knowing your isolated, per month vega position.

- Vega is an isolated measure of a static price. It does not take into consideration the impact of a changing implied volatility or other greeks.

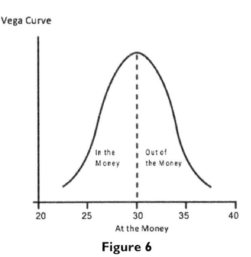

Figure 6

Vega and its Relationship to Gamma

Vega is related to options gamma in an odd way since they seem to develop in different ways. As way of example, when implied volatility on an underlying is low, the gamma of at the money options will be high, while the gamma of deep out of the money options will be very low. This is because, when volatility is low, deep out of the money options will have very little value as the time premium is so low. However, option prices rise dramatically on a relative basis, as you move back along the option chain towards the at the money strikes.

When implied volatility is high, and option prices are higher across all strike prices, gamma tends to be more stable across the option strike prices (see Chapter 4). When implied volatility is high, the time value embedded in the out of the money options will rise and can do so dramatically. Consequently as you move from the outer strikes back towards the at the money strikes, the increase in time value is less dramatic.

Gamma always has the same sign as vega. In fact, gamma is the realization of vega. A fast moving market gives the trader the chances to profit from a long gamma as his delta will move favorably whichever way the market moves.

Vega and Time Decay

Options are contracts - a wasting asset that can contain both intrinsic value and extrinsic value. The loss of extrinsic value (theta – see Chapter 6) occurs due to the passage of time as all options – at expiration – must equal their intrinsic value or zero.

One of the mistakes traders make is confusing "time decay" or "theta" as a move lower in implied volatility and thus a reduction in options vega.

One way to guard against this is to use a general, hand-calculated theta/vega ratio. The theta/vega ratio is computed as options theta divided by options vega. This ratio allows the trader to control how much theta they are receiving relative to the amount of vega in the position. The higher the theta/vega ratio, the higher the amount of theta the trader obtains comparative to vega risk, and the more optimal a situation it develops for short option premium strategies.

Application of Options Vega

A solid understanding of options vega is a good start and yet a small fraction of options trading. With options vega, one must understand the subtleties of implied volatility and how that relates to options vega. If the market moves up or down, what happens to option prices? What happens to the implied volatility? What happens to the vega implied by those option prices?

Consider the meager example of an at-the-money one-year option on SPY with a spot and strike of 190. If the market trades higher 20 points, to the 210 strike, will the value of that option increase in proportion to its delta, which presumes that its implied volatility will remain constant? Or will it go up by more or by less on the basis of one-time factors? In relative terms, the at the money option's implied volatility will go down by the difference in volatilities between the two strikes. But trading isn't relative and a trader must embrace the multi-dimensionality of an option's vega.

Experienced traders understand not only vega, but also the relationship of underlying movement and its effects on implied volatility and vega. Where are your net long and short strikes concentrated along the volatility curve? If implied volatilities go up or down pointedly, how is your long or short vega going to vary?

What might happen if you're short a ratio of out of the money strikes (versus at the money) and implied volatility abruptly goes up? You may have thought you were comfortably within your personal risk limits when the markets were dull, but when things get a little more volatile, you may find that you're suddenly short volatility—and all of those out of the money options suddenly have lots of vega. Now you're short lots of volatility, more than you bargained for.

CHAPTER 6

Option Theta

Option theta, otherwise referred to as "decay" or "rent" is a mathematical estimation that measures the loss in extrinsic value of an option resultant of one-day's passage of time. More exactly, theta – like all greeks – is stationary, it provides an approximation of time value without any regard to underlying movement or any change in implied volatility or term structure.

The option's theta specifically measures the option's time decay. The theta quantifies the rate at which options lose their value, specifically the time value or premium, as the expiration date draws near. A trader who is "positive theta" is actually "net short" options premium (extrinsic value) and hopes to collect premium as the option position deteriorates.

A trader who is "negative theta" is actually "net long" options premium (extrinsic value) and hopes other factors (i.e. underlying movement or a spike in implied volatility) will bring enough value to the option – subsequently offsetting the rate of decline in the options time-premium. An underlying long or short securities or futures position has zero theta as its value does not change with a change in date.

- Long (purchased) calls and puts contain negative or short theta.
- Short (sold) calls and puts contain positive or long theta.
- Underlying futures and securities contain zero theta.

Put-Call Parity and Options Theta

Generally speaking, due to put-call parity (see chapter two), a call and put with identical strike prices and expiration dates will – more or less – have the exact same rate of decay. That means the decay of a VIX March 10 dollar call (.80 delta) will have the same theta as the VIX March 10 dollar put (.20 delta).

However, in the case of options theta and securities, there can be slight theta variation between a same strike call and put. The theta difference between same strike (same month) calls and puts depends on the underlying securities cost-to-carry. Therefore, an underlying asset without a dividend or an implied dividend yield (i.e., stock index future) will have call and put thetas that are equal.

When the cost of carry for a stock is positive (i.e., dividend yield is less than the interest rate), theta for the call is higher than theta for the put. When the cost of carry for the stock is negative (i.e., dividend yield is greater than the interest rate), theta for the call is lower than that for the put.

- **Positive (security) "cost-of-carry":** the dividend yield is LESS than the interest rate; option theta for the call is higher than the corresponding put.

- **Negative (security) "cost-of-carry":** the dividend yield is GREATER than the interest rate; theta for the call is lower than the corresponding put.

Regarding "cost to carry" and "theta differences" - it should be noted that if a professional options trader incurs "cost to carry" via "theta difference" (between same strike call and put), the price of the theta will be enhanced by the interest paid on the premium, making it entirely neutral. In other words, a risk management system may show unequal theta yet that difference should be reflected in the premium of the option. If carry costs are 5.0% (they can also be a dollar figure), options theta should fall by 5% (or the amount of the perceived carry) of the total extrinsic value.

Theta Graph

Type	Theta Value	Effect of Time Decay
Long Call	Negative	Negative
Short Call	Positive	Positive
Long Put	Negative	Negative
Short Put	Positive	Positive
Underlying Asset	Zero	Zero

Figure I

Theta Distribution and Same Month Strike Prices

Consider the options chain for the 30-day SPY. Like options gamma and vega, theta reaches its highest point with at the money options and arithmetically decreases as the strike price moves further away from the at the money strike. This is due to at the money options holding the largest amount of extrinsic value, having a lot more time premium to lose in comparison to an in the money or out of the money option.

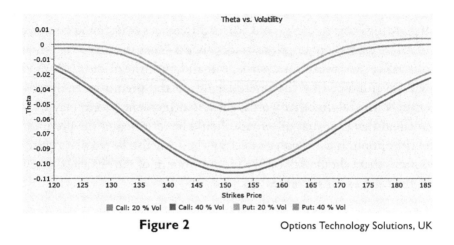

Figure 2   Options Technology Solutions, UK

In the world of classroom textbooks – a world without an implied volatility skew - a 10% out of the money put should have equal rate of theta as compared to a 10% out of the money call of the same month. However, implied options skew (see Chapter 11: Skew) muddies the waters.

Observe in Figure 2 the distinct amount of theta difference between equidistant calls and puts of the same month. This does not make mathematical sense but it's the current reality of options trading. The key takeaway is to understand the textbook answer (equidistant calls and puts will have equal theta) but embrace reality. Options skew is fluid and will challenge what the textbooks suggest. This will be discussed in detail in subsequent chapters.

Option Theta and Time

An option with more days to expiration will have more extrinsic value compared to an option with fewer days to expiration. However, even though there is more time premium in deferred options, the rate of decay is much quicker in shorter dated options. Other words, options decay is not constant, and the impact of time on options pricing may be more non-linear in nature than most would believe.

An option's rate of decay (theta) is arithmetically sloped, indicating that option theta will quicken as expiration draws nigh. (Particularly when options approach 30 days or less to expiration.)

However, it should be noted that decay accelerates (i.e. theta increases) as expiration approaches for at-the-money options while it actually slows down for both in the money and out of the money options.

THETA	Further to Expiration	Closer to Expiration
ATM Option	Lower Theta	Higher Theta
ITM & OTM Options	Higher Theta	Lower Theta

Figure 2a

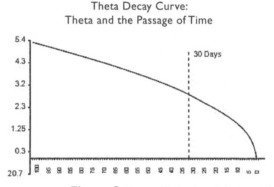

Theta Decay Curve:
Theta and the Passage of Time

Figure 3 Options Technology Solutions, UK

For example, the SPY July 190 put is worth $4.00, has twenty days until expiration, and has a theta of (-.20). The SPY September 190 put is worth $5.75, has eighty days until expiration, and has a theta of (-.05). with one-day passage of time – provided the price of SPY doesn't change, assuming there is no change in the implied volatility of either option, the value of the SPY July 190 put will drop by $0.20 to $3.80, whereas the value of the SPY September 190 put will drop by $.05 to $5.70.

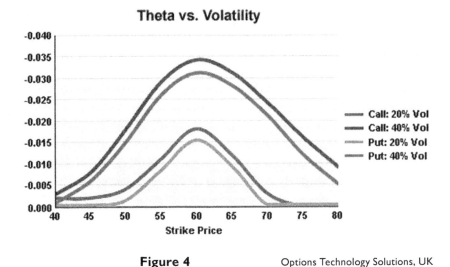

Figure 4   Options Technology Solutions, UK

Option Theta and Implied Volatility

What goes up must (eventually) come down. The higher the volatility level, the greater the extrinsic value added to an options price and thus a higher theta.

At-the-money options are the most vulnerable to time decay. And as Figure 5 shows below, options that are either deep, in the money or far out of the money will have relatively less decay (compared to at-the-money options) as they have less time premium. Consequently, changes in implied volatility (assuming everything else remains the same) will profoundly affect at the money options – spilling over to a lesser degree to both in the money and out of the money options.

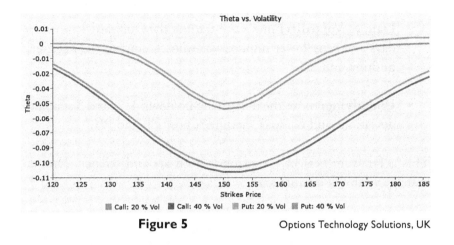

Figure 5   Options Technology Solutions, UK

Theta and its Practical Application

Double Whammy of Theta:

Most traders would agree that over the course of a trading career, losses incurred from negative theta (net long option premium) have the tendency to be larger than anticipated. This is owing to quiet or even range-bound markets (i.e. markets where underlying is not moving far enough to offset cost of decay) which, many times cause a reduction in implied volatility. Thus, the trader gets "double-whammy'd" with both decay and costs associated with being long implied volatility.

There are different types of solutions to this real-life risk of being negatively affected by both theta and volatility of which will be discussed in (Chapter 10: Volatility and Trading Decisions) and (Chapter 23: Practical Risk Management Solutions). However, for the purposes of this chapter, I will say an options trader must review his current greeks and compare them with:

- **Date:** move the trading date forward 1, 3, and 7 days (everything else constant) and compare net greek position and P/L.

91

- **Date & Volatility:** move the trading date forward 1, 3, and 7 days and raise/lower implied volatility. Compare the net greek position and P/L.

- **Underlying:** move the underlying up/down 1, 2, and 3 standard deviations and compare net greek position and P/L.

This is far from perfect – trading is both art and science. How to manage your risk is more art.

Theta – Volatility Flip

The new trader fails to remember that theta becomes more important as expiration draws near, whereas volatility becomes uniformly less important. Professional option market makers recognize that the risk in short-dated options is more theta, whereas the risk in back-month options is chiefly volatility. And that relationship and importance flips as expiration draws closer.

Those who don't fully expect or grasp the implications (and how their importance swaps places) of theta (time) and vega (implied volatility) are subject to pricy mistakes. Say you think the SPX will trade up from its current price of $1910. You decide to buy a one-month call with a strike price of $1925 for a premium of $1.00. As the days pass, the price for SPX moves up to $1912, but the call option is now worth only $1.50. Why? What happened?

In this very basic example, even though the SPX went up, implied volatility went down. Although the underlying index moves up $2, the option will not necessarily mirror that movement. Also, the option loses value as it nears expiration; it has less time to move toward being in the money. Both of these factors affect the movement of the option independently from its underlying.

Many traders don't understand (or don't care to know) how important the greeks are; therefore, they become dejected by the seemingly haphazard movement of the option even though their predictions about the underlying were correct. Options are non-linear and there are complexities at work that may reward you even though you were wrong about the movement or, more often, cause you suffering even when you were right about direction.

It is not overly far-fetched for vega and theta to sometimes work against you. In a volatile market, you're short a put while the underlying goes up, and your option still loses money! You see vega beat theta! If you asked professional traders whether they make more money trading delta, direction, or vega, most of them would say that their money was made through vega.

Theta and the Real World

We know that an at the money option includes the most negative theta – it has the highest rate of decay. Theta is also a certainty—the certainty lies in that options are wasting assets and, if adequately out-of-money, will shed value the closer they get to their expiry. What's not certain is although theta is a path-independent measure – it's not a proxy for a market that continually makes moves yet ultimately reverts back to the mean.

Theta is Inevitable – a game of musical chairs

In either a rising volatility environment or a large move in the underlying it's often difficult to comprehend that one day theta will start producing decay in options. Consider a trading environment where volatility spikes day after day—even with small moves in the underlying— the projected theta will rise, but it won't be necessarily realized.

Recall, implied volatility is just that—implied. The options are suggesting that the market will have a larger variance compared to the past. When trading or managing options, think on the plain and simple insurance industry scenario. The buyer of options is paying a premium (negative theta) to transfer his risk to another and that premium erodes with time. The seller of option premium is the insurance underwriter – they are assuming the risk and receive potential premium as payment.

Theta – no right answers

Some traders will show their position thetas representing one day's worth of time decay; others show thetas giving three or even seven days' worth of decay. Some keep days constant and focus on decay vs. changes in implied volatility. There may be differences on when decay is being experienced – for example, decay may be bigger on a Friday since you will lose two more days over the weekend when there is no trading. In some cases, the decay may occur in the morning rather than at the end of the day, as the market anticipates a loss in value to the option due to the passage of time.

Theta as an asset class boils down to cautiously constructing the risk you will be managing. Extensive experience and a deep knowledge of trading in options markets can only help because theory, as everyone knows, has its drawbacks.

Recognize danger and react quickly. Thetas when combined with moves in underlying and/or volatility are strange bedfellows. Unlike some other theoretical values, volatility is based solely on opinion, fear, and supply and demand. Theta, though, is eventually certain— the certainty lies in that options are wasting assets and, if sufficiently out of the money, will lose value the closer they get to their expiry.

CHAPTER 7

The "other option Greeks": Secondary Option Greeks & Greeks of the Second Order

AJS on trading and the knowable:

A concise awareness that the future is not-knowable is paramount yet, what can be knowable is how your perceived or not-perceived risks can be − to a degree − accounted for through a thorough understanding of the option greeks and their many implications to you and your risk management.

Being able to manage risk is a key element in trading success. However, an often overlooked or dismissed component involves the identification and the foreknowledge of that risk. A concise awareness that the future is not-knowable is paramount yet, what can be knowable is how your perceived or not-perceived risks can be − to a degree − accounted for through a thorough understanding of the option greeks and their many implications to you and your risk management.

This chapter will highlight the definitions of some of the minor greeks including – Rho, Omega, Vanna, Vomma, and Charm. These lesser-known greeks are used as various measures of change and should be understood as second-nature to the options participant.

Managing risk is a nice concept on a conceptual basis - the difficulty often revolves around its measurement. Options risk management always requires a person who recognizes there are both embedded risks and the risk of change. This chapter is by no means exhaustive; the intention is to give the reader a foundation to build upon in subsequent chapters on strategy and risk management.

Rho

Definition

Rho is the sensitivity of option value to change in interest rates. Rho indicates the absolute change in option value for a one percent change in the interest rate.

Rho is particularly pertinent to securities whereas due to margining, futures contract don't require a cash outlay and that amount deposited earns interest - a change in interest rates will have a zero effect on futures options.

For example, you're pricing a call option with a theoretical value of 5.50 that is showing a Rho value of .10. If interest rates increase from 2% to 3%, then the price of the call option, theoretically at least will increase from 5.50 to 5.60.

As seen in the below graph (Figure 1), option rho for calls and puts react in a polar opposite direction; calls move from zero to a positive number as the underlying rises while puts move from a negative figure towards zero under the same conditions.

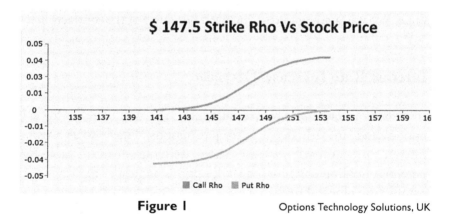

Figure I Options Technology Solutions, UK

Rho and Put-Call Parity

Unlike the other greeks discussed thus far, rho and its influence on same strike, same month, calls and puts differ. To understand the valuation differences between same strike, same month call and puts, one must first understand forward pricing and how it relates to options valuation.

Forward Price

In simple terms, when a trader calculates the "fair-value" of an option, he must make an assumption (whether he knows it or not) of what the underlying will be worth at expiry. This is known as the "forward price" and it can be expressed in terms of the current price of the underlying including any cost of carry (e.g. interest, dividends). Although one can never know exactly what this price will be, all other things being equal, it must be worth at least the cost of holding the underlying until the expiration date. This value basically replicates what it would cost someone to borrow funds and invest in the asset until the expiration date.

What is the estimated value of an option on a present-day basis? When you think on it, the price of an option today is based on its perceived future value. What is it going to cost you over the course of the contracts life?

Interest Rate Increase/Decrease

In a rising interest rate environment, the rho will increase for call options and similarly decrease for put options. This is so as a rising interest rates similarly increases the underlying's forward price (or, potential holding cost) making call options a cheaper replication to owning the physical underlying.

In a falling interest rate environment, the opposite takes effect where rho will drop for call options and increase for put options. As borrowing costs fade so do the costs of owning or replication – thus, calls become less of an attractive alternative.

- Increasing interest rate environment – call premiums increase put premiums decrease.

- Falling interest rate environment – call premiums decrease put premiums increase.

- Calls on a security will have a positive rho as a rise in interest rates indicates a call option will be relatively cheaper to own then the underlying security and vice versa for the put options, which have a negative Rho.

Rho and Same Month Options Chain

In polar-opposites to other greeks, rho depends not on distance from the at the money strike but how deep the option is in the money relative to the underlying. Rho is largest for deep in the money and steadily decreases as the option moves out of the-money. This should make sense as rho reflects cash-flow replication costs. A participant who wishes to replicate the SPX cash index will be more likely to purchase 1.00 delta calls and not .50 delta calls or .10 delta calls.

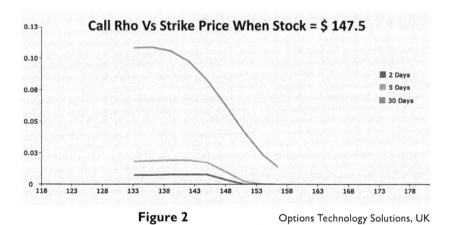

Figure 2   Options Technology Solutions, UK

Rho and Time to Expiration

More time to expiration equates to more unknowns and greater risk of cost-of-carry. With that, and similar to vega - options rho will generally increase with more time to expiration. Not only is the time of cost to carry longer, so is the time of uncertainty of the yield curve.

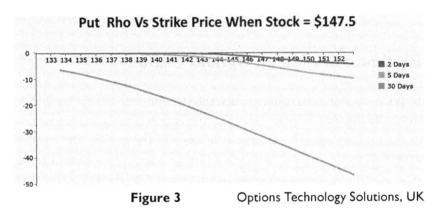

Figure 3   Options Technology Solutions, UK

Rho and Practical Application

Over the years, and over mistakes made, it becomes engrained in a trader's mind that any options position producing short deltas (i.e. a position where the trader needs to purchase underlying) would generally have a negative reaction to rising interest rates. Other words, a trader who is net short (sold) calls or long (purchased) puts will be vulnerable if interest rates rise. Conversely, a trader whose position requires short hedging (i.e. an option position of net long calls and short puts) would benefit from a rising interest rate environment.

- The higher the price of the security, the higher the interest costs. Financing a $1,000 security will cost more than a $20 security.

- The longer time until expiry will translate to greater sensitivity to changes in interest rates and thus higher rho values.

- Due to margining, futures contract don't require a cash outlay and that amount deposited earns interest - a change in interest rates will have a zero effect on futures options.

- One of rho's limitations is it assumes a parallel shift in the interest rate yield-curve one with a smooth and continuous line.

- Rho is expressed as a positive number for calls and negative number for puts.

Option Omega or Lambda

Definition(s) of Omega

Omega is a measure of the change in an option's value with respect to the percentage change in the underlying price. The omega gives option traders an estimate of how their options positions and the asset price that underlies it move together. Omega is the third derivative of the option price, and the derivative of gamma.

Omega symbolizes the percentage change in an option's value with respect to the percentage change in the underlying price. Omega is one of the greeks, used chiefly in large options portfolios, to help provide clarity to the trader on the positions current leverage factor.

Omega – also referred to as "lambda" or leverage factor" is used as a measure of leverage to the participant.

Example

As way of example, if SPX underlying increases 3% during a specific, defined period of time and an SPX call option increases 1% during that same period, the omega of the call option would be 1 divided by

3 or 0.33%. The omega infers that for every 1 percent SPX underlying move, the call option will move 0.33%.

Practical Application

Omega is really a by-product of the delta since it is basically the result of the delta multiplied by the ratio of the underlying price over the option price. In other words, equivalent to the mathematical derivative of the option price with respect to the underlying price.

Because of its straightforward relationship with the delta and its non-direct correlation with hedging, the omega is not a very widely used greek. Traders prefer to use the delta as this provides them their risk profile directly. Lambda can be a useful measure for a leverage indication but is fairly redundant otherwise.

Options Leverage and Risk

Leverage is both the beauty and danger of options – more leverage (i.e. deep out of the money options) means more exponential upside potential (buyer) but can also denote exponential amounts of risk for the options seller. An Omega of 30 would generally infer that the participant would need to trade 30 times the premium of the option (notional value) to mimic the same gain or loss using the underlying future or security.

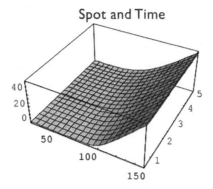

Figure 4   Options Technology Solutions, UK

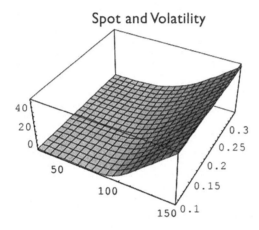

Figure 5   Options Technology Solutions, UK

The bottom line is an options position can give participants similar/ same exposure as the underlying yet with much less up-front capital costs. Additionally, the leveraging power of options can both magnify gains and losses as compared to a direct position in the underlying.

AJS Key Takeaway on option risk management:

Option risk management always requires a person who recognizes there are both embedded risks and the *risk of change*.

Some Second Order Greeks

Simply and practically speaking, second-order greeks measure how quickly first-order greeks (i.e. delta, vega, theta, rho) are going to change with regards to changes in:

- Underlying movement

- Implied volatility

- Passage of time

- Interest rates

Vanna

Vanna measures the movements of the delta with respect to incremental changes in implied volatility (1% change in implied volatility). Alternatively, it can also be interpreted as the fluctuations of vega with respect to small changes in the underlying asset price. Call options have positive vanna, and puts have negative vanna. This is because an increase in implied volatility raises market expectancies of the chance of any particular call or put expiring in-the-money. Recall (Chapter 3: "Options Delta") the discussion on delta and its convergence towards .50 delta. Additionally, vanna can provide the trader with an estimate of the distribution of option premium along various strike prices along the curve.

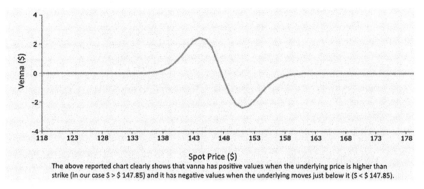

Spot Price ($)

The above reported chart clearly shows that vanna has positive values when the underlying price is higher than strike (in our case S > $ 147.85) and it has negative values when the underlying moves just below it (S < $ 147.85).

Figure 6   Options Technology Solutions, UKFigure

Vomma

Vomma measures how vega is going to change with respect to implied volatility and it is normally expressed in order to quantify the influence on vega should the volatility oscillate by 1 point. As displayed in the above graph, out of the money options generally contain the highest vomma, while at the money options have a low vomma. This indicates that vega remains almost constant with respect to volatility. Options traders know this is definitely NOT reality!

The shape of vomma is something that every options trader should be mindful of while trading because it explicitly proves that the vega that will be most influenced by a variation in volatility will be the out of the money options while, on the other hand, the relationship with the at the money options will remain fairly static. This makes sense (going back to the chapters on first-order greeks and their behavior) since a change in implied volatility would increase the likelihood of out of the money options to expire in the money and this is exactly why vomma is the highest around the out of the money portion of the options curve.

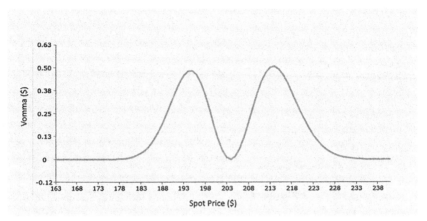

Figure 7   Options Technology Solutions, UKFigure

Charm

Charm (or Delta Bleed): Charm measures an options delta's sensitivity to a small movement in time passage. In practical terms, it shows how the delta is going to change (all else being equal) with one or more days in the future. Option charm is one of the "other greeks" used on a regular basis by those managing large or complex options positions.

Similar to vanna, options charm reaches its highest absolute value when the options are near or around at the money. Practically and with some experience noted, marginally in the money or out of the money options will have the highest charm values.

This hopefully will begin to resonate as common sense given the greatest impact of theta (time-decay) is on at the money or near at the money options. The closer one gets to expiry, the more deep in the money options will replicate underlying and deep out of the money options replicate worthlessness. Consequently, the deltas of at-the-money or slightly in the money or out of the money options will be the most eroded by time.

As discussed in chapter three (Chapter 3: "Options Delta") options charm is a mix of art and science yet crucial to options traders

– especially those with multi-month, multi-strike positions. An experienced (and, honest) options trader will attest to the sheer agony of option charm – especially as one gets closer to expiration. Only experience will give the trader wisdom on when and how to view charm when hedging an options portfolio. How to think about hedging with deltas that you may or may not have is one of the hardest questions to answer.

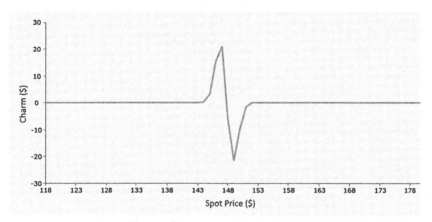

Figure 8   Options Technology Solutions, UKFigure

CHAPTER 8

Greek Behavior – Time & Space

The intent of this chapter is to combine concepts learned in Chapters 3 through 7 and to begin applying them in real-life trading situations. Although we have yet to cover option trading strategies, we can – at the very minimum – begin to make sense how options traders think about the greeks when applying risk management or trading implementation. As previously mentioned, the greeks are simply an estimate and the successful application thereof requires a balance of artistic impression and scientific notation. The chapter will look at greeks with changes in time and space.

Greeks and the passage of time

SPY	188.00		Expiry	90 Days	
Call Strike	Value	Delta	Gamma	Vega	Theta
178.00	12.80	77	0.017	0.21	0.036
183.00	9.60	64	0.023	0.32	0.046
188.00	6.80	50	0.25	0.33	0.047
193.00	4.30	38	0.027	0.33	0.045
198.00	2.70	26	0.021	0.24	0.035

Figure I SPY Options Chain with 90-days until expiry

90-Days till Expiration: Take notice of the above table and focus particularly on the various differences with regards to the strike prices and their greek values. As way of review, take note:

- At the money call strike (188.00) delta will be somewhere near .50-delta.

- There is a slight implied volatility skew (Chapter 11: "Option Volatility Skew") as judged by the disparity of extrinsic value and greeks between equidistant strikes.

- The 178.00 strike is $10.00 away from the at the money strike (188.00) and has $2.80 of extrinsic value. Compare that to the 198.00 strike – also $10.00 away from the at the money strike (188.00) yet has $2.70 of extrinsic value (Extrinsic Value is also known as Time Value).

- Delta: due to the apparent implied volatility skew, the equidistant strike deltas will vary as well. Notice the 178.00 strike has a .77 delta. Due to put-call parity rules, that would imply a put delta of (-.23) as the absolute value of a strike price will be 1.00. However, if you compare the 188.00 strike, it shows a .26 delta.

This would imply a 188.00 put delta of (-.74). The delta difference is the result of the implied volatility skew.

- Gamma: With regards to skew, observe that gamma does not line up properly between equidistant strike prices. Take special notice that the gamma for the beneath the money strikes (i.e. 178 & 183) is lower than the gamma for the above the money strikes. Recall from Chapter 4: "Options Gamma" where it was explained that higher implied volatility will REDUCE gamma and vice-versa. Here is a perfect example as the SPY beneath the money strikes are being artificially inflated with premium – thus the reduction in gamma relative to the above the money strike prices.

- Vega: With implied volatility skew in mind, the vega differences between equidistant strikes is barely noticeable – a result of a "relatively" high implied volatility level. A very common phenomenon for an equity index option with 90-days remaining till its expiration. Take notice that although vega is at its greatest point with at-the-money strikes, this doesn't yet fully apply as both the 183 & 193 strikes have similar vega to the 188.00 strike at this stage. Recall the old trading floor saying, "Front month has gamma and back-month has volatility." It applies with this much time till expiration.

- Theta: With 90-days until expiry, options decay is not much of a factor. At this implied volatility level and skew levels, you may notice that theta is fairly well distributed amongst the options curve. This will remain so unless skew continues to rise OR with the passage of time.

SPY	188.00		Expiry	60 Days	
Call Strike	Value	Delta	Gamma	Vega	Theta
178.00	11.60	80	0.02	0.14	0.051
183.00	8.30	68	0.03	0.22	0.059
188.00	5.60	50	0.047	0.29	0.066
193.00	3.59	33	0.041	0.24	0.057
198.00	2.20	18	0.027	0.165	0.042

Figure 2 SPY Options Chain with 60-days until expiry

60-Days till Expiration: Moving time (keeping everything else constant) forward 30 days, compare this options chain with the 90-day chain.

Noteworthy observations include:

- Delta: In the money strike deltas are climbing towards 1.00, while out of the money deltas are falling towards 0. Notice the 188.00 strike (at the money) is still being published as a .50-delta option.

- Gamma: As we get slowly closer to expiration, gammas will begin to bunch towards the at-the-money strike. Notice that all strike gammas increased although only meaningfully so with the strikes nearest to the money.

- Vega: Options vega has decreased across all strikes – that should make sense as vega becomes less of an issue (relative to gamma), the closer one gets to expiration. Notice that the at the money strike still contains the most vega. To reiterate, vega is an important metric but not so on a comparative basis to a 90-day option.

- Theta: With 60 days until expiration, you are starting to detect some decay separation between strikes. At this point, theta is slowly increasing amongst all strike prices. Take special note of the theta of the 178.00 strike (-.051) versus the equidistant 198.00 strike (-.042) Due to the implied volatility skew, the downside (below the money strikes) has a higher implied volatility and thus, more extrinsic value to potentially lose.

SPY	188.00		Expiry	30 Days	
Call Strike	Value	Delta	Gamma	Vega	Theta
178.00	10.50	87	0.02	0.04	0.07
183.00	5.60	75	0.04	0.08	0.10
188.00	2.80	51	0.06	0.1	0.17
193.00	0.45	20	0.03	0.06	0.09
198.00	0.06	4	0.02	0.02	0.03

Figure 3 SPY Options Chain with 30-days until expiry

30-Days till Expiration: Again, we move time forward another 30-days without altering implied volatility levels, skew, or movement in the underlying.

- **Delta:** In the money strike deltas are rapidly climbing towards 1.00 delta, while out of the money deltas are quickly falling towards 0. Similar to previous examples, the at the money strike (188.00) has a delta stuck at .50.

- **Gamma:** A divergence is quickly taking place whereas gamma is becoming more concentrated at the 188.00 strike and precipitously falling on the outer strikes (178.00 & 198.00). Due to options skew, you may notice a variation between the gamma of the 183.00 (0.04) and 193.00 (0.03) strikes. Skew is keeping an inordinate amount of extrinsic value of the 183.00 strike (relative to the 193.00 strike) and thus, "gamma decay" is occurring at a slower rate.

- **Vega:** The passage of time has decreased vega along each strike – yet, it is still highest along the at the money strike. At this stage, it's easier to appreciate the impact of implied volatility skew on strike vega. The vega for the in the money strike(s) – 178.00 (.04) and 183.00 (.08) are noticeably higher than the equidistant out of the money strikes 193.00 (.06) and 198.00 (.02).

- **Theta:** 30-days till expiry tend to be the inflection point for theta. Recall in Chapter 6: "Options Theta" how options decay follows a fairly arithmetic formula until about 30 days out when it becomes more exponential in nature. In this example, you can plainly see how quickly decay has increased relative to the example with 60 days until expiry. Also worth noting is the decay estimate of the 198.00 strike. According to the estimate, the 198.00 call will be worthless in two trading days. This is possible but not likely as the 198.00 call will most likely hold some value much longer than what theta dictates.

SPY	188.00			Expiry	10 Days	
Call Strike	Value	Delta	Gamma	Vega	Theta	
178.00	10.05	95	0.00	0	0.01	
183.00	5.15	82	0.02	0.02	0.03	
188.00	1.00	50	0.42	0.1	0.30	
193.00	0.10	10	0.02	0.02	0.02	
198.00	0.01	1	0.00	0	0.01	

Figure 4 SPY Options Chain with 10-days until expiry

10 Days till Expiration: An options chain with 10 days until expiration is the most straightforward and simple to understand. The situation becomes a lot more black and white in terms of an option expiring either in the money or out of the money. Greeks become less and less of a factor – it's all about the expiring strike price at this stage.

Delta: With 10 days remaining options will be quickly moving towards 1.00 or 0 delta. The significant difference is the at-the-money strike (188.00) which will remain at 50-delta up through and including expiration day if the underlying remains at 188.00.

Gamma: At this point – with 10 days remaining and the underlying SPY stuck at 188.00 - the vast majority of gamma will be concentrated on the 188.00 strike. This should be clear as the 188.00 strike will either be a 1.00 or 0 delta at expiration. Recall, gamma is at its highest point amongst a .50-delta option. It's also very worth noting that strike gamma – with 10 days to go – can change rapidly. A $1.00 move in SPY would cause gamma to begin falling in the 188.00 strike and transferring it to the strike the SPY is approaching.

Vega: As we know, with 10 days remaining until expiration, implied volatility will have little effect on option prices. This can be plainly seen as options vega has all but evaporated from the strike prices along the options curve.

Theta: An important point to reiterate is options decay is now highly concentrated on the 188.00 strike while much less on the strikes away from the money. Perhaps not intuitive, it must be remembered that both the in the money and out of the money strikes have lost (on a real basis) most of their extrinsic value; the remaining premium will typically "drip" very slowly and methodically throughout the last 10 days remaining till expiration.

Greeks and Space

SPY	185.00		Expiry	30 Days		
Call Strike	Value	Delta	Gamma	Vega	Theta	IV
187.00	3.35	43	0.04	0.20	-0.08	24.00
189.00	2.44	35	0.04	0.19	-0.07	22.50
191.00	1.66	27	0.03	0.17	-0.06	21.50
193.00	1.04	20	0.03	0.15	-0.06	20.75
195.00	0.60	13	0.02	0.11	-0.04	20.00
SPY	191.50		Expiry	30 Days		
Call Strike	Value	Delta	Gamma	Vega	Theta	IV
187.00	6.85	66	0.03	0.19	-0.07	24.00
189.00	5.45	59	0.03	0.20	-0.07	22.50
191.00	4.19	52	0.04	0.21	-0.07	21.50
193.00	3.07	43	0.04	0.21	-0.06	20.75
195.00	2.12	35	0.04	0.21	-0.05	20.00

Figure 5   SPY Option Greeks within Space

Option greeks are very straightforward estimates yet should not be used on a stand alones basis. Successful trading requires disciplined risk management which requires a good mixture of estimation and mathematics. The next part of this chapter will focus on greeks and profit/loss estimates with regards to movement in the underlying.

The next examples will balance both the theoretical and practical application. We will be looking at:

SPDR: S&P 500 ETF (SPY)

- 30-day American Option.

- Compare metrics at a SPY underlying price of $188.00 versus an ending price of $191.50.

- Option multiplier = $100.00. If you purchase a SPY option for $2.00, you are paying $200.00 per option.

SPY	185.00		Expiry	30 Days		
Call Strike	Value	Delta	Gamma	Vega	Theta	IV
187.00	3.35	43	0.04	0.20	-0.08	24.00
189.00	2.44	35	0.04	0.19	-0.07	22.50
191.00	1.66	27	0.03	0.17	-0.06	21.50
193.00	1.04	20	0.03	0.15	-0.06	20.75
195.00	0.60	13	0.02	0.11	-0.04	20.00

Figure 6   SPY Option Greeks within Space – 185.00

Starting Point: SPDR: S&P 500 ETF (SPY) - $185.00

Take notice of the following details:

- The example is out of the money calls from the 187.00 through 195.00 strike prices.

- Expiration is 30 days away.

- Gamma – fairly smooth gamma curve yet slightly higher (as it should be) with strikes nearer to the at-the-money strike.

119

- Vega – highest vega with strike nearest to the at the money strike, option vega arithmetically descends with distance from the at the money strike.

- Theta – options are decaying at fairly similar rates at this stage in the cycle. Strike theta will begin to become much more distinct with each passing day.

- Implied Volatility – notice the volatility difference between strikes. Other words, there is currently 1.5 volatility points between the 187.00 and 189.00 strike prices but only .75 volatility points between the 193.00 and 195.00 strike prices.

SPY	191.50		Expiry	30 Days		
Call Strike	Value	Delta	Gamma	Vega	Theta	IV
187.00	6.85	66	0.03	0.19	-0.07	24.00
189.00	5.45	59	0.03	0.20	-0.07	22.50
191.00	4.19	52	0.04	0.21	-0.07	21.50
193.00	3.07	43	0.04	0.21	-0.06	20.75
195.00	2.12	35	0.04	0.21	-0.05	20.00

Figure 7   SPY Option Greeks within Space – 191.500

Ending Point: SPDR: S&P 500 ETF (SPY) - $191.50

Take note of the following changes from $185.00 to $191.50. Also, bear in mind, a one-day $6.50 point move in SPY would be considered a very large move. This would translate into a +60.50 up-move in the S&P 500 futures. A dramatic move was necessary to help better demonstrate various points.

Take notice of the following details:

- The example is out of the money calls from the 187.00 through 195.00 strike prices.

- A significant one-day move with 30 days until expiration.

- The implied volatility curve (between $185.00 and $191.50) did NOT shift. This is definitely not realistic however necessary for our purposes.

- Delta – has shifted up in synchronization with the markets up-move. Note that the $6.50 move has basically shifted the option deltas accordingly. Thus, the 187.00 strike originally had a. 43 delta. With the move, the 193.00 strike now has a .43 delta.

- Gamma – with the up-move, gamma moves as well. It increases with strikes nearest-to-the-money and reduces the further the strike is from the underlying price.

- Vega – continues to be highest with near-the-money strikes. This simply shifts with the new underlying price.

- Theta - continues to be highest with near-the-money strikes. This simply shifts with the new underlying price.

Profit-Loss Example and Points for Consideration:

Details:

- Purchase 100 calls

- Hedge accordingly (e.g. purchasing 100 .43 delta calls would require you to sell 4,300 shares; the current amount estimated by "delta" to replicate the underlying).

In the Figure 8 below, it goes without saying that any one of these call purchases could be a very profitable trade indeed. Sadly, this is theoretical – there is more to it than meets the eye.

$6.50	P/L		
Call Strike	Call P/L	Hedge P/L	Net P/L
187.00	$35,000	-$27,950	**$7,050**
189.00	$30,100	-$22,750	**$7,350**
191.00	$25,300	-$17,550	**$7,750**
193.00	$20,300	-$13,000	**$7,300**
195.00	$15,200	-$8,450	**$6,750**

Figure 8

P/L - Implied Volatility Change

Using history and experience as a guide, a $6.50 up-move in SPY would generally cause implied volatility to drop. To further complicate matters, the market would most likely see a drop in implied volatility along with a shift in implied volatility skew (not covered in this chapter – see Chapter 11: "Options Skew") causing out of the money call values to languish.

Generally speaking this type of market up-move would force implied volatility down approximately 3.0 volatility points. Figure 9 below table shows each strikes profit-and-loss with a $6.50 up-move AND a reduction of 3.0 in implied volatility.

(-3) Vols	Static Skew	P/L	
Call Strike	Call P/L	Hedge P/L	Net P/L
187.00	$29,000	-$27,950	**$1,050**
189.00	$24,400	-$22,750	**$1,650**
191.00	$20,200	-$17,550	**$2,650**
193.00	$15,800	-$13,000	**$2,800**
195.00	$11,900	-$8,450	**$3,450**

Figure 9

P/L – Implied Volatility and Theta

Assume the SPY has just finished making its +6.50 point move and implied volatility has come down -3.0 volatility points. It's now mid-day – the market is sitting still and one-day theta begins to come out of each option. Below is the P/L of fully hedged call trades with movement, implied volatility reduction, and full theta being expressed.

(-3) Vols	1-Day	P/L	
Call Strike	Call P/L	Hedge P/L	Net P/L
187.00	$28,300	-$27,950	$350
189.00	$23,700	-$22,750	$950
191.00	$19,500	-$17,550	$1,950
193.00	$15,200	-$13,000	$2,200
195.00	$11,400	-$8,450	$2,950

Figure 10

In this final (theoretical yet not terribly out of the ordinary) example, you will see the final P/L numbers have been significantly reduced.

- 187.00 strike (-95%) to $350

- 189.00 strike (-87%) to $950

- 191 strike (-75%) to $1,950

- 193 strike (-70%) to $2,200

- 195 strike (-56%) to $2,950

Important and Practical Takeaways:

- These examples are realistic yet also highly theoretical. Every market environment is different.

- This exercise demonstrates the importance of hedging correctly. Imagine the P/L difference if you were off by a few deltas.

- The importance of strike selection is highlighted as you can compare the difference in leverage between purchasing the 187.00 strike and the 195.00 strike.

- This example shows a +$6.50 "gap" move with stark before and after greeks. Imagine if this had been a slower move – would you have sold long deltas (accumulated due to the positive gamma position) earlier? Obviously doing so would have been detrimental when considering the subsequent implied volatility move and decay.

PART III

Volatility Surface

CHAPTER 9

Introduction to Option Volatility

As an intern and young trader/market maker working for as well as representing Saliba Partners LLC on the floor of the Chicago Board of Options Exchange I learned from Tony Saliba, and other senior traders, the unwritten company motto: "staying spread is staying alive". Ultimately what defines a successful trader is the profit and loss that shows up on the daily trading sheets, but managing risk and adapting to the ever-changing nuances of the market place is what keeps the doors open.

-John Saliba

The Journey of Volatility

Volatility is a fundamental market force. It is a statistical measurement (a number) of the probability dispersion or variability of a random variable known as standard deviation or sigma. It measures changes in prices, not direction.

Fischer Black and Myron Scholes, while creating the option pricing enigma in the early 1970s, followed more or less the same reasoning and thought process as Einstein. The math and the physics was precisely the same. Only the context was different and certain broad (and sweeping) suppositions were made about the economy and the investors in relating the problem in physics to that in financial economics. Going from a statistical measurement, to becoming an exchanged traded asset is the story of volatility. From Harry Markowitz to Milton Friedman, to the Chicago Board Options Exchange (CBOE) is a very short distance. But it's been a long and fascinating journey in time.

From the when option trading began on the CBOE in 1973, participants traded options for their value, which was captured mainly by the volatility of the underlying. Therefore, traders were buying and selling volatility using options and options strategies (indirectly at least).

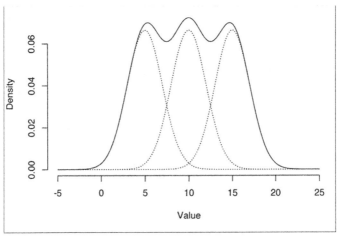

Mixed Probability Distribution

Volatility on a Conceptual and Mathematical Basis

First and foremost, volatility is an essential concept in determining the value of an option and it can be viewed from two angles: conceptually and mathematically.

- Conceptually, volatility is essentially the measurement of an underlying's tendency to move up and down in price over a given period of time. It is also the only variable in an option pricing model not known with certainty in advance.

- Mathematically, volatility can be defined as *the annualized standard deviation of daily returns of a given underlying.*

It is crucial to understand that volatility has a straightforward relationship with an option's price: as the percentage of volatility increases, the price of the option likewise increases. Why?

1. First, options volatility is tied to the price movement of the underlying instrument.

2. Second, a higher volatility means that the underlying has a greater likelihood of movement.

3. Third, an underlying with a greater likelihood of movement has a higher probability of reaching the exercise price.

4. Fourth, an underlying with a higher probability of reaching its exercise price will have a relatively higher price than one with a lower probability of reaching the exercise price. (Note that all this can be demonstrated mathematically and graphically by a look at low medium and high volatility distribution curves).

Below are three statistical tendencies of volatility that are crucial for the trader to understand. All of these tendencies can greatly assist the trader in deciding when, or at what point, to execute trades.

A. Mean Reversion: Volatility tends to be mean reverting. Over the short and intermediate terms, when markets become imbalanced, volatility fluctuations can be violent. But when the underlying market finally achieves balance, volatility will tend to revert back to its long term mean. This is a hugely important fact for volatility traders, those who buy and sell chiefly by looking at a stock's volatility levels. In other words, if for whatever reason the market (or an individual stock) has experienced a significant rise or dip, and volatility levels have changed drastically from what has been established as the "norm" (here the mean), it is most likely that the levels will eventually revert back to the long-term mean.

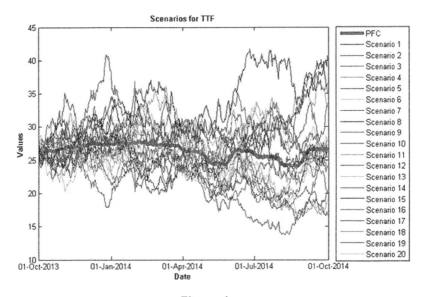

Figure I

B. Serial Correlation: Volatility over a given time period is highly correlated to the volatility of the previous identical time period. In other words, the volatility of the next 30 days is statistically likely to be similar to the last 30 days. This interesting characteristic is referred to as serial correlation. This is an important piece of information for the trader wishing to go long or short volatility. The volatility trader will always check movement in volatility against previous period's parameters.

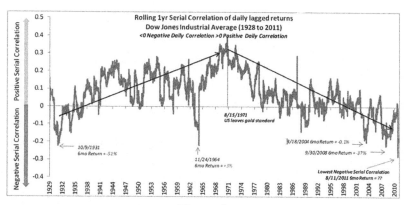

Figure 2

C. Relationship to Time: Volatility fluctuates inversely with respect to time. As short term volatility is moved away from the mean by various and sundry short term events, it has less chance to return to the mean because of time restriction. Longer term volatility, on the other hand, has a greater amount of time to revert to that mean. Options are wasting assets - their value diminishes over time. Thus, the volatility trader must always be simultaneously aware of current and past volatility levels, as well as the time value of the option he is trading.

Definitions of the Types of Volatility

It is important to note that options professionals actually describe volatility in four different ways. Equally important is to introduce the notions of volatility using minimum mathematics.

- **Historical Volatility** is the measure of price changes of an instrument (a stock, index, etc.) over a given period of time. Think of it as the instruments "up and down-ness", for a short and pithy definition. Historical volatility can also be defined mathematically as the stock's annualized standard deviation of daily returns.

131

- **Expected Volatility** is more subjective. In essence, this simply refers to the trader's best guess as to what volatility will be. Of course, these aren't blind guesses: most traders study historical charts and look at market conditions to come up with the expected volatility value. But they are estimates nonetheless.

- **Realized volatility** is the volatility that will be realized between the present date and a certain time in the future (expiration date). It is essentially future volatility, and is unknown.

- **Future Volatility** is a statistical/mathematical concept. By definition it is the annualized standard deviation of daily returns during a yet to be specified future period of time. This period typically extends from the present to the option's expiration. Most importantly for our purposes, future volatility is the number needed to plug into an option pricing model in order to determine an option's theoretical value.

- **Implied Volatility** is the volatility value (expressed in % form) that justifies or implies the current market price of the option. In other words, it is the value for volatility that the market implies at its present trading range. Other words, implied volatility is a number derived from the option prices for a given strike price and maturity.

A Non-Mathematical Approach to Historical and Implied Volatility

Options traders generally look at two measures of volatility: *historical* and *implied* volatility. Professionals think of them in this fashion:

Historical volatility measures the change in the value of an underlying based on historical prices over a distinct period of time. Generally, traders determine historical volatility by calculating the daily average percentage change in price for an underlying over a pre-defined time period. This average is then presented as an annualized percentage. Historical volatility is often referred to as actual volatility or realized volatility and is discussed in detail in Chapter 10.

- Historical volatility is measured by taking the daily (close-to-close) percentage price changes in an underlying and calculating the average over a given time period. This average is then expressed as an annualized percentage.

- Professional traders tend to use shorter time periods for measuring historical volatility, the most common being five-day, 10-day, 20-day and 30-day. Retail investors tend to use longer time periods, most commonly 60-day, 180-day and 360-day.

Implied volatility is the current volatility of an underlying, as shown by the changes in the price of the option based on that asset. To calculate the price for an options contract, traders use the following values:

- Strike price
- Expiration date
- Current price of the underlying
- Projected dividend payments
- Current interest rates

Implied volatility acts as a proxy for option value. It is the only parameter in option pricing that is not directly observable from the market, and cannot be "hedged" or offset with some other trading instrument. A wise, experienced options trader knows that an option's implied volatility is merely an estimate and should be treated as such.

Practical Example on Predicting Volatility

Imagine we are all traders and we must make a prediction of a future volatility value. To do this, we are going to have to look at some data concerning historical volatilities. Most traders find it easiest to plot the data and view it graphically. For conceptual purposes, I will forgo the graph and use some bare numbers.

Historical Volatility Values for Underlying ABC

Past 30 trading	days	20%
Past 60 trading	days	18%
Past 120 trading	days	16%
Past 250 trading	days	14%

First of all, if we were predicting the volatility for a long-term option, then we are justified in appealing to the mean reversion tendency. In this case, we might just look at the 250-day, long-term historical volatility value, and call this the mean. In other words, for long-term options the volatility over the life of the option should be close to 14%.

For shorter-term options we are not justified in using this value. How can we use the data on historical volatility that we have while also utilizing the pattern of serial correlation to our advantage? One way that traders do this is to assign a weight to each historical volatility value, assigning greater weight to the most recent historical information. Remember the best predictor of the value of options volatility over a given (short) period of time, is the value that it exhibited over the same, most recent period of time. Thus, the 20% figure may be assigned the greatest weight. Let us use the short-term 30-day option for this example:

(Note: the weighted percentages I have assigned below are estimates, and are for the purpose of this example).

45% x20 + 25%x18 + 20%x16 + 10% x14 =18.1%

The future volatility value that a trader might use for a very short-term option (30 days here) given the above data here would be 18.1%.

Similarly, if we were valuing a slightly longer term option, say a 60 day (2 month) option, we could assign the value from the past 60-day period the highest value, (Serial Correlation again!) and then rank the weights in virtue of their proximity to that time period, here 60 days.

Following the data from our table:

(35% x 20) + (45% x 18) + (20% x 16) + (10% x 14) = 19.7%

The above examples are somewhat crude, but I have only tried to introduce the conceptual background behind the way traders predict or "forecast" volatility. Note that I did not factor implied volatility into my equation, and every trader will, of course, want to factor in what the "market says".

Volatility in the Real World

- **Historical volatility and implied volatility may be correlated but in a very non-linear way.** Implied volatility should move in lock-step with historical volatility. However, future volatility tends to follow the volatility observed more recently, especially when the time periods involved are short. But implied volatility can sometimes spike in response to unusual market events.

- **Historical volatility is often disproportionate.** Most markets tend to fall much faster than they rise. Sell orders tend to intensify in falling markets. On the other hand, rising markets tend to attract participants who see a trend; most don't flock to rising markets with the same fury they bring to falling markets. Therefore, falling volatility does not necessarily look like rising volatility.

- **Volatilities tend to trade in regimes.** A period of volatility for a security or market, either high or low, can continue for a very long time before slowly returning to the historical norm. For instance, it seems that periods of low volatility are generally followed by comparable periods of high volatility before returning to more standard levels. With that in mind, making an educated guess as to near-term volatility in the future may be as simple as considering the most recent historical volatility.

- **Correlations and probabilities simply don't matter.** In options and in life, probabilities don't really matter. In fact, you could argue that the idea of probability doesn't make sense. In the end, it matters little whether an event has a 1 percent chance or a 99 percent chance of occurring. Whether or not the incident actually happens, it's the ultimate payoff or loss, is what counts. That potential payoff or loss is what should motivate options traders, clearinghouses, and investors alike.

- **Option volatility or any correlation between them aren't necessarily efficient and can't be explained with rational analysis.** Sometimes the price of equities under- or overreact and are either too low or too high as compared with essential numbers related to the corporate or industrial sector. This happens because traders are not rational, but emotional. Volatility represents the collective emotions of all participants motivated by the availability of inadequate information. This volatility—based on emotion—eventually decides the price of equities and their corresponding option prices.

CHAPTER 10

Volatility and Trading Decisions

"I've known Tony Saliba as a colleague, partner, and friend for more than two decades. Tony exemplifies clear and concise decision making with integrity always, and especially when facing volatility in everyday life along with trading and dealing with the markets."

-Michael McGuire

Volatility is simultaneously a philosophical concept and an extraordinarily straightforward one as well. The options industries pursuit of a clear explanation exists solely because volatility seems to represent different things to different people. To some it's a measure of fear, while to others volatility is nothing other than a statistical estimation. To some it's an asset class! The fact is that volatility embraces all of the above making it both confusing and misunderstood.

Recall the concept that historical volatility gauges the change in the value of an asset based on (backwards looking) historical prices over a pre-determined period of time. Historical volatility is expressed as an annual percentage of the underlying and is easily calculated for any instrument for which historical data is available. This average is then presented as an annualized percentage. Historical volatility is often referred to as actual volatility or realized volatility.

While historical volatility can be calculated monthly or yearly, options traders usually measure daily or weekly. Additionally in the options industry, daily volatility is often preferable to weekly volatility as five times as many information points are available.

Calculating volatility

Standard Deviation (volatility): measures the probability dispersion or variability of a random variable (measurement of volatility)

Variance Formula: Var (y) = ∑ (y − E (y))2 Py (y)
Probability weighted average of squared deviation from the mean (expected value)

sd = square root of Var (y)

Example

Steps	1	2	3	4
y(value)	Py(y)	(y-E(y))	(y-E(y))2	(y-E(y))2×Py(y)
-0.20	.10	-0.20	.04	.004
-0.10	.20	-0.10	.01	.002
0	.40	0	0	0
0.10	.20	0.10	.01	.002
0.20	.10	0.20	.04	.004
			5 Var(y)	.012

Figure I

Steps: * = multiply

1. Find expected value E (y)

   $(-.20*.10) + (-.10*.20) + (0*.40) + (.10*.20) + (.20*.10) = 0$

2. Subtract $y - E(y)$

3. Square $(y - E(y))^2$

4. Multiply by probability $(y - E(y))^2 \times Py(y)$

5. Sum = variance

6. Square root of Var(y) = standard deviation $= \sqrt{.012} = .110$

Confidence Intervals

Example: Annual volatility: 19%

What is one standard deviation? $.19 * 50 = +/- 9.5$

1 standard deviation = 68%	9.5
2 standard deviations = 95%	19
3 standard deviations = 99%	28.5

One would be 68% confident that a stock with annual volatility of 19% and a current price of 50 would be in the range of 40.5 to 59.5 in one year.

Converting an Annual Volatility

Monthly Volatility: Annual / square root 12
                               19% / 3.4641 = 5.48%

Weekly Volatility:	Annual / square root 52
	19% / 7.2 = 2.64%
Daily Volatility:	**Annual / square root 256**
	19% / 16 = 1.19%

Implied Volatility

Implied volatility is the current volatility of an asset, as revealed by the changes in the price of the option based on that asset. Implied volatility is using backwards-looking data to predict the future. That said, many traders assume implied volatility is an unbiased estimate of future realized volatility. That is one hundred percent incorrect!

To calculate the price for an options contract, traders use the following values:

- Strike price
- Expiration date
- Current share price of the underlying asset
- Projected dividend payments (securities)
- Current interest rates

If a trader can come up with all of the above values for an options contract, except volatility, he can use them, plus the price of the contract itself, to change his pricing model and calculate the implied volatility for the options contract.

Option Pricing Models

Evaluating an option's value through the use of a pricing model allows one to determine the **theoretical value (TV)** of an option. The TV of an option is the price one would expect to pay in order to breakeven in the long run. Once the TV is known, one can then evaluate whether the option's current market price is overpriced or underpriced.

An option pricing model is only a prediction of how an option might perform. Since the inputs can be inaccurate, there is no assurance that the model's TV will be accurate. One should take advantage of the insights a pricing model offers but be aware of its limitations. The following is a brief look at two models; the **Black-Scholes Model** and the **Cox-Binomial Model**.

Black-Scholes Model

In 1973, Fischer Black and Myron Scholes introduced an uncomplicated and practical option pricing model known as the Black-Scholes model. The model assumes that stock prices change continuously, stock returns follow a lognormal distribution, and the prices of assets adjust to avoid arbitrage.

After the crash in 1987 ("Black Monday") option participants quickly learned the shortcomings of the Black-Scholes model including the models assumptions that there exists a continuous and known volatility along with the idea that a participant would be hedging and re-hedging the options position on a continuous basis. Thirty years removed from "Black Monday" participants still use the Black Scholes model or an aberration thereof. The difference today is most participants know that the model is a great tool but markets cannot ever fit inside of a normally distributed world!

The Black-Scholes call option pricing Model:

$$C = S * N (d_1) - Ke\text{-}rT * N (d_2)$$

The Black-Scholes put option pricing Model:

$$P = Ke^{-rT} * N(-d_2) - S * N(-d_1)$$

where:

$$d_1 = \frac{\ln(S / K) + (r + \frac{1}{2} * variance) * T}{standard\ deviation * \sqrt{T}}$$

$$d_2 = d_1 - standard\ deviation * \sqrt{T}$$

ln is the natural logarithm
e is the exponential (2.718)
N(.) is the normal distribution function

Black-Scholes Inputs:

S: Current stock price.

Characteristically, the last stock price traded can be used. However, in cases where the stock has not traded recently, it may be inappropriate to use the last traded price.

K: Strike (exercise) price of the option.

This input is known and requires no calculation.

T: Time until expiration.

This input is calculated as a fraction of a 365 day based year. For example, an option with 100 days left until expiration has T = 100/365 = 0.2739.

r: Risk-free interest rate.

Treasury Bill rate can be used as a good estimate with a maturity closest to the expiration of the option. The average between the bid and ask can be used to obtain a simple T-Bill risk-free interest rate.

Example:

T-Bill: 65 days left to maturity
Bid yield: 6.83%
Ask yield: 6.77%

Price of a T-Bill = 1 − 0.01 * (Bid yield + Ask yield) / 2 * (days left to maturity / 365)

= 1 − 0.01 * (6.83 + 6.77) /2 * (65/365)

= 1 − 0.0121

= 0.9879

Next, find continuously compounded rate:

erT= 1 / Price of T-Bill

er(.18)= 1 / 0.9879

T = 65/365

.18r = ln (1.012248) = 0.01217

r= 0.01217 / .18 = 0.0676

Thus, in this example we have obtained a risk-free rate of 6.76% for our model.

Cox-Binomial Model

The Cox Model assumes that over a certain period of time a stock can move up or down by a particular amount. An up move's probability is given **p** while the possibility of a down move is given **1 − p**.

For example, in the simplest case of only one period left until expiration, assume a stock with value of 50 can either move up to 55 or down to 45 with a 50% chance of either outcome. At expiration, the value of the 50 call will either be worth 5 (stock at 55) or 0 (stock at 45). The expected value of the 50 call can be calculated by:

$$(0.5 * 5) + (0.5 * 0) = 2.50$$

In multiple periods the expected return of the option is the sum of the outcomes where the option is in-the- money multiplied by the outcome's probability. Out of the money outcomes are given a value of zero.

Example:

Probability of outcome:	.1	.25	.3	.25	.1
Stock at expiration:	140	145	150	155	160

Expected value of 150 call =   .1(0) + .25(0) + .3(0) + .25(5) + 1(10)

=   2.25

What does implied volatility uncover, if anything??

Implied volatility is the one input in an options price that is not "known" or "defined" – yet implied prices are made around the clock in hundreds of instruments around the world. Is there anything to learn by reviewing implied volatility levels?

It would be intuitive to suppose that implied volatility levels are directly linked to what the market believes about the variance and/or pathway of that asset in the future. Along those lines, it would make sense to think that relatively high levels of implied volatility would suggest the anticipation of a large move in the underlying. And relative low levels of implied volatility would point to a market stagnating within a small range.

Yet, experience has shown me that implied volatility can move for any reason or no reason at all. That being said, there are some tendencies of implied volatility:

- Implied volatility has a tendency to overshoot on both extremes.

- Implied volatility skew is generally "overpriced" due to demand for hedges.

- Implied volatility skew tends to rise when implied volatility drops significantly.

- Implied volatility tends to be at its highest point both at the opening and closing bell.

The link between historical and implied volatility

- Historical volatility = past movement

- Implied volatility = future movement (according to market participants)

- Volatility is serially correlated

- Past behavior correlated with future behavior

- Past behavior impacts future expectations

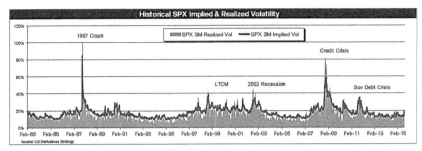

Figure 2   Credit-Suisse Equity Derivatives (US)

It appears to be the case that over longer periods of time, the historical volatility of the underlying seems to be dictating parameters for the options implied volatility. Yet, over shorter time horizons, other real and otherwise contrived factors can and do have a considerable impact. A geopolitical event or surprise government report are prime examples that – in the short-term – affect any correlation between historical and implied volatility. Indeed, any imminent event that could have unforeseen consequences can have an effect on implied volatility despite the underlying's historical volatility.

Any experienced options trader will admit that most of the time, implied volatility tends to trade at a higher level than historical volatility. A common rookie mistake would be to think that implied volatility is simply overpriced.

The perceived aberration of implied trading over historical has a couple well-entrenched reasons behind it. First, there exists a steady demand for protection via out of the money puts (holders of large equity portfolios) or out of the money calls in some of the agricultural products. This steady demand for hedging needs to be sold by options traders and it should make sense they would charge additional premium to be continuously negatively skewed. Additionally, there appears to be a constant bid for far out of the money calls and puts given their attractive risk-reward opportunity for investors.

146

Options Strategies in Various Volatility Environments

Within optionality, there are strategies in which volatility is uniformly long or short and the vega, gamma, and theta are all on the same side of the market—all three are positive or all three are negative. There are also trades involving both buying and selling options – combining various strike prices or expiry dates. Lastly there are strategies that attempt to capture the "volatility of volatility" in that ratios of long and short options are combined along the implied volatility skew.

Position management rule: When trading volatility spreads think and communicate your risks – including volatility – in terms of your range of risk. This is crucial as options strategies can and do flip from long to flat to short.

Directional anti-volatility spreads

Ratio Call Spread

- Direction: Up

- Magnitude: Small to moderate

- Velocity: Slow to moderate

- Current implied volatility levels: Rich

- Expected implied volatility levels: Declining

- Risk: Downside if debit, unlimited to upside, rising implied volatility

Ratio Call Spread

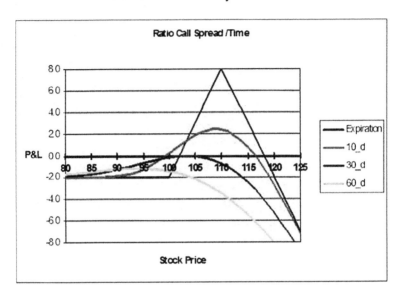

Long the XYZ 100/110 1 X 2 ratio call spread at 2.00 debit

Figure 3

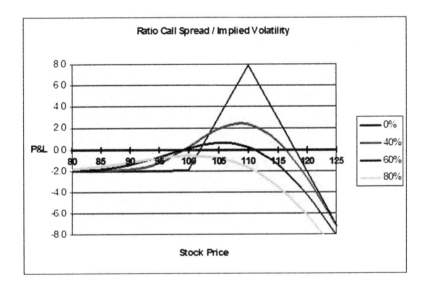

Long the XYZ 100/110 ratio 1 X 2 call spread at 2.00 debit

Figure 4

Ratio Call Spread Structure

CALLS	STRIKE	PUTS
+1	100	
	105	
-2	110	

Figure 5

Ratio Call Spread – Expiration

With a call ratio spread, the risk and profit potential must be broken down in terms of upside and downside

- Downside risk: Premium paid, if any

- Upside risk: Unlimited beyond breakeven

- Upside profit potential: High strike – Low strike +(-) credit (debit)

- Downside profit potential: Credit if any

- Up Breakeven: [(#short calls * short call breakeven) – (#long calls * long call breakeven)] /(#short calls - #long calls)

Ratio call spread breakeven calculation example:

- Buy 1 100 call at 4.50

- Sell 2 110 calls at 2.00

- Long the 100/110 1 X 2 call spread for .50 Debit

149

- Upside Breakeven: [(# short calls * short call breakeven) – (# long calls * long call breakeven)] /(# short calls - # long calls)

- [(2* 112.00) – (1* 104.50)]/1 = 119.50

Put Ratio Spread

- Direction: Down
- Magnitude: Small to moderate
- Velocity: Slow to moderate
- Current implied volatility levels: Rich
- Expected implied volatility levels: Declining
- Risk: Upside if debit, unlimited to downside (zero), rising implied volatility

Ratio Put Spread

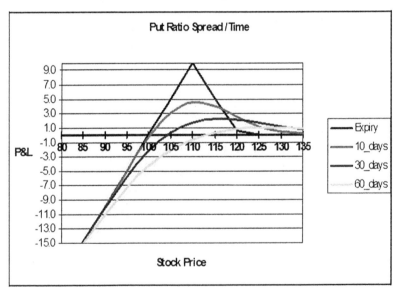

Long the XYZ 110/120 1 X 2 ratio put spread at 0.00

Figure 6

Ratio Put Spread (Continued)

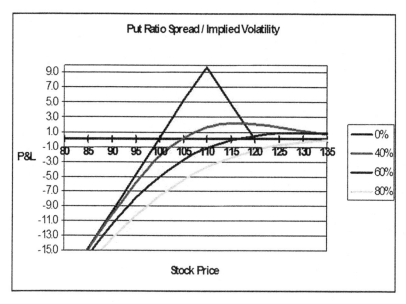

Long the XYZ 110/120 1 X 2 ratio put spread at 0.00

Figure 7

Ratio Put Spread Structure

CALLS	STRIKE	PUTS
	110	**-2**
	115	
	120	**+1**

Figure 7

Ratio Put Spread at Expiration

Due to a put ratio spread's construction, the risk and profit potential must be broken down in terms of upside and downside

- Downside risk: Unlimited to zero

- Upside risk: Debit, if any

- Downside profit potential: High strike –Low strike +(-) credit (debit)

- Upside profit potential: Credit if any

- Downside Breakeven: [(# short puts * short put breakeven) – (#long puts * long put breakeven)] /(# of short puts - # of long puts)

Ratio Put Spread breakeven calculation example

- Buy 1 120 put at 10.00

- Sell 2 110 puts at 5.00

- Long the 110/120 1 X 2 put spread for 0.00 ("even")

- Downside Breakeven: [(# short puts * short put breakeven) – (# long puts * long put breakeven)] /(# short puts - # long puts)

- [(2* 105.00) – (1* 110.00]/1 = 100.00

Directional Volatility Spreads

Call Backspread

When to Use a Call Backspread

- Direction: Up

- Magnitude: Large!

- Velocity: Fast!

- Current implied volatility levels: Low

- Expected implied volatility levels: Rising

- Risk: Slow move up, collapsing volatility

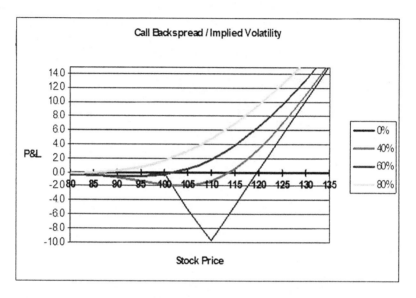

Long the XYZ 100/110 2 X 1 call backspread at 0.00, 30 days to expiry

Figure 9

Call Backspreads

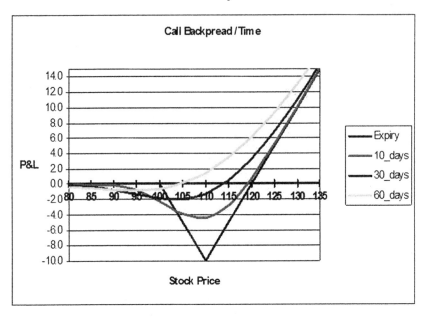

Long the XYZ 100/110 2 X 1 call backspread at 0.00, 30% implied

Figure 10

Call Backspread Structure

Calls	Strike	Puts
-1	100	
	105	
+2	110	

Figure 11

Call Backspread at Expiration

With a call backspread, the risk and profit potential must be broken down in terms of upside and downside

- Downside risk: Premium paid, if any

- Upside risk: Difference between strikes +(-) credit (debit)

- Upside profit potential: Unlimited

- Downside profit potential: Credit if any

- Upside Breakeven: [(#long calls * long call breakeven) – (#short calls * short call breakeven)] /(#long calls - #short calls)

Put Backspread

When to use a put backspread

- Direction: Down

- Magnitude: Large!

- Velocity: Fast!

- Current implied volatility levels: Low

- Expected implied volatility levels: Rising

- Risk: Slow move down, collapsing volatility

Put Backspreads (Continued)

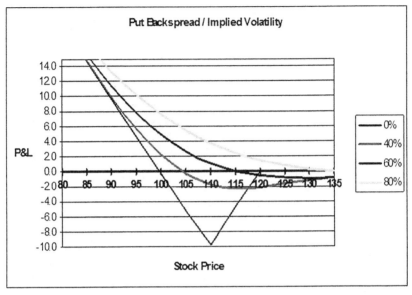

Long the XYZ 110/120 2 X 1 put backspread at 0.00, 30 days to expiry

Figure 12

Put Backspread Structure

Calls	Strike	Puts
	100	+2
	105	
	110	-1

Figure 13

Put Backspread at Expiration

With a put backspread, the risk and profit potential must be broken down in terms of upside and downside

- Upside risk: Premium paid, if any

- Downside risk: Difference between strikes +(-) credit (debit)

- Downside profit potential: Unlimited

- Upside profit potential: Credit if any

- Downside breakeven: [(#long puts * long put breakeven) – (#short puts * short put breakeven)] /(#long puts - #short puts)

Backspread Fodder: Continuation Patterns

- The underlying forms a consolidation pattern that indicates a breakout may be imminent (symmetrical triangle, ascending or descending wedge, triangle, the handle portion of a "cup and handle" formation.)

- Implied volatility usually drops during the consolidation phase

- As the pattern approaches maturity, initiate a backspread in the direction of the trend.

The prevailing trend has stalled out into a declining implied volatility consolidation phase

Trader believes that the market will move sharply out of the consolidation pattern

Figure 14

- The prevailing trend has stalled out into a declining implied volatility consolidation phase.

- Trader believes that the market will move sharply out of the consolidation pattern.

Non-directional Volatility Strategies

The Long Straddle

When to consider a long straddle

- Direction: Either

- Magnitude: Large

- Velocity: Rapid

- Current implied volatility levels: Cheap

- Expected implied volatility levels: Rising

- Risks: Sideways movement, falling implied volatility

The Long Straddle

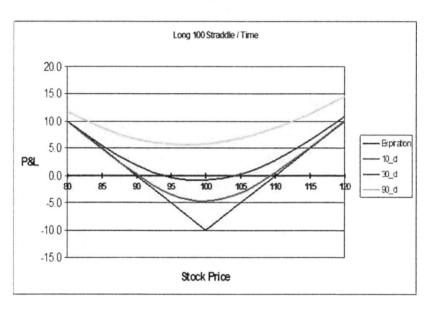

Long the XYZ 100 straddle at 10.00

Figure 15

The Long Straddle (Continued)

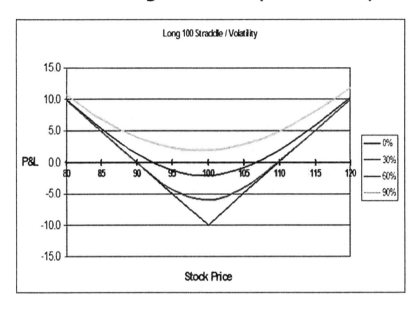

Long the XYZ 100 straddle at 10.00

Figure 16

Long Straddle Structure

CALLS	STRIKE	PUTS
	95	
+1	100	+1
	105	

Figure 17

Long Straddle at Expiration

The profit potential of a long straddle is slightly asymmetrical because a long call has unlimited profit potential and a long put does not, therefore, profit potential must be broken down into upside profit potential and downside profit potential.

- Risk: Premium paid
- Upside profit potential: Unlimited
- Downside profit potential: Strike – premium paid
- Breakeven: Strike +/- premium paid

Short Straddle

When to consider a short straddle

- Direction: Either
- Magnitude: Small
- Velocity: Slow
- Current implied volatility levels: Rich
- Expected implied volatility levels: Falling
- Risks: Strong directional movement, rising implied volatility

The Short Straddle

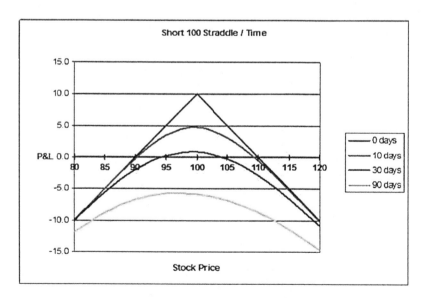

Short the XYZ 100 straddle at 10.00

Figure 18

The Short Straddle (Continued)

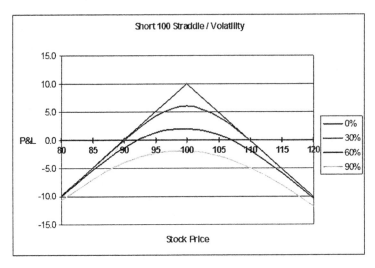

Short the XYZ 100 straddle at 10.00

Figure 19

The Short Straddle (Continued)

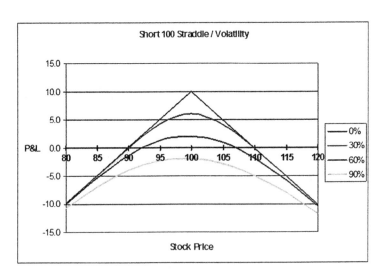

Short the XYZ 100 straddle at 10.00

Figure 20

Short Straddle at Expiration

The profit potential of a short straddle is slightly asymmetrical because a short call has unlimited risk and a short put does not, therefore, risk must be broken down into upside and downside risk.

- Upside risk: Unlimited

- Downside risk: Strike price minus premium received

- Profit potential: Premium received

- Breakeven: Strike +/- premium received

CHAPTER II

Volatility Skew

Thoughts from experience...

"When one has to think quickly about the market impact on a longer dated option or option spread, thinking about a one day option – which is easy to visualize—illustrates how the Greeks will work for the option which might be more difficult to intuitively understand."

-Ernest Jaffarian

CEO & CIO Efficient Capital Management

The Volatility Skew

From the beginning of exchange option trading through the mid-1980's traders used the Black-Scholes pricing model to calculate the theoretical fair value of an option. At the time, most traders presumed that the same implied volatility would apply for all options contracts based on a single underlying and with the same expiration date. It was also presumed that all options based on a specific underlying should trade with the same measure of volatility, and at the money calls and puts with the same strike price and expiration date should have precisely the same volatility.

But that was before "Black Monday" on October 19, 1987. On a single day, the Dow Jones Industrial Average fell by 508 points, or 22.6 percent. During that month the index lost nearly one third of its value. Since then, it was noticed in the market that implied volatility of options differed across strike prices for a given expiry date. From October 1987 onwards, it was observed that at least for equity index options, almost always, implied volatilities increase with decreasing strike – that is, out of the money puts trade at higher implied volatilities than out of the money calls. This feature is often referred to as "negative" skew, where skew is just another characterization of smile.

Black Monday 1987 also gave us what we now label as a term structure of volatility, i.e. implied volatility varied across different maturities; another key observation was that long-term implied volatilities exceed short-term implied volatilities. From this, the notion of volatility surface was born. This was a surface – a two dimensional matrix – where implied volatility was plotted against strike prices and time to maturity. From this surface, implied volatility of any arbitrary option can be incorporated.

Volatility Skew – a graphic interpretation

The Volatility Skew or Smile is the graphic representation of the implied volatilities of an option (Y-axis) as a function of its strike price (X-axis). Recall that an option's implied volatility is the volatility value, expressed in percentage form that justifies or is implied from the current market price of the option. If one used a pricing model such as Black Scholes, implied volatility is the value required in order for the theoretical value of the option to equal the actual market price of the option.

Implied Volatility Skew for an Equity Stock Index

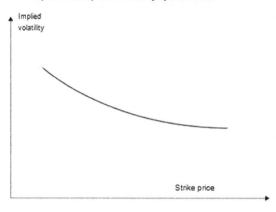

Figure 1

Volatility skews are the result of the fact that the assumptions behind a theoretical pricing model are not 100% accurate. If all the assumptions behind a pricing model were perfectly accurate, then the implied volatilities of all the options on the same underlying contract with the same maturity would have the same value.

For example, if all assumptions behind my pricing model were 100% correct, then all SPY Calls ought to have the same implied volatility. This conclusion follows from an examination of the pricing model. Logically, because the underlying contract can have only one volatility per life of the option, then all options on that underlying contract should follow suit. (Recall the variables in the Black Scholes model include: exercise price, underlying price, time to expiration, interest rates, dividends, and volatility).

However, in the real world, this is not the case. Some options on the same underlying contract - with the same expiration - trade at repeatedly higher volatilities, and some trade at consistently lower volatilities. This fact is known as volatility skewing.

A Volatility skew, when plotted graphically, can roughly resemble a shape like a "U ", thus the name "smile". The bottom point of the "U" is where the at-the-money strike falls. The upward curve on both sides of the "U" is caused by the tendency of far out of the money options to have higher implied volatility values. The shape and magnitude of the skew vary with time to expiration, market conditions, and type of underlying.

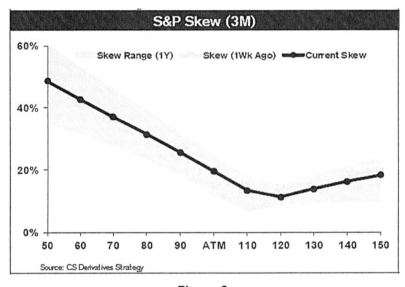

Figure 2

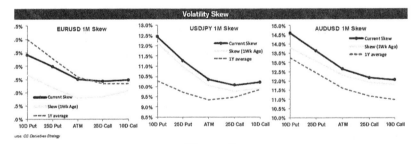

Figure 3

Some volatility skews can resemble an "S" and other skews can slope in various shapes, based on supply and demand. In verbal form, the "U" graph is saying that the further away an option's strike price is from the actual market price of the underlying stock, the higher is the option's volatility. This is because far out of the money options have a higher probability of a significant price move (collapse) compared with an equivalent rise and fall in the underlying market. High volatility, in effect, represents a higher level of "anxiety" amongst traders and investors. There are numerous reasons, such as:

- Traders prefer to sell at the money options to take advantage of time decay.
- There is greater demand for, thus less liquidity in far out of the money options.
- Traders demand a higher premium to sell small, very far out of the money options.
- Early exercise for American-style options could cause options to trade at different volatilities.
- Market imperfections that do not allow options to take their true Black-Scholes values.

The volatility skew is a reading that, in my opinion, should be used as a remote indicator for those not trading professionally. It is too sensitive and contains too many variables to use it to trade against, per se. As you will see, the skew has a purpose for those trading in a book that can take advantage of the seemingly fleeting changes in the curve. And it has value, as a reference, for those doing strategies that have a time horizon longer than a day. I can't say that it would be wise to trade off of it solely, though.

However, I firmly maintain that every trader-professional or retail must grasp the fundamental concept of and nuances behind volatility. By studying the phenomenon of the "skew" you will come to grips with an essential tool the professional volatility trader uses in his day-to-day career. I have always advocated the saying "knowledge is power", and it is my fervent desire to increase the firepower of your trading armamentarium.

Constructing the Basic Skew

Traders are constantly looking for any kind of information that will prove useful in valuing options for their trading decisions. As you know, most professional traders rely heavily on pricing models, such as Black Scholes, to generate an option's theoretical value. They then compare the market price of the option to their theoretical value to determine if it is over, or under-valued.

Recall, however, that the theoretical values generated by these sophisticated pricing models are in the end merely estimates, or "educated guesses" based upon historical market data. Key variables from the current market situation are fed into the model, and it then spits out a theoretical value.

I have seen instances, for example in the case of implied volatility values, where the trader utilizes the actual real-time prices in the market as a pricing tool instead of his theoretical values. The trader can make sense out of the price differential between what his model says an option is worth and what the actual market price of the option is by calculating the option's implied volatility.

The use of the skew is merely a continuation of this utilization of implied volatility values. After deciding on a particular pricing model, the trader then renders all theoretical options prices in terms of their implied volatility values. Then he simply plots these values against their respective exercise prices, and the curve smoothens out. The trader will want to make markets that are consistent with the volatility skew, as against the theoretical values.

With the basic smile in place, the trader can adjust the skew as market conditions then shift.

For example, if the underlying increases 3 points in value, then the trader would shift the entire skew up three points on the X-axis. If the underlying price moves down 10 points, he would move the skew down 10 points on the X-axis.

The Y-axis represents graphically the implied volatility values of an option.

Consequently, if the trader has reason to believe the option's implied volatility value is 5 percentage points too high, he would simply shift the whole skew downward 5 points for adjustment.

Implied Volatility Skew Examples

The table below offers a sample of option settlement prices and their corresponding volatilities for 30-day SPY options. The table reflects both prices and levels that option traders have learned to become accustomed.

Strike Price	Call Price	Put Price	Strike Volatility
$970	$98.00	$4.00	29.0%
$990	$80.00	$6.00	27.5%
$1,010	$63.00	$8.85	26.0%
$1,030	$47.00	$13.05	24.5%
$1,050	$33.35	$19.35	23.0%
$1,070	$21.80	$27.80	21.5%
$1,090	$12.95	$39.00	20.5%
$1,110	$7.25	$53.00	20.0%
$1,130	$3.60	$69.40	19.5%
$1,150	$1.75	$88.10	19.0%
$1,170	$0.80	$106.50	19.0%

SPX = $1,064.00, cash settled. Thirty days to expiration, interest rate = 2 percent.

Figure 4

Reviewing this table, it's clear that the implied volatilities at various exercise prices do not line up. This is a problem if one believes that the Black-Scholes or any other model is supposed to be flawless in predicting option prices. In fact, the projected prices don't make sense.

If the SPX is trading at $1,064 and expires in thirty days, how can it be that the $1,070 call should have a volatility of 21.5 percent, whereas the $1,110 call should have a volatility of 20 percent? Why should the call contract with the higher strike price have nearly identical volatility, given that it is so far out of the money? And why should the volatility for both put and call contracts fall within a range of 18.5–29 percent across a range of $200 in strike prices?

Positive Skew or Forward Skew

In the forward or positive skew pattern, the implied volatility for options at the lower strikes are lower than the implied volatility at higher strikes. This would suggest that out of the money calls and in the money puts are in greater demand compared to in the money calls and out of the money puts.

The forward skew pattern is common for options in the commodities market. When supply is tight, businesses would rather pay more to secure supply than to risk supply disruption. For example, if weather reports indicate a heightened possibility of an impending frost, fear of supply disruption will cause businesses to drive up demand for out of the money calls for the affected crops.

The most common place to find a positive skew is in the futures market, particularly the grains (Corn, Wheat, or Soybeans) although others such as Coffee, Sugar, and so on normally have a positive skew as well.

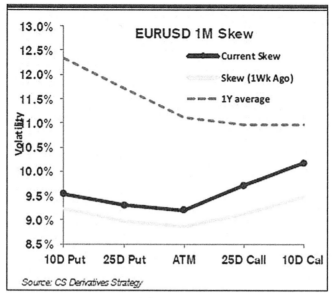

Source: CS Derivatives Strategy

Figure 5

Non-Mathematical Approach to Understanding Skew

IVT is presently trading at $800 a share. Using exchange parameters, a three-month at the money straddle costs about $68. The implied volatility of this price is about 21.5%, which (not) coincidentally is nearly 10% above its three-month actual volatility of 19.5%. Using coincident exchange parameters, a three-month strangle with strikes of 700 and 900 would trade at $12; the Implied Volatility here is a blended 23.0%, about 7% above the at the money level.

In both cases, the buyer can only lose the premium paid with the potential for an unlimited gain. On the other hand, the seller's profit is limited to the premium received while exposed to a potentially huge loss. The pricing model is supposed to produce prices that will have comparable, net present values, but the reality is that while the strangle does have 100 points of "cushion" over the straddle, they both ultimately have the possibility for "unlimited" loss.

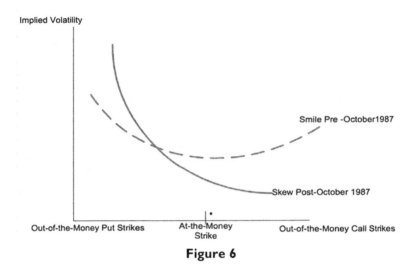

Figure 6

As such, since the potential losses are similar (infinite) yet the strangle seller books a premium barely one sixth as large as the straddle seller, a risk averse strangle seller will demand a higher net present value, and thus its implied volatility is elevated above that of the straddle. While slightly drawn-out, this is the best non-mathematical way I can describe the classic "smile" one sees for many option profiles.

Kurtosis and Options Skew

Option models employ normal or lognormal distribution curves for ease and simplicity. The problem is that over time – this is not reliable! Subsequently, the far left and right sides of the distribution tend to be "fatter" in reality than expected under classroom conditions. Kurtosis is the mathematical term for measuring the "fatness" of the tails in a distribution. Ultimately, traders give up on the "implicit" solution of "fitting" the distribution via tweaking the Kurtosis setting to alter model option values. Instead, market convention is to employ an "explicit" method of arching the skew profile to change the implied volatility input in such a manner that the model value more closely matches the market price.

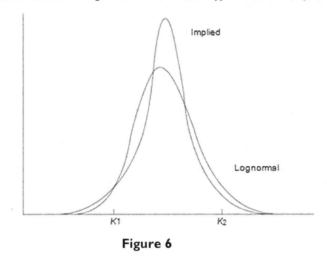

Implied Distribution and Lognormal Distribution for a Typical Stock Index Option

Figure 6

"Fitting" and the Moments of a Probability Distribution

The concept of "moment" in mathematics developed from the concept of "moment" in physics. The moments articulate the nature of the distribution. Any distribution can be characterized by a number of features, such as the mean, the variance, the skewness, the kurtosis, and so forth. Whether you like it or not, you are forced to live with these higher moments every single trading day. So what are these moments and how do they affect our options trading decisions?

<u>**First moment of a normal distribution:**</u> Finding the Mean. Options traders are all concerned with the problem of figuring out the likelihood or expectation of a certain outcome. One trader, after hours of research, places a value on a commodity for a future period. A local market maker may take the average of the last three months of an ETF and quickly conclude that it will trade at such and such a price. In this case, both traders are toying with the expected value of an asset—the first moment of a normal distribution. You may, for example, take the average of a price for the last six months and use that to develop a

175

value. You aren't forecasting a price for a specific future date or series of dates; you are simply finding the average for past performance and using that to get an idea of where the underlying price might go next.

Second moment of a normal distribution: Estimate the variance or volatility of that asset over time. Next, options traders try to estimate the odds that the stock price will trade between, for example, $50 and $70 over the next 30 days. They seek to refine an estimated future price into the variability of that price over time. The standard deviation— or implied volatility, in financial terms—is the second moment. The second moment tries to capture the dispersion of values around the single expected value that you estimated in the first moment described above. So, the second moment captures the risk or volatility of a financial underlying.

The second moment—the volatility—of the distribution is one of the most valuable concepts in financial philosophy. Financial derivatives are based on this second moment. The second moment of the normal distribution is the "stress" in the orderliness which prompts asset prices to diverge from what everyone assumes them to be, thus stirring up risk in the system.

Third moment of a normal distribution: The skew or shape in the distribution. Sometimes - option traders - confront sizeable positive or negative returns. This is the skew. If a distribution has a skew—and all normal distributions in actuality do—it insinuates the ever-present possibility of large negative returns. This is actually negative skew.

Skew is the contour, or the unevenness, in a distribution, the dent in the bell curve. A negative skew suggests that the left half of the normal distribution (the left side of the mean) is twisted in such a way that the prospect of achieving negative returns is superior to that of achieving large positive returns. Recall that in a theoretically precise, ideal normal distribution, positive returns and negative returns of equivalent magnitudes have more or less equivalent probabilities. Hence the distribution is symmetrical, or balanced. Of course, a distribution can possess positive skew as well, which signifies the prospect of a large positive return.

When dealing with skew, traders strive to resolve how frequently in the trading time horizon they will obtain negative returns rather than positive returns. A skew demonstrates the relationship between the movement of an underlying asset and its volatility.

Fourth moment of a normal distribution: Kurtosis or varying variance, the volatility of volatility. Statisticians have a fearsome term for the fourth moment of a normal distribution—kurtosis. The fourth moment is a measure of whether the distribution curve is tall and skinny or short and squat, measured up to the normal distribution of the same exact variance. It means varying volatility or, more precisely, varying variance.

The fourth moment is something that all options traders can relate to, although they may not know its name or be able to offer details. It signifies volatility of the volatility of an underlying asset. What happens to the distribution of the curve when volatility changes? What occurs to the extreme downside skew if volatility changes? A changing volatility can cause the tails of the normal distribution to become "fatter" or "skinnier" than otherwise projected, thereby increasing the potential risk. This is the work of the fourth moment.

Trading Skew – Managing Skew

Equity markets almost always exhibit a "smirk" or a "negative skew". Levels of fear aside, there are well -established industries (e.g. insurance companies) that are regular sellers of calls and buyers of puts. As such, professional options participants are typically long out of the money calls and short out of the money puts. FX markets typically exhibit a true "smile" while commodity options will exhibit different levels of "positive skew".

There exists no sure way to estimate what the skew will be for a given underlying; the out of the money implied volatility can be positive, negative, or even flat to its at the money implied volatility.

When the market skew is steep (or, very negative)—out of the money puts are priced higher than equally distanced out of the money calls—does that indicate the market is going down? When market skew is deemed steep or expensive, the market is more than likely to trade higher. Major market downturns or other rare events seem to occur as shocks. When you have an exceptionally steep skew, it means that an event or crash has been built into the market; people are willing to shell out this risk premium (or crash premium) with the fear of the impending crash. And that's precisely why it doesn't happen, since the aspect of surprise is gone.

CHAPTER 12

The Volatility Surface

I've spent years attempting to study implied volatility through a quantifiable lens with the hopes of looking for information that truly mattered. Through years and thousands of trades, I've found it is far more important to consider why that information matters, and if the reason why that information matters is conveniently consistent with what I consider important. In other words, I realized that keeping up with quantitative research was important, but it needed to be balanced with both intuition and common sense. Decades of experience has shown me that finding traders who can appropriately balance theoretical analysis and instinct is a trader who will be successful as trading demands both.

Beyond the path dependency of the underlying, most experienced traders will agree that they think of "greek" risks as the key exposures of an options position. That initial reaction makes a great deal of sense because when an option position loses money it typically means that the trader was hurt by the gamma, and ultimately the delta, of a position.

The risks associated with the pathway of the underlying along with the associated greek risks are real and should never be dismissed.

However, the risks and complications of both implied volatility skew and term structure can be equally as important and should be learned and defended against. In real life, implied volatility for a particular underlying asset at a particular time is not an identical constant for all options on a given underlying asset observed at a given time. Rather, implied volatility differs for options with different strike prices and days to expiration, and this leads to both implied volatility skew and term structure.

Traders should always ask questions including – what is the best measure of implied volatility skew, how should one compare skew for a 15 percent volatility equity ETF against skew for a 40 percent commodity? Additionally, traders should actively weigh the relevance of measuring term structure of implied volatility. What type of weight should a trader place on what's considered a rising, falling, or flat term structure environment?

Implied Volatility Skew + Term Structure = Volatility Surface

In 1973 Black-Scholes option pricing model was advanced in the financial markets. The formula produced put and call values as following a geometric Brownian motion – a Gaussian diffusion process – with a static volatility parameter. The point that volatility is constant is extremely important (and later cataclysmic) in a Black-Scholes world, because it simplifies the quandary of option pricing enormously.

The Black-Scholes honeymoon ended dramatically with the stock market crash "Black Monday" of 1987 when option traders and risk-managers quickly realized that volatility is not constant. The notion of volatility skew – a varying implied volatility across strike prices and volatility term structure – a varying of implied volatility across maturities – was born. And, in the three decades since "Black Monday" was born an entire cottage industry relating to the trading and measurement of the volatility surface.

Today the implied volatility curve presented by the options market in equity related securities has taken the general form as seen in Figure 1 below.

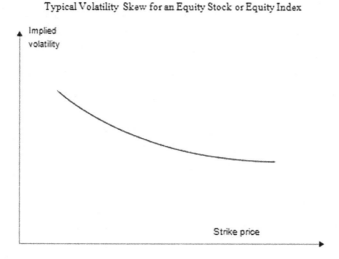

Typical Volatility Skew for an Equity Stock or Equity Index

Figure I

You will notice that the implied volatility (per strike price) increases as the underlying asset price decreases. In addition, as the underlying asset price rises, the implied volatilities fall. In other words, the implied volatility of a lower strike option (i.e. deep in the money calls or deep out of the money puts) is higher when compared with a higher strike price option (i.e. far out of the money call or deep in the money put).

The nuance of the "implied volatility skew" correlates directly to the probability distributed described by the dotted line in Figure 2 while the standard lognormal distribution is depicted with the solid line. Notice the severe difference! The dotted line curve (real life prices) has a heavier left tail and much less heavier right tail – especially when compared to the textbook (solid line) lognormal distribution.

Implied Distribution and Lognormal Distribution for a Typical Stock Index Option

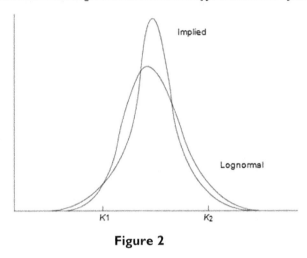

Figure 2

The crucial take-away in all of this can be seen in Figure 3 where, day-to-day life, implied volatility skews are almost an asset in and of themselves. Implied volatility skew can and do rise (steepen) or fall (flatten) depending on market sentiment, supply and demand, and where the underlying is relative to recent history.

SPX 30-day Skew Structure

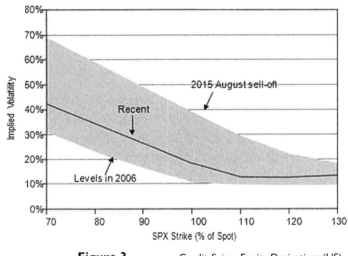

Figure 3   Credit-Suisse Equity Derivatives (US)

Equity Skew:

- Rising or Steepening Skew: the implied volatility of the deep in the money calls and far out of the money puts will consequently rise relative to the out of the money calls and in the money puts.

- Falling or Flattening Skew: the implied volatility of the in the money calls and out of the money puts would drop relative to the out of the money calls and in the money puts.

Implied Volatility Skew and Option Greeks

It should come of little surprise that shifting skew levels can and will affect your greek values. And, the changes can be dramatic when combining a shift in skew, the passage of time, and levels of implied volatility. One way to limit skew exposure is keeping your long options close to your short options. The further your longs are away from your shorts the greater your skew becomes. See the following table to get a firm idea on what happens to greek values with a significant change in skew.

Delta	ITM calls less positive	OTM calls less positive
	OTM puts more negative	ITM puts more negative
Gamma	ITM calls up	OTM calls down
	OTM puts up	ITM puts down
Theta	ITM calls higher	OTM calls lower
	OTM puts higher	ITM puts lower

The Effect of Implied Volatility Skew on Greek Values ; Rising Skew

Figure 4

183

Delta	ITM calls more positive	OTM calls more positive
	OTM puts less negative	ITM puts less negative
Gamma	ITM calls down	OTM calls up
	OTM puts down	ITM puts up
Theta	ITM calls lower	OTM calls higher
	OTM puts lower	ITM puts higher

*The Effect of Implied Volatility Skew on Greek Values ; **Falling Skew***

Figure 5

Option position considerations in rising skew environment (assuming no other parameter changes)

In equity related options, skew is typically most volatile in the .35 delta area of the curve. Thus, in a rising skew environment, the implied volatility of the .35 delta put will rise faster relative to the .60 delta put. Additionally, in a rising skew environment (assuming no other parameter shifts) the implied volatility of the .35 delta put area will rise while the implied volatility of the .35 delta call area will fall (although not necessarily and not necessarily by the same amount).

A rising skew environment will impact "skew" options and their greeks exactly the same way they do in rising volatility or in a more "time to expiration" environment. In position management, utmost attention should be made with regards to your net greeks relative to your skew level. This is especially so if your inventory includes: wide vertical spreads, risk-reversals, or ratio vertical spreads.

Example: in its simplest form, assume you purchased 100 SPY .32 delta puts and you hedged them with the purchase of 3,200 shares of SPY underlying ETF. After hedging, skew steepens significantly and your .32 delta puts now have a .35 delta (all other parameters unchanged).

184

Instead of being theoretically flat deltas, you now find yourself -300 shares? What should you do?

This doesn't sound like a major problem however; imagine your positions getting bigger and more complex? What delta do you trust?

Remedies:

- Avoid skew trades as much as possible. Do not make skew trades for "perceived edge's sake". Over time, professional traders will inevitably inherit the anxiety of the market. Poor options traders will wind up with the bad side of skew – guaranteed!

- Neutralize skew trades as much as possible. An options position with skew needs to be quantified. What range of strikes are you long or short skew – that's the risk you need to communicate.

- Review your net "greeks" at various skew levels. Recall, this is something I encouraged traders to do with regards to various volatility levels and time-to-expiry.

- Don't overthink skew levels – skew can often be high at low volatility levels due to excessive call selling. Skew can often be low at high volatility levels due to profit taking in downside puts. Vice-versa applies as well.

Option position considerations in flattening skew environment (assuming no other parameter changes)

In equity related options, skew is typically most volatile in the .35-delta area of the curve. Thus, in a flattening skew environment, the implied volatility of the .35 delta put will fall faster relative to the .60 delta put. Additionally, in a falling skew environment (assuming no other parameter shifts) the implied volatility of the .35 delta put area will fall while the implied volatility of the

.35 delta call area will rise (although not necessarily by the same amount).

A flattening skew environment will impact "skew" options and their greeks exactly the same way they do in falling volatility or less time to expiration environment. In position management, utmost attention should be made with regards to your net greeks relative to your skew level. This is especially so if your inventory includes: wide vertical spreads, risk-reversals, or ratio vertical spreads.

Implied Volatility Term Structure

The term structure of implied volatility is the curve showing the differing implied volatilities of options with differing maturities. The term structure is curved, since the volatility implied by short-dated option prices typically changes quicker than that implied by longer-term options. Take note that according to the Black-Scholes model, term structure should not exist, or more precisely, it should be a long boring flat line.

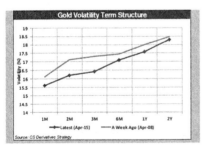 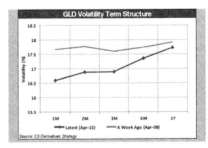

Figure 6

In actual trading, the term structure of volatility can and does slope upward or downward. The underlying causes of term structure shifts are not always straightforward. Whatever the influences for causing the implied volatility term structure to slope—whether it be supply and demand, macroeconomic risk expectations, or a built-in jump fear component—it is important to know how it can and does affect the greeks of your options position. Term structure—like implied volatility skew—is hard to predict and harder still to manage.

S&P 500 ATM Implied Volatility Term Structure

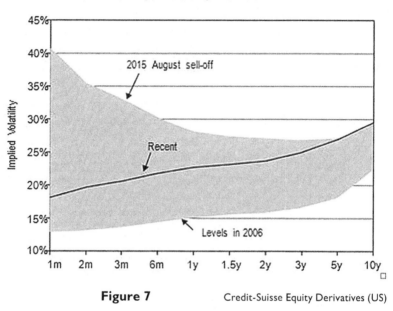

Figure 7   Credit-Suisse Equity Derivatives (US)

Practical Application of Term Structure

The "front-month" option series has little – if nothing – to do with the rest of the term structure. This is a bold statement yet options professionals will all agree. Why? When the front month begins as the "front month" it initially has a modest amount of vega and about an equally modest amount of gamma. As time passes closer and closer to expiry, the vega declines more rapidly. Meanwhile its gamma becomes stronger. Within two weeks of expiry, front-month vega will all but disappear. Yet its gamma (depending on location relative to the underlying) will increase. On the other hand, the "back-month" options contain much more vega than gamma relative to the front-month. Additionally, the back-month has far less theta.

Term Structure and its Upward Slope

Typically when there is a shock in the market, "front month" volatility tends to spike likewise as the market expects the volatility to continue in the short or intermediate-term. That is precisely why further out implied volatilities tend to rise by fractional amounts compared with short-dated implied volatilities. However, events that are considered quickly mean-reverting could potentially have far less effect on shorter-dated options compared with longer-dated ones.

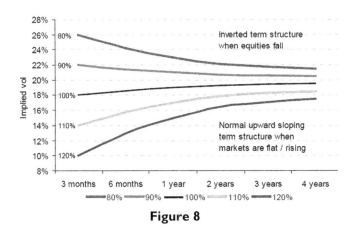

Figure 8

Correlation between skew and term structure

A steady decline in near-dated, at the money implied volatility will lift implied volatility term structure along with implied volatility skew. This is not a phenomenon per se. Rather, it's a simple function of far out of the money puts and far-dated implied volatilities tend to be "sticky". That said, both implied volatility skew and term structure can and are often correlated as a fall in short-dated at the money implied volatility lifts both of them accordingly.

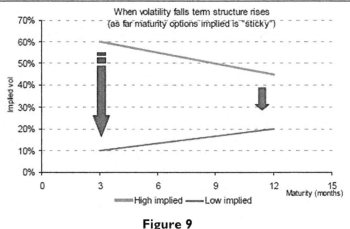

Figure 9

Calendar Spread, Vega, and Term Structure of Implied Volatility

The phrase term structure, or 'yield curve', is nothing new amongst interest rate products. Those who trade interest rate derivatives are constantly assessing the term structure, or the differences in interest between short and long-term bonds, for example. For options, we will be concerned about the different volatilities of the at the money options of different maturities.

Time spreads (also known as horizontal or calendar spreads) can be very sensitive to changes in the term structure. Remember vega is the greatest for at the money options with more time to maturity. So, a long time spread (buying the deferred month and selling the near month) will be a long vega, or a long volatility play.

Let's look at an example in Microsoft (MSFT). The January 2016 75 put has a premium of $11 with a vega of .22 and the December 75 put has a premium of 14.50 and a vega of .35. If we purchased this spread, our position would be net long .13 cents of vega. If volatility increases by one point in both months, then the spread will expand by 13 cents to $3.63 from $3.50. So, anticipating an increase in volatility should increase the value of this spread, right?

Unfortunately, it's not that easy. In practice it's rare that the volatility changes by the exact same amount in both months. The volatility will change by some amount so the value of the time spread will stay consistent. If volatility increases, characteristically it will not be by one point in both months. To keep the value of the time spread consistent, the volatility of the December 75 put would move only by 0.6%.

The relationship in volatility between expiration months can be assessed in a similar way to that of individual options in one month. We know that if the volatility of one strike price increases, then those around it must as well. The same thing happens between months. If large buy orders come in for one month in particular, the surrounding month's volatility should also increase by some amount to keep the relationships in line. The trick is when and by how much to move the volatility.

Below is a graph of the term structure a couple of months ago. Notice the extreme hump in May. Is this consistent? Should we just sell May and buy the surrounding months expecting them to normalize again? When something looks too good to be true, it usually is. Upon further investigation, we learn that May is an earnings month and we already know what happens to option volatility in anticipation of announcements. In addition to that, the announcement occurred during expiration week, so how much volatility is 'really' there? Knowing this, traders may be quite hesitant to sell this month.

Every spread you ever construct will have a unique risk or twist, so remember to analyze them properly.

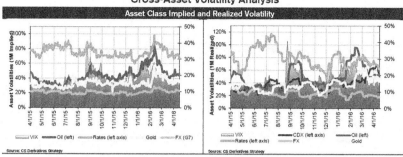

Figure 10

PART IV

Option Strategy

CHAPTER 13

Selling Premium – "Covered Call", "Covered Write", "Buy-Write"

Baseball has a saying, "The ball will certainly find you." Meaning that the one time you are playing out of position, playing hurt or not at full concentration, inevitably the ball will be hit to you – at the most crucial moment – causing embarrassment for you and misery for your teammates.

This old saying can be equally – almost perfectly – applied to options trading. Be certain that volatility will inevitably strike when you are not ready, over extended, or not thinking clearly in terms of risk and objectives. Be ready at all times as that "rare event" – both good and bad could occur when you are least prepared.

The Covered Call

It's no doubt, when one begins to learn about options strategy, the first strategy you learn is to sell covered calls – it's a natural extension for the investor, brokerage house, and the trader. For the investor who owns underlying, using covered calls offers the chance for supplemental income, and a limited amount of protection. The covered call strategy is widely heralded as a "secure investment" from the perspective of a brokerage house, the financial system, and the investor who is eager to generate additional income. It is indeed "safe" as the investor has a clearly articulated risk-reward basis and, the brokerage house won't be left holding any bag as they have the shares and will deliver them upon potential assignment. However safe doesn't always equal smart.

Definition & Practicality of the Covered Call Strategy

Basically, an investor or trader who owns (long) underlying sells a near at the money call or slightly out of the money call. The seller of this call collects premium (extrinsic value) in return for assuming the guarantee of underlying delivery if the underlying winds up above the sold (short) call strike. This strategy is called "covered" as the investor owns the underlying and will automatically deliver such if assigned by the owner of the call option. A pure "covered call" sells one option for each unit of underlying owned.

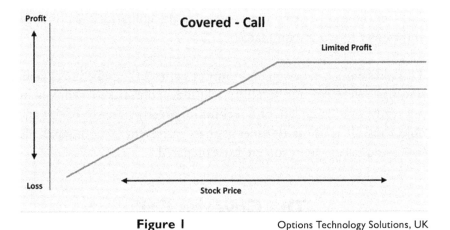

Figure I　　　　　　Options Technology Solutions, UK

Structure of the Buy-Write or Covered Call

The buy-write is constructed by purchasing underlying and selling a call against it on a one-for-one basis. For example, buy 100 shares of stock and sell 1 call against it. The strike of the call chosen is up to the investor, depending on their opinion of the stock and their opinion of the implied volatility of the options involved.

By studying the theoretical payout diagrams of the components of a buy-write (below), we can see that the combination of long stock and short call emulates the behavior of a single option position, the short put. (See Figures 5 and 6).

Theoretical Payout Diagrams

Below we see the breakdown of payout diagrams of individual components of a buy-write, and the combined position. We are going to purchase the IBM April $150 buy-write by purchasing IBM stock at 148.52, and selling the April 150 calls at 1.83. Therefore we are purchasing the IBM April 150 buy-write for 146.69 (148.52 – 1.83):

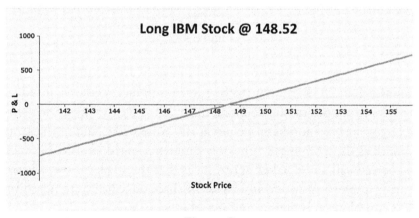

Figure 2

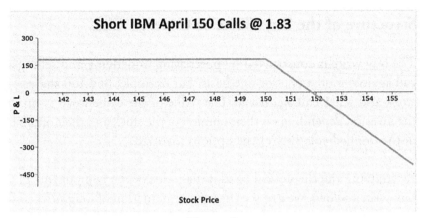

Figure 3

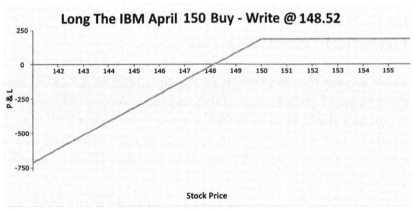

Figure 4

Figures 4 and 5 reveal that the buy-write is in fact synthetically equal to a short put position! Therefore, the quick and easy way to "lock in" a buy-write is to purchase the put at the same strike, and in the same month as the written call. The only difference in risk profiles between a covered call and a naked short put is that the stock (in the covered call example) will not expire. So as the share price begins to nosedive, it will prolong your agony and increase your losses.

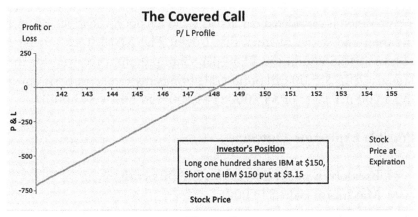

Figure 5

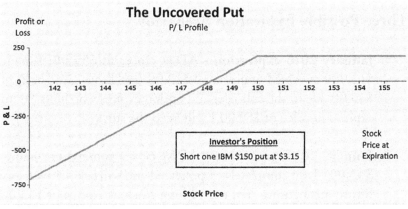

Figure 6

A Real-Life Example of the Covered Call Strategy

Let's suppose I'm enthusiastic about the long-term prospects of **Archer Daniels Midland (NYSE: ADM)** and buy one thousand shares at $44.50. I want to sell a call option that offers a satisfactory amount of premium within my investment time horizon. Holding a long-term bullish conviction on ADM stock, I find a January 2016 $55.00 call option that is trading at $1.50 per share and subsequently sell ten of these call options.

This position is considered covered as I sold ten option contracts against the thousand shares of stock that I own. The ADM stock purchase cost me $44,500 and the $1.50 per share premium received for the January 2016 $55.00 call option sale brings my total cost basis down to $43.00 per share or $43,000 ($44,500 – $1,500 = $43,000).

Possible Expiration Outcome

- **Breakeven point downside:** $43.00 per share.
- **Maximum risk:** $43,000
- **Maximum return:** $12,000

Three Possible Expiration Scenarios

1. **January 2016 expiration - <u>ADM closes at $55.00!</u>** I made $12,000 as ADM appreciated $12.00 (recall new cost basis of $43.00 due to the call sale) and option expires worthless. At an expiration price of $55.00 I will keep the stock.

2. **January 2016 expiration - <u>ADM closes somewhere below $43.00</u>** - I am completely unprotected and will lose 1:1 with any future misfortunes. I'm naked long stock at a price of $43.00 per share.

3. **January 2016 expiration - <u>ADM closes somewhere above $55.00!</u>** – Whether the stock expires at $60, $90, or $250, I will have been "stopped out" at $55.00 per share. My 1,000 shares of ADM stock will have been "called away" from me at $55.00 per share, allowing someone else to enjoy the profit.

Greeks and the Covered Call

Covered Call and Delta

<u>Delta of a Covered Write:</u> The delta of a covered-call position is the sum of the deltas of the elements.

<u>Example:</u> What is the delta of a covered-call consisting of 100 shares of long stock and short 1 .65 delta call?

100 + (100*-.65) = 100 + (-65) = 50 shares

Note that the delta of the call is inverted because it is a short call.

Covered Write and Gamma

<u>Gamma of a Covered Call:</u> The Gamma of an option is not linear, and is also sensitive to market circumstances.

<u>Example:</u> Consider a covered-call position involving 100 shares of long stock and short 1 .65 delta call. The call has a gamma of .15. What is the delta of the overall position if the stock rises 1.00?

+100 + (100 *-(.65 +.15)) = +20 net deltas

What is the delta of the overall position if the stock falls 1.00?

+100 + (100*-(.65 -.15)) = +50 net deltas

Note that the gamma solely increases or decreases the delta of the option as the underlying price varies; it does not change the sign of the delta.

Covered Call and Vega

Vega of the Covered Call: As discussed in chapter 5 "Option Vega" we know long option positions have a positive vega and short option positions contain negative vega. Given a covered-write has a short call as its option it will always have a negative vega.

Example: Consider the covered-write position containing 100 shares of long stock @ 50.00 and short 1 call @ 3.00. The call has a vega of .15. With the stock unchanged, what is the change in value of the overall position if:

Implied volatility rises 5%...

The price of the call will change from 3.00 to 3.75 (3.00 + 5*.15), so the value of the position will change from an original value of 47.00 to a new value of 46.25.

Implied volatility falls 5%...

The price of the call will change from 3.00 to 2.25 (3.00 - 5*.15), so the value of the position will change from an original value of 47.00 to a new value of 47.75.

Covered Call and Theta

Theta: As discussed in chapter 6 "Options Theta" long option positions have a negative theta and short option positions have a positive theta. Since a covered-call has a short call as its option piece it will have a positive theta.

Example: You have a covered-call position consisting of 100 shares of long stock @ 50.00 and short 1 call @ 4.00. The call has a theta of .03. With the stock unchanged and implied volatility unchanged, what is the change in value of the overall position if:

5 trading days pass...

The price of the call will change from 4.00 to 3.85 (4.00 - 5*.03), so the value of the position will change from 46.00 to 46.15

Note that time decay works in favor of a covered call.

Covered Call – Objectives, Strike Selection, and Trade Management

First, a covered-writer must know his objective. Is the participant a "long-term strategist" who uses the covered-write as a long- term plan against a long-term core portfolio? A long-term strategist will sell calls to create income, and, over time, potentially reduce the cost basis of the portfolio. Or, the "short-term strategist" - who executes the covered-call as a way of expressing his conviction(s) - of either a stagnating underlying or relatively high implied volatility levels.

Before you choose which call strike price to sell you must first come to terms with your investment intention. Your strike selection should be motivated to whether your conviction is based on supplemental income, limiting the risk of loss, or a perspective on implied volatility. Questions including where you do think the underlying is headed or how much protection you are looking for will help determine which area of the curve should be targeted.

Market Outlook:

<u>Neutral Outlook:</u> You would generally maximize your conviction through writing an at the money call.

Writing at the money calls generally offers the highest return and provides some degree of downside protection while preserving a little upside potential. Just how much an at the money call reduces your risk profile depends solely on how much extrinsic value you receive. Additionally, being short volatility—even when covered and the risk/reward is quantified—is potentially risky in that the investor simply doesn't know the course of future volatility and undoubtedly isn't receiving enough advantage (premium) for taking on the risk.

<u>Slightly bullish:</u> If you are expecting a slight rise through expiration, you would be best served to write a call that is slightly out of the money.

Writing a slightly out of the money call will increase your upside profit potential and the further out of the money the strike price is, the higher the upside cap will be placed. However, writing an out of the money call diminishes downside protection. Like a seesaw, the higher the strike price you write, the less downside protection you will have.

<u>Reasonably Bullish:</u> If you are anticipating a more substantial rise in the underlying price through expiration, one would want to write a call that is further out of the money to realize maximum returns.

Even in a high-volatility environment, the premium received for an out of the money strike needs to be weighed against the potential you may receive from it. Other words, you are receiving a small amount of premium yet locking your risk/reward profile – is it worth the risk?

Risk Tolerance

Holding a covered call is kind of like playing chicken - as long as the market moves sideways to slightly higher, you are making money, and because you are short premium, every tick of the clock puts a little more money in your pocket. Because of this there is a tendency amongst holders of buy-write positions to stay a little too long at the party. When the music stops, and the market begins to retreat, and implied volatilities begin to climb, holders of buy-writes often find themselves scrambling and making a not-too-elegant exit from their positions.

Having an exit strategy in place ahead of time will save unnecessary slippage and confusion when it is time to exit from any position, and this is especially true with a buy- write. Because a buy-write is a so-called "complex" position consisting of two legs, many investors find it difficult to execute, wasting valuable time when the market is moving against the position.

Lower Risk Tolerance: Generally includes those who desire more downside protection and thus tend to sell slightly in the money or at the money options. This type of strategy will enhance the downside protection but reduce the potential for upside appreciation. Another lower-risk tolerance call write would include those solely interested in the potential return of the covered-write as a trade, and are drawn to environments where high volatility (higher call premiums) are throwing off high potential rates of return. This type of participant is very sensitive to risk because a loss in the position cannot be recouped over time as it might be with a long-term covered-call writer.

Higher Risk Tolerance: A participant with a portfolio of stocks who intends to hold them in perpetuity. They pursue the covered-call strategy in order to generate income and lower the overall cost-basis of their holdings. They are not predominantly interested in the downside protection aspect of the covered-call since they are going to hold their stocks regardless of what the market might do, therefore, they are less sensitive to risk. Those with a high tolerance to risk can afford to collect less premium for downside protection; this affords them the chance to write calls that are further out of the money or of shorter duration.

Trade Management Thoughts and Considerations

Whether you fall into the high-risk or low-risk category, one thing is certain – after any trade is executed it will need to be managed due to shifts in the underlying, implied volatility, or movement in the underlying. The covered call is definitely not a complacent strategy - even if you are 100% correct with your conviction – it needs to be managed.

The Covered Call and Thoughts from Experience

- **"Everyone's Doing It"** Investors and portfolio managers are natural owners of stock and they typically sell out of the money calls for additional income or feel pressure to meet a benchmark. Whatever the case, this natural supply of repetitive call selling can and does reduce the implied volatility of the out of the money call price – especially as compared to equidistant out of the money put prices. We call this options skew (Chapter 11: "Options Volatility Skew"). **Bottom line:** Due to the natural inclination of public call selling, you will rarely – if ever – receive enough options premium to satisfy the risk-reward of giving up your upside potential.

- **"Bad Way to Sift Wheat from the Chaff"** Think about it. You have 10 stocks in your portfolio all of which you sell call options against. After the passage of time, some of the stocks have gone up, some have gone down, and some have not changed. The stocks that went up (the goods ones) got called away. The ones that have gone down are most likely well below the call strike sold. What inevitably remains is a portfolio off poorly performing stocks.

- **"Violating one of the Primary Principles of Trading Risk Management"** The primary objective of long-term trading success is to maximize income while using leverage to limit portfolio risk. The covered call violates this premise as you are layering an options strategy that caps upside potential while slightly reducing the downside exposure. Surely, there are circumstances where the covered call makes good sense but, the investor must be fully aware of the risks involved. It's a comparatively negative skewed trading bet – one that you want to stay away from over the long-term.

- **"Risking Dollars to Make Pennies"** In trading it's absolutely paramount to continually cut your losses and let your winners run. This is instinctual to some of the world's best traders – for the rest of us it's an acquired trait – one that requires tons of discipline and practice. From personal trading and/or investment experience, I can tell you that some of my very best stock convictions – the home run trades (JPM -early 1990's, AMZN – late 1990's) were reduced to mediocrity as I was forced to deliver stock immediately before the stock catapulted to the upper atmosphere.

The Covered Call and Considerations from Experience

<u>You Have a Change in Market View:</u> Once again, the covered-write is a strategy that is meant to be applied in a neutral to moderately bullish environment. If one's market view suddenly shifts away from neutral to moderately bullish (i.e., becomes bearish or rampantly bullish) then the covered-write is an inappropriate strategy and should be liquidated.

There are actually two ways to exit a covered-write quickly. One is to liquidate (i.e. buy back the short call and sell the underlying) the original position. The second technique is to utilize a synthetic relationship that exists between a covered-call position and the put of the same strike and expiration. Recall, a covered-call is actually the synthetic equivalent of a short put of the same strike and expiration of the short call component of the covered-write. This means that the covered-call behaves exactly as short put in terms of risk, reward, and breakeven points of the position.

So a quick way to "neutralize" a covered-call position is to buy the put of the same strike and expiration date as the short call in the covered

–call position. Implementing this leaves a residual arbitrage position known as a "conversion". The conversion has very little risk, but still may require some capital to hold, and may or may not have to be managed at expiration regarding the exercise of the long put.

Long Underlying Moves up through Your Short Call Strike

Once the underlying moves up through the strike, the upside profit potential of the covered-write is capped. In order to give the position some additional upside potential, the short call has to be "rolled up" to a higher strike.

Rolling Up: This can be achieved by buying a vertical call spread, covering the short call and selling a higher strike call in the same expiration month. The purchase of a long call spread will cost the investor some money, adding to the cost basis of the position. Assume you sold $21.00 calls when the stock was trading at $20.00. If the stock rises to $21.50 for example, you might consider buying back the short $21.00 calls and selling the $22.50 strike.

Long Underlying Moves down through Your Short Call Strike, More Protection Desired

The covered-call does offer a modest amount of downside protection for long underlying positions. The amount of this protection is equal to the premium collected when writing the call. If additional protection is desired, additional premiums must be collected. This can be accomplished by "rolling down" the short call to a lower strike by selling a vertical call spread in the same expiration month.

Rolling Down: Assume you sold $21.00 calls when the stock was trading at $20.00. If the stock drops to $19.00 per share, you might want to buy back the $21.00 calls and sell the $17.50 calls. As the stock drops, even if implied volatility rises, the short calls ($21.00 calls) may become cheaper, making it possible for the investor to buy them back for less than they originally sold for. Rolling down your strike will provide you with more downside protection and provide you with a new short strike with more value.

Instant action is not the same as contemplative action. Exercising both together is ideal, but acting too hastily may hurt you more than acting too slowly.

CHAPTER 14

The "Cash-Write" or "Cash-Secured Put"

"Correlations and betas change. When building a portfolio, one has to account for the increasing correlation that occurs with downside shocks. Further, risk factors leading to correlation come in and out of the market. After 9/11, a travel factor became dominant with cruise ships, airplanes, hotels, and entertainment venues showing similar weakness. After the Long-term Capital issue, a super-premium appeared based on the liquidity of an asset. Factor defining risk change, and therefore correlations change."

-Peter J. Layton, Principal

Blackthorne Capital Management, LLC

The Volatility Skew

Consider the sturdy Midwestern bank that for generations earned a stable income loaning money to credit-worthy companies and families. Generations removed from its origins, the bank grows bold and begins lending a lot of money to a diverse host of business concerns all with prime credit. And, to the delight of the board and applause of its shareholders, the bank kept on earning steady interest and kept boosting its bottom line. One day, one of the company's abruptly defaulted on one of the loans. And, all of a sudden, within one week, there was a cascading effect and a large number of these borrowers defaulted and the banks vault, once chocked-full of sure profits, simply vanishes! Over the decades what appeared to be a safe, steady stream of earnings on the balance sheet suddenly gets transformed into a huge crater.

The bank, in effect, was short a put option. Like short options, the loaning of money has a lop-sided payoff. Perhaps a 99.0% probability of making a gain however, it's the 1.0% that eventually will catch up to you. Remember, in options trading, odds and probabilities DO NOT matter. What does matter is the impact to you and your portfolio should you fall prey to that 1.0%.

The "Cash Write" with Puts

The buy-write is a sensible and time-honored strategy for investors holding equities. Writing (selling) calls against long stock positions may generate additional income, enhance portfolio returns, and, depending on location and expiration date of the strike written, provide a degree of downside protection to the portfolio.

As the market declines and cash levels of portfolios rise, investors need to recognize that writing puts against cash in a portfolio is just as sensible, and may be just as lucrative. How does one write puts against cash? It is simply a matter of understanding relationships:

Every trade has its inverse side. Whether obvious or not every long position generates a short position, and every short position generates a long position.

Think of the currency markets. If I buy USD/EUR, I am long the US dollar and short the Euro. It is the same with equities and cash, when you buy stock, you become short of cash, when you sell stock, you become long cash.

For example:

Buy 100 XYZ @ $100/Share, resulting position, long 100 XYZ, short $10,000.

-OR-

Long XYZ @ $100/Share = Short dollars @ .01 Shares/$.

As the market rallies, XYZ should appreciate in terms of the dollar, or the dollar should depreciate in terms of XYZ. If the market were to sell off, XYZ should depreciate in terms of the dollar, or the dollar should appreciate in terms of XYZ.

Seeing this inverse relationship between cash (dollars) and equities, one can now see that calls on equities = puts on cash (if you exercise an equity call, you pay cash to receive the equity), and puts on equities = calls on cash (if you exercise an equity put, you sell the equity to receive cash).

Writing Puts

Therefore, writing puts on equities is the same as writing calls on cash. Just as with a buy write program, where one must have the securities to deliver if called, with a cash write program, one must have the cash to deliver if put. Selection of the strikes and expiration cycle of puts to be written is exactly the same as call writing in reverse. Let's examine a couple of scenarios:

An investor is sitting on some cash and decides that ABC, currently trading at $50/share would be very attractive at $40/share. The investor decides to sell the ABC 40 puts (the same as selling calls on his cash). Let's examine some possible outcomes:

- The market declines and the puts are exercised; the investor delivers the cash and is now long ABC at $40 minus the premium collected in selling the put.

- The market trades sideways, the puts expire worthless, and the investor pockets the premium, enhancing the return on his cash position. Another put could now be written if desired.

- The market rockets upward, the puts expire worthless, the investor pockets the premium enhancing the return on his cash position BUT he is left holding cash as ABC rallied sharply.

As the buy-write gives limited protection against equities going lower, so writing puts against cash only gives limited protection against equities going higher. For this reason, this strategy is not appropriate for a strong bullish view.

The conditions suitable for covered call writing are suitable for cash-covered put writing: High implied volatilities and a market view that the stock will drift either sideways or slightly higher.

Textbook Definition of the "Cash-Secured Put" or "Cash-Write"

The investor simultaneously sells a put contract and deposits in a brokerage account the <u>full cash amount</u> for a potential purchase of underlying shares. The point of depositing this cash is to ensure that it's obtainable should the investor be assigned on the short put position and be required to purchase shares at the put's strike price. The net price paid for the underlying shares on assignment is equivalent to the put's strike price minus the premium received for selling the put in the first place. For this reason, the strike price selected, less the premium amount, should replicate the investor's target price for purchasing underlying shares.

Cash Write Breakeven

The breakeven point for the cash write is an underlying price equal to the put's strike price less the premium received for selling the put. If the underlying declines below the strike price by expiration, on assignment, the trader will be "put" the underlying, i.e., purchase underlying well above its present price level. However, this loss will be unrealized as long as the participant holds the underlying. Anybody whose motivation in writing a cash-secured put is to buy underlying should therefore be committed in advance to a target price for a possible purchase and select a strike price accordingly.

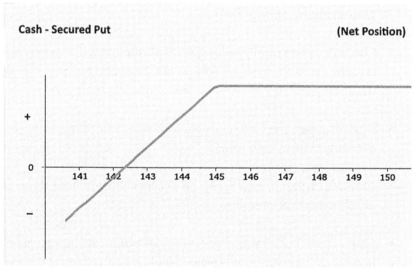

Figure I   Options Technology Solutions, UK

Cash Secure Put and its Synthetic Equivalency to the Covered Call

Bear in mind that writing puts on equities is the same as writing calls on cash. Just as with a covered call, where one must have the securities to deliver if called, with a cash-write program, one must have the cash to deliver if put. Selection of the strikes and expiration of puts to be written is exactly the same as call writing in reverse. As the covered call gives limited protection against equities going lower, so writing puts against cash only gives limited protection against equities going higher. The conditions suitable for covered call writing are suitable for cash-covered put writing: High implied volatilities and a market view that the stock will drift either sideways or slightly higher.

Who Should Consider the Cash-Secured Put?

- One who is 100% resolute in their conviction to buy the underlying in which the put is written.

- One who is potentially willing to give up potential gains in the underlying by selling the put.

- One who is potentially willing to buy underlying that is beneath current market prices and will potentially persist to trade lower than the put strike at which it was originally sold.

- One who perceives the cash-secured put trade as payment for entering a stock limit order.

- One who fully understands and accepts the potential dangers of selling option premium.

- One who is both taking advantage of observed high levels of implied volatility and/or elevated implied levels of options skew.

Example of Cash-Secured Put Trade and Profit-Loss

Example: Suppose you like the long-term prospects of **Weight Watchers International (WTW)** yet, the current price of $27.37 per share is a little rich for your blood – you'd feel much more comfortable owning the stock in the low $20's.

Setup:

- Sell 1 November $22.00 put for $0.80/per share or $80.00 per hundred shares. From your vantage point, this seems like an appropriate amount of premium as judged by the perceived risk.

- Deposit $2,120 (cash) with the brokerage house. ($22.00 x 100 shares = $2,200 - $80.00 (premium received) = $2,120).

Potential P/L Scenarios:

- **Best Case #1**: On November expiration, WTW settles anywhere between $22.00 and $28.17 ($27.37 + $0.80) in which case you keep the $80.00 of premium.

- **Best Case #2:** On November expiration, WTW settles just below $22.00 and above $21.20. In this case, you will be assigned the stock (recall your conviction) at an attractive price and will also – depending on where it settles between $21.21 and $22.00 keep part of the original premium sold.

- **Worst Case #1:** On November expiration, WTW catapults to the stratosphere - far above $27.37. You were 100% correct with your conviction however dead-wrong about your investment time frame! Believe me, the $80.00 earned (the put premium collected) will feel hare-brained in comparison of "what could have been" if you would've simply bought the stock instead of selling that measly put!

- **Worst Case #2:** On November expiration, WTW falls victim to some outlier, rare event subsequently pushing the stock down the basement steps with no hopes of stopping. Your original sincerity of "feeling more comfortable purchasing the stock in the mid-$20's," seems ill-advised and misplaced. You are stuck buying stock well above the current market price – all with the courtesy of that $80.00 worth of premium and an idea just gone plain bad!

Expiry Price	November 22.00 Profit/Loss	Post Expiration Stock Position
$0.00	($2,120)	100 @ $22.00
$5.00	($1,620)	100 @ $22.00
$10.00	($1,120)	100 @ $22.00
$15.00	($620)	100 @ $22.00
$20.00	($120)	100 @ $22.00
$21.00	($20)	100 @ $22.00
$22.00	$80.00	0
$27.37	$80.00	0
$28.17	$80.00	0
$30.00	$80.00	0
$35.00	$80.00	0
$50.00	$80.00	0

underlying WTW = $27.37

Figure 2

Many investors avoid selling puts because of the large downside risk; a stock can always fall to zero. However, these same investors are usually willing to buy stock and hold it through a lengthy decline, far beyond the point at which it should have been sold in the name of prudent risk management. The key to success with this procedure is to understand its unique drawbacks and to implement the strategy correctly in the appropriate market conditions.

An Expensive (Cash-Write Put) Lesson

Imagine that you were once a proud shareholder of the large insurance concern – AIG. Throughout that time, you were steadfast and unmovable in your devotion as a stockholder. And, your affection grew ever fonder as the company nearly scuttled through 9/11 and shook violently during the 2005 loss of its coveted AAA, US Government-like credit rating. That tumultuous eight-year affair had cost you $20.00 per share as the stock seeped lower with each passing year.

Yet, you were infatuated with the company, hypnotized with its potential and star-struck with your own personal trading ability. With every tick lower in AIG stock, you twisted yet another fantasy on why everyone else had it wrong. You had Stockholm syndrome to the nth degree. And, you set out to prove yourself right and everyone else wrong!

Trade Selection Lead to Undesirable Consequences

"Stand up and be counted!" "Consensus is wrong!" "The market is over-emphasizing its AAA rating!" With that mindset, you produced a plan. You were going to sell puts naked on AIG and either:

- **Best-case scenario** – Watch AIG stock rally (which you were fully expecting) and enjoy seeing your short puts expire worthless providing me you a little extra income!

- **Worst-case scenario** – AIG stock expires beneath your short put strike in which case you would be "put" the stock (i.e. buy the stock) at the puts strike price. If you liked the stock at $80.00 (original purchase price) you will love it at $55.00! That best describes the boldness of your approach.

The downward spiral started in late October 2007; you sold 10 December $55.00 puts for $2.00 with AIG trading at $58.00. Your profit and loss details were as follows:

<u>Trade #1:</u> **Sold 10 AIG December '07 $55.00 puts at $2.00 per share. AIG reference: $58.00**

- **Best-case scenario** -If at expiration AIG closed $55.01 or higher – you would keep the entire $2,000. (Recall, you sold 10 puts at $2.00. This equates to 10 x 100 shares x $2.00 premium = $2,000).

- **Breakeven scenario** – If at expiration AIG closed at $53.00. (Recall, you sold the $55.00 put for $2.00. $55.00 strike price - $2.00 premium= $53.00). You would be "put" stock at $55.00 however, your theoretical purchase price would be $53.00 given the premium I received for selling the put.

- **Worst-case scenario** – If at expiration AIG closed at $53.00 or lower, your loss would be 1:1 with the downward stock move.

Conclusion on Trade #1:

In short, if AIG settled at $55.00 or below, you would be assigned the stock (i.e. you would own 1,000 shares at $55.00 however, given the original $2.00 premium you received, you would be insulated from loss until the stock went below $53.00).

December expiration day arrived with AIG stock expiring at $58.00. Your account grew by $2,000 due to your put sale expiring worthless. Feeling justified in your conviction, you repeated the same strategy. This time around, you sold the February '08 $55.00 put at $2.50 per share ($2.50 x 100 shares x10 contracts = $2,500) with AIG stock trading near $58.00.

Expiry Price	December 55 Put Profit/Loss	Post Expiration Stock Position
$10.00	($43,000)	1000 @ $55.00
$40.00	($13,000)	1000 @ $55.00
$45.00	($8,000)	1,000 @$55.00
$50.00	($3,000)	1000 @ $55.00
$55.00	$2,000	0
$58.00	$2,000	0
$60.00	$2,000	0
$65.00	$2,000	0
$70.00	$2,000	0
$75.00	$2,000	0
$105.00	$2,000	0

Underlying AIG = $58.00

Figure 3

<u>Trade #2:</u> **Sold 10 AIG February '08 $55.00 puts @ $2.50 per share. AIG reference: $58.00**

- **Best-case scenario** – If at expiration AIG closed $55.01 or higher – you would keep the entire $2,500. (Recall, you sold 10 puts at $2.50. This equates to 10 x 100 shares x $2.50 premium = $2,500).

- **Breakeven scenario** – If at expiration AIG closed at $52.50. (Recall, you sold the $55.00 put for $2.50. $55.00 strike price - $2.50 premium = $52.50). You would be "put" stock at $55.00 however, your theoretical purchase price would be $52.50 given the premium you received for selling the put.

- **Worst-case scenario** – If at expiration AIG closed at $52.50 or lower, your loss would be 1:1 with the downward stock move.

Conclusion on Trade #2

This is when things went horribly wrong! AIG stock expired in February '08 at $47.00 – leaving you straddled somewhere between dumbstruck and shell-shocked! "How could've you possibly allowed yourself to lose $5,500 on top of what you were already losing on your original stock investment!" "Where was the discipline, the stop-loss mechanisms, the exit plan?"

In a random flash of awareness, you recognized you had no plan and, if you did, it was stubbornness peppered with stupidity. You distinctly recall feeling captured in a frozen, hypnotic state likened to a nightmare - one where you're desperately attempting to run from danger yet, you simply cannot move your legs. No matter what, you were now the proud owner of 1,000 additional shares of AIG at $52.50; (You were assigned on the $55.00 put strike that you sold price minus $2.50 premium collected).

In March '08, your near ten-year affair came to an abrupt end. Your love had turned to sadness then to anger as you finally came to terms with your laundry list of shortcomings. You finally jettisoned your stock at $43.00 per share having lost a small fortune and never looked back.

Expiry Price	February 55 Put Profit/Loss	Post Expiration Stock Position
$10.00	($42,500)	1000 @ $55.00
$40.00	($12,500)	1000 @ $55.00
$47.00	($5,500)	1000 @ $55.00
$50.00	($2,500)	1000 @ $55.00
$55.00	$2,500	0
$58.00	$2,500	0
$60.00	$2,500	0
$65.00	$2,500	0
$70.00	$2,500	0
$75.00	$2,500	0
$105.00	$2,500	0

Underlying AIG = $58.00

Figure 4

CHAPTER 15

The Collar Strategy

The collar (also called a fence) is frequently used by those who are looking to limit their downside risk on a long underlying position. Its name comes from its ability to contain or "fence in" potential risk and reward.

Collar and reverse collar strategies can fall into two categories. They can be used as bullish or bearish, stand-alone speculative strategies or they can be used to hedge and/or modify the risk in an existing bullish or bearish position in the underlying market.

When used as an options spread strategy, the collar and reverse-collar are usually employed for very specific market scenarios:

- To capture persuasive directional moves to the upside or downside.

- To play contingent "if/then" types of scenarios.

- To play particular breakout/ breakdown situations.

A collar merges a covered call and a protective put. Both the covered call and the protective put. As an investor, you would establish a collar primarily to protect your positions against loss if market values fall. But you can also use the collar to allow for growth in market values, and all of this protection comes at a discreet cost. The money you earn from selling a covered call can be used to cover most or all of the costs to buy the protective put.

To create a collar, you buy a put option (a married put) and sell or write a call option (a covered call) at the same time. Both are based on the same underlying, both are out of the money, and both expire on the same date. Generally, you buy the puts and sell the calls for a stock position that you already own to completely cover that position.

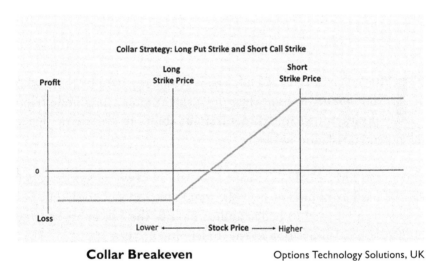

Collar Breakeven   Options Technology Solutions, UK

Composition of the Collar

To establish a collar, the trader simultaneously purchases an out of the money put and sells an out of the money covered call. For example, if XYZ, a fictitious stock, currently trades at $50, buying 100 shares of XYZ, selling the XYZ 55 call and buying the XYZ 45 put creates a collar.

Example of the Collar

Suppose you have one thousand shares of XYZ common stock, currently trading at $30 per share. You are familiar with using married put contracts to protect this stock if the stock falls, but you don't want to spend the money to buy the ten put contracts you would need to cover those thousand shares.

To lower the net cost of your risk strategy, you could buy ten six-month $27.50 put contracts for $3 each, and at the same time sell ten six-month $35 calls for $2.50 each. Your net cost is 50 cents per contract.

> ## Risk
> Risk = underlying price – put strike +/- cost of collar
> ## Reward
> Reward = call strike – underlying price +/- cost of collar
> ## Breakeven
> Breakeven = underlying price +/- cost of collar

Collar Strategy	Instrument	volume	price per share
own	stock	1000	$30.00
buy	put	10	$3.00
sell	call	10	$2.50
net premium paid per share			$0.50

Call Strike = $35.00 ; Put Strike = $27.50 ; Expiry = 6 months

Figure I

Consider Three Potential Expiry Scenarios

- XYZ common shares close above the short call strike of $35
- XYZ common shares close below the long put strike of $27.50
- XYZ common shares close between the collared strikes of $27.50 and $35.00

XYZ Is above the Short Call Strike of $35 at Expiration

If XYZ is trading above $35 at expiration, the call options contracts you sold will be exercised against you, forcing you to sell the thousand shares of stock to the other investor at $35 a share. In this example you are selling the stock at $35 a share, making a profit of $5 a share over your original purchase price, but less the 50 cents per share cost for the collar. So your profit is $4.50 a share.

XYZ Is below the Long Put Strike of $27.50 at Expiration

If XYZ is trading below $27.50 when the contracts expire, you will exercise the put contracts forcing the seller to buy the shares from you at $27.50. You end up losing $3 a share. You originally bought the stock for $30, so you lose $2.50 per share in the sale, plus the net cost of the collar, 50 cents per share. But in this case you limit your total loss to $3 per share.

XYZ Is Trading between $27.50 and $35 at Expiration

If the price of a share of XYZ is between $27.50 and $35 when the contracts expire, both the put and call options will be out of the money and will expire as worthless. You get to keep your shares of XYZ, you protected yourself against excessive loss, and the only cost to you is the 50 cents per share in insurance premiums in the form of the put and call contracts.

Figure 2 below shows the likely results of your investment strategy based on the price of a share of XYZ stock at the put and call contracts' expiration date.

Collar Strategy Profit and Loss Table at Expiration (Long 1,000 Shares XYZ @ $30 per Share; Long 10 XYZ $27.50 Puts; Short 10 XYZ $35 Calls)

XYZ Price Expiry	Collar P/L	Stock P/L	Net P/L
$50.00	($15,500)	$20,000	$4,500
$36.00	($1,500)	$6,000	$4,500
$35.50	($1,000)	$5,500	$4,500
$35.00	($500)	$5,000	$4,500
$34.00	($500)	$4,000	$3,500
$33.00	($500)	$3,000	$2,500
$32.00	($500)	$2,000	$1,500
$31.00	($500.00)	$1,000	$500
$30.00	($500.00)	$0.00	($500)
$29.00	($500.00)	($1,000)	($1,500)
$28.00	($500.00)	($2,000)	($2,500)
$27.50	($500.00)	($2,500)	($3,000)
$27.00	$0.00	($3,000)	($3,000)
$26.00	$1,000	($4,000)	($3,000)
$25.00	$2,000	($5,000)	($3,000)
$10.00	$17,000	($20,000)	($3,000)

Figure 2

Dynamics of the Collar Strategy

A trader who is moderately bullish on a stock but lacks a strong conviction is likely to consider establishing a collar. I say *moderately bullish* because the covered call caps the profit potential on the stock. Take note that the strike price of the call determines the degree of bullishness of the strategy. This strategy becomes more bullish the farther the call moves out of the money.

To fully appreciate the potential cost effectiveness of the collar we must first understand the dynamics behind a more basic hedging strategy, the protective put.

Basic Hedging: The Protective Put

Let's take a step backwards for a moment: What is a hedge? A hedge is established to protect an existing position. The trader who establishes a hedge effectively acquires an insurance policy for that position.

The most straightforward means of protecting a long stock position is to purchase a protective put. In this hedge, the trader buys one put for every 100 shares of stock owned. A put option permits the trader to sell underlying stock at a specified price for a predetermined period of time. By purchasing a put, the hedger is perfectly protected, or insured against an unforeseen move in the underlying at any price at or beyond the exercise price of the purchased option.

Imagine a trader owns 100 shares of XYZ stock currently trading at $40. After careful reflection, the trader decides that a loss on the stock down to $35 is tolerable. What can be done to add a measure of protection here? Simple: Purchase 1 XYZ 35 put to hedge every 100 shares of stock. With the puts in place, the trader has the right, but not the obligation, to sell all 100 shares of stock for $35, no matter how far down the stock drops.

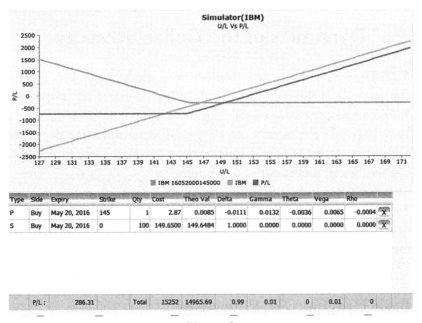

Simulator(IBM)
U/L Vs P/L

Type	Side	Expiry	Strike	Qty	Cost	Theo Val	Delta	Gamma	Theta	Vega	Rho
P	Buy	May 20, 2016	145	1	2.87	0.0085	-0.0111	0.0132	-0.0036	0.0065	-0.0004 X
S	Buy	May 20, 2016	0	100	149.6500	149.6484	1.0000	0.0000	0.0000	0.0000	0.0000 X

P/L:	286.31		Total	15252	14965.69	0.99	0.01	0	0.01	0

Figure 3

XYZ	25	27.5	30	32.5	35	37.5	40	42.5	45
35 put	10.00	7.50	5.00	2.50	0.00	0.00	0.00	0.00	0.00
Premium	(0.75)	(0.75)	(0.75)	(0.75)	(0.75)	(0.75)	(0.75)	(0.75)	(0.75)
Total	9.25	6.75	4.25	1.75	(0.75)	(0.75)	(0.75)	(0.75)	(0.75)

Note: Commission costs are not included in these examples.

Figure 4

Hedging at a Reduced Cost: The Collar

So what is the downside, if any, to buying protective puts? Why wouldn't every trader with a stock position purchase a put to hedge against an adverse movement in the market this way? The answer is that the premiums on these options can be expensive.

We are now in a position to appreciate the practicality of the collar. The trader establishes a collar can finance part or all of the cost of the put with the premium received from the sale of the call. In some instances, the short call can be sold for a premium equal to or greater than the cost of the put. In this scenario, the strategy is essentially put on for free, and sometimes even for a credit.

If the puts being purchased trade at a higher implied volatility than the calls being sold, as many currently are, the underlying may have to be higher than the mid-point between the strikes to execute the collar for zero-cost.

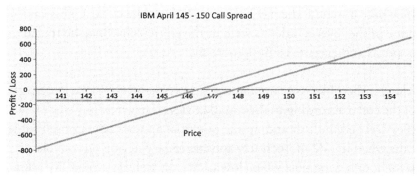

Figure 5   Options Technology Solutions, UK

Applying a collar to a long underlying position simply converts it to a limited risk/limited return bull spread. In the following example, the trader sacrifices any gains above 10% on the upside, in return for protection from any losses exceeding 10% on the downside.

Application of the Collar

When is it best to use a collar? Looking at the payout summary in Figure 2 for the collar versus the simple long underlying position, we see that the collar position outperforms the long underlying position below the strike price of the put, performs the same between the strike price of the put and the strike price of the call, and under performs above the strike price of the call. Therefore, since a collar limits the upside of a long stock position, it is best to apply them when potential upside looks limited and downside risk is a concern.

Other Considerations

One of the best things about the collar is its flexibility. Since there is a long option component and a short option component, traders can put on the strategy in stages (also referred to as "legging in", taking advantage of implied volatility fluctuations. For example: When implied volatility is high, they may sell the out-of-the-money call against the underlying (constructing a buy-write) and when volatility comes down, they may purchase the put (which completes the collar.) This can be done in the reverse order as well, or the entire collar may be traded as a spread and executed simultaneously.

Many traders like to swing their positions in and out of various stages of the collar according to their market view. They may buy stock when they feel very bullish and upside potential appears large; or sell some calls when upside momentum appears to be petering out or volatility is high; or buying puts when downside risks appear or volatility is low.

Collar Strategy Strike Selection

Strike selection is very subjective and largely depends on your goals and risk tolerance. Strikes can be implemented close to at the money or far out of the money. If you are a long-term perspective, you want the stock price to stay within the range you set—the strike price for the put contracts you plan to buy and the call contracts you plan to sell. Fortunately you can adjust your strategy on the basis of how much risk you can tolerate, the cost for the premiums over time, and how volatile the share prices are likely to be in the months to come.

Defensive Collar

Consider the defensive collar strategy if your primary concern is your downside exposure.

The defensive collar involves buying an at the money or near–at the money put while also selling an at the money or near–at the money call contract. This strictly limits on your risk and reward profile. The tighter you make the collar—that is, the closer the put and call contracts are to being

In the money—the more restricted your profit or loss will become.

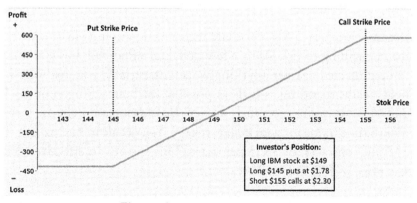

Figure 6   Options Technology Solutions, UK

As seen in Figure 6, your total profit or loss from the combinations of these positions is limited to $3 per share. This means that if your stock explodes to $100 per share, the most you will receive is $41. Conversely, if your stock tanks to $1 per share, the least you will receive is $38.

The Appreciating Collar

An appreciating collar is used as a milder risk management technique to provide a downside stop, yet upside potential as well. A standard appreciating collar is the coinciding purchase of an out of the money put against the sale of a further out of the money call. Typically, the appreciating collar strikes are not equidistant (where the call strike is further out of the money than the put strike) from the underlying stock price. The wider the collar strikes chosen, the wider your profit/ loss profile will be.

To illustrate this strategy, suppose that about a year ago you bought XYZ during the midst of a selling panic at $30 per share, and since then the stock has risen to about $40 per share. You may be either neutral or optimistic about the long-term prospects for this company's stock, but in the short term you're concerned about overall market volatility. More important, you have substantial unrealized gains in the stock ($10 per share), and you don't want to lose that. So you need to consider your strategy before setting up a collar trade on the stock.

Because you have a $10 per share unrealized gain in your stock, you may be willing to risk losing a few dollars if values fall, but you want to be protected against anything worse. Essentially, you just want to hold steady, spending as little as possible, without selling your stock and without losing too much money. In addition, you choose a six-month time frame for your collar strategy. You decide to buy six-month $37 put contracts for $3.15 per share. This ensures an effective XYZ sale price of $33.85 per share:

$37.00 strike price - $3.15 per share put premium = $33.85

To help pay for the put contracts and increase your potential sale price per share, you choose to sell a six-month $45 call for $1.80 per share. This sale will obligate you to sell the stock at $45 if the contracts are exercised against you, but the sale also reduces your put premium cost. Your total collar cost is as follows:

Long six-month $37 put - short six-month $45 call
Or
$3.15 per share - $1:80 per share = $1.35 per share

The $1.35 net purchase price of the six-month $37/$45 collar provides you with the following results:

- If the share price falls, your effective sale price will be $35.65 per share, or $37 per share strike price on the put contract minus $1.35 per share net cost to set up the collar. No matter how low the stock goes, you know you will be able to sell the shares for the next six months for $35.65 per share.

- If the share price climbs, your effective sale price will be $43.65 per share, or $45 per share strike price on the call contract minus $1.35 per share net cost to set up the collar. No matter how high the stock goes over the next six months, you know that you will not be able to sell your stock for more than $43.65 per share.

Call Strikes	Price	Put Strikes	Price
$41.00	$3.30	$39.00	$4.05
$42.00	$2.90	$38.00	$3.60
$43.00	$2.50	$37.00	$3.15
$44.00	$2.15	$36.00	$2.75
$45.00	$1.80	$35.00	$2.35
$46.00	$1.55	$34.00	$2.05
$47.00	$1.35	$33.00	$1.80
$48.00	$1.10	$32.00	$1.50
$49.00	$0.95	$31.00	$1.30
$50.00	$0.80	$30.00	$1.10

XYZ = $40.00 ; 120-day options

Figure 7

Summary

- As previously noted, choosing the correct strike prices for your matching put and call contracts for your collar trade is highly subjective. In the example of the $37/$45 collar, a few issues become clear: With a $1.35 per share cost, this collar apparently does provide insurance but at a hefty price. According to Table 1508, you are risking $4.35 to make, at the most, $3.65. In the long run, this may not be a good gamble.

- Notice in Figure 8 below that the prices are not equal in terms of call and put as well as the distance to the strike. For instance, with the stock at $40 per share, the $5 out of the money call contract trades at 55 cents less per share than the $5 out of the money put. This disparity between call and put prices is common, and the cause is directly caused by volatility, skew, dividends, and supply and demand.

- Weigh the cost/benefit of the strike prices you choose for an appreciation collar. As the old adage says, "You get what you pay for."

- You may decide that this $37 put/$45 call collar is too expensive for the amount of security it provides. Yet, consider the alternatives shown in Figure 9.

Stock Price at Expiry	Stock P/L at $40 per Share	Long $37 Put Value	Short $45 Call Value	Collar Debit	Net P/L per Share
$100.00	$60.00	$0.00	($55.00)	($1.35)	$3.65
$50.00	$10.00	$0.00	($5.00)	($1.35)	$3.65
$45.00	$5.00	$0.00	$0.00	($1.35)	$3.65
$43.65	$3.65	$0.00	$0.00	($1.35)	$2.30
$40.00	$0.00	$0.00	$0.00	($1.35)	($1.35)
$37.00	($3.00)	$0.00	$0.00	($1.35)	($4.35)
$35.65	($4.35)	$1.35	$0.00	($1.35)	($4.35)
$30.00	($10.00)	$7.00	$0.00	($1.35)	($4.35)
$15.00	($25.00)	$22.00	$0.00	($1.35)	($4.35)
$0.00	($40.00)	$37.00	$0.00	($1.35)	($4.35)

Long XYZ Stock @ $40 per Share ; Long XYZ $37.00 Puts ; Short XYZ $45.00 Calls at a Net Debit of $1.35 per Share

Figure 8

Collar	Strikes	Net Cost	Collar	Protected	Range
43 call	39 put	$1.55	$41.45	$37.45	$4.00
44 call	38 put	$1.45	$42.55	$36.55	$6.00
45 call	37 put	$1.35	$43.65	$35.65	$8.00
46 call	37 put	$1.20	$44.80	$34.80	$10.00
47 call	35 put	$1.00	$46.00	$34.00	$12.00

Range of Protection Implementing Various Strkie Prices

Figure 9

In Figure 9 you can see a sample of collars that could be implemented against the long XYZ position. The suggested collar strikes are all, for practical purposes, a mathematical extension from the original $45 call/$37 put example. A collar can be chosen with any combination of strikes, but note the following:

- You really do get what you pay for. Choosing the collar with the least cost or with no net cost at all may not provide you with the protection you want.

- Weigh the factors that matter most to you. Are you simply trying to avoid a loss if the market falls? Or do you have a wider tolerance for risk if you can also gain more opportunity for profit if share prices rise?

The Reverse Collar Strategy

The reverse collar is constructed by selling an out of the money put, and using the premium received to purchase an out of the money call (same expiration cycle) at the same time. In order for this combination to be zero-cost (call premium = put premium), the options need to be more or less equidistant from the current price of the underlying stock.

For example, if XYZ is currently trading at $50, selling the XYZ 45 put, and buying the XYZ 55 call could construct a reverse collar. The cost of the collar, *however, is dependent on market conditions. If the puts to be sold are trading at a higher implied volatility than calls to be purchased, one may actually receive a credit (take in money) by executing the reverse collar. If the puts to be sold are trading at a lower implied volatility than calls to be purchased, one may have to pay to execute the reverse collar.*

Theoretical Payout Diagrams

A reverse collar applied to a short underlying position has three components: short underlying, short puts (out-of-the-money), and long calls (out-of-the-money). By breaking this position down into its components, we can see the payout of the complete structure. The following is a breakdown of a 90 put /110 call reverse collar applied to a short underlying position (short stock at 100.00):

The "Reverse Collar" components:

Short Stock @ 100:

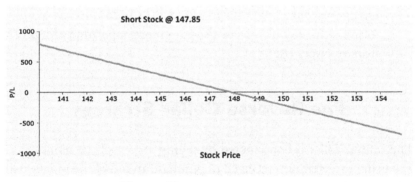

Figure 10   Options Technology Solutions, UK

The "Reverse Collar" components: Long 110 Call @ $5.00

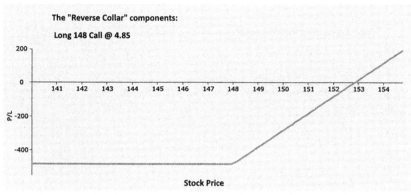

Figure 11   Options Technology Solutions, UK

Short $90 Put @ $5.00

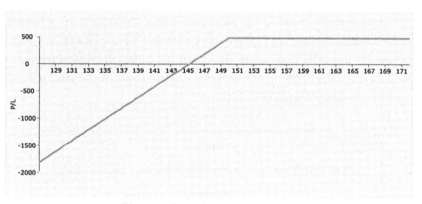

Figure 12   Options Technology Solutions, UK

The "Reverse Collar" with Short Stock: By combining all three of these separate positions together, you are left with:

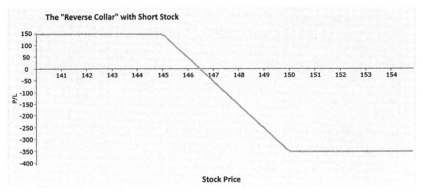

Figure 13   Options Technology Solutions, UK

Notice that we have also created a bear spread! Applying a reverse cost collar to a short underlying position simply converts it to a limited risk / limited return bear spread. The investor has sacrificed any gains below 10% on the down side, in return for some protection from any losses exceeding 10% on the up side. Calculations of the risk, reward, and breakeven points are as follows:

> **Risk**
>
> Risk = Call Strike – Underlying Price +/- cost of collar.
>
> **Reward**
>
> Reward = Underlying Price – Put Strike +/- cost of collar.
>
> **Breakeven**
>
> Breakeven = Underlying Price +/- cost of collar.

When is it best to apply a reverse collar to a short position? Looking at the payout in Figure 13 of the combined reverse collar/ short underlying position versus the simple short underlying position, we can see that the reverse collared position will outperform the short underlying position

238

above the strike price of the call, perform equally between the strike price of the put and the strike price of the call, and under-perform below the strike price of the put. Therefore, since application of a reverse collar limits the profit potential of a short stock position, it is best to apply one when potential downside looks limited versus upside risks.

Scaling

Like the collar, the reverse collar can be a very flexible vehicle. Since there is a long option component and a short option component, traders can put the strategy on in stages, taking advantage of implied volatility fluctuations.

For example, when implied volatility is high, traders could sell out of the money puts against their short underlying positions, and when volatility comes down, traders could purchase the out of the money calls, which would complete the reverse collar. This can also be done in the reverse order, depending on market conditions, or the entire collar may be traded as a spread and executed simultaneously.

A reverse collar may be an excellent stopgap strategy for shorts. When squeeze potential is high (pre-earnings, pre-Fed Announcement) traders might want to put a reverse collar on their short positions, ride out the storm, and then remove it when the coast is clear.

The Naked Reverse Collar Strategy

The naked reverse collar is constructed by selling an out of the money put, and using the premium received to purchase an out of the money call (same expiration cycle) at the same time. In order for this combination to be zero-cost (call premium = put premium), the options need to be more or less equidistant from the current price of the underlying stock.

For example, if XYZ is currently trading at $15, selling the XYZ 10 put, and buying the XYZ 20 call could construct a naked reverse collar. The cost of the collar, however, is dependent on market conditions. If the puts to be sold are trading at a higher implied volatility than calls to be purchased, one may actually receive a credit (take in money) by executing the reverse collar. If the puts to be sold are trading at a lower implied volatility than calls to be purchased, one may have to pay to execute the reverse collar.

There is also an interest rate component to the put premium vs. call premium equation. Option prices are based on the forward price of the underlying, not the spot price. Therefore any underlying with negative carry will have a forward price higher than the spot price, and the forward price will increase over time. This means that as you move out in time to more distant expiration cycles, the calls will trade at an increasing premium relative to puts.

Theoretical Payout Diagram

A reverse collar has two components: Short Puts (out of the-money), and Long Calls (out of the money). By breaking this position down into its components, we can see the payout of the complete structure. The following is a breakdown of a 10 put / 20 call naked reverse collar:

The "Naked Reverse Collar" components

Long 20 Call @ 1.50

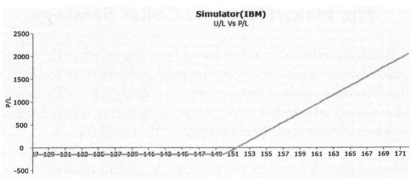

Figure 14   Options Technology Solutions, UK

240

Short 10 Put @ 1.50

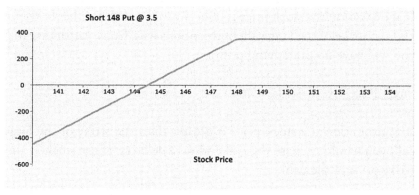

Short 148 Put @ 3.5

Figure 15   Options Technology Solutions, UK

The "Naked Reverse Collar"

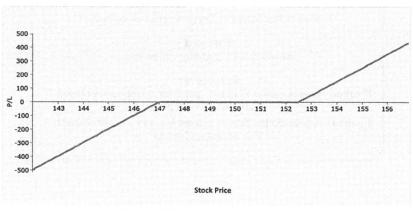

Figure 16   Options Technology Solutions, UK

At expiration there are three possible outcomes

<u>Stock Price < Put Strike</u>

If at expiration the stock price is less than the strike of the short put, you will be assigned and take delivery of the stock at the strike price of the put.

<u>Put Strike < Stock Price < Call Strike</u>

If at expiration the stock price is in between the strike of the short put and the strike of the long call, both options will expire worthless, and you will have no underlying position.

<u>Stock Price > Call Strike</u>

If at expiration the stock price is greater than the strike of the long call, you would exercise the call and take delivery of the stock at the strike price of the call.

Risk / Reward / Breakeven:

Risk

Risk = Put Strike – Zero +/- cost of collar.

Reward

Reward = Potentially Unlimited.

Breakeven

If naked reverse collar was executed for a debit, breakeven =
Call Strike + Debit;

If naked reverse collar was executed for a credit, breakeven =
Put Strike – Credit.

Application of the "Naked" Reverse Collar

The Zero Effect

When is it best to apply a naked reverse collar? Because of the semi-open ended risk of the short put (risk to zero), the investor has to have enough capital to absorb a move, theoretically, to zero. That is why it is usually best to apply a naked reverse collar to lower priced stocks. On the upside, it is important to have a stock that exhibits a certain amount of volatility, so there is the possibility that the stock could explode through the strike price of the call.

That is why this strategy is popular with traders who specialize in low-priced high-tech stocks. Whenever the tech stocks take a beating, these investors will put on naked reverse collars, knowing that they may get put the stock at a really low price, or catch it on a strong rebound like the one we just experienced.

Scaling

Since there is a long option component and a short option component, traders can put the strategy on in stages, taking advantage of implied volatility fluctuations.

For example, when implied volatility is high, traders could sell out of the money puts, and when volatility comes down, traders could purchase the out of the money calls, which would complete the naked reverse collar. This can also be done in the reverse order, depending on market conditions, or the entire naked reverse collar may be traded as a spread and executed simultaneously.

Collar and Trading Risk Management Objectives

The typical reason a collar or reverse collar is used to trade a directional forecast rather than another option strategy is that the trader is unsure of their timing. Because the collar and reverse collar have the "one long option/one short option" structure, the timing issue is softened as the time decay and implied volatility risks largely offset one another, allowing the trader to stay with the position longer while he or she waits for the forecast directional move.

In addition to a large-scale bullish or bearish forecast, choosing the structure of a collar or reverse collar requires an analysis of several market parameters:

What is your current short or intermediate market forecast? Bullish, bearish, or stagnant?

What is the prompt price for the forecast move? This is important information because, ideally, the long put (in the case of a collar) or the long call (in the case of the reverse collar) portion of the position should be located as close to the prompt price as possible to capture the majority of the forecast move.

What is the length of the forecast move? Although the collar and reverse collar are intentionally structured to allow for some inaccuracy in timing, it is still significant to have an idea – however it is arrived at – regarding when the underlying is going to make its move. The expiry selected for construction of the collar or reverse collar should comfortably cover this time horizon

What are current implied volatility and skew levels? Implied volatility surface can sometimes be the determining factor when a trader is contemplating several different strategies to address a market view.

What is your risk appetite? If the trader has plenty of capital to work with and okay with the possibility that he or she might end up with a position if the underlying moves in the opposite direction – getting long delta with the market moving lower or getting short delta with the market moving higher – then there is not a problem. The trader is simply getting long on weakness or short on strength instead of the other way around.

Successful Position Risk Management

If your trade is profitable it is important to vigorously manage the long put or long call component of the trade to squeeze the maximum profitability out of that portion of the position, while either closing out or deciding what to do about the lingering short option component of the trade that is now out of the money. This is frequently accomplished by "rolling" the long option position along with the underlying by selling vertical spreads. Rolling a long option position is an excellent way to manage a position that is "going your way". Rolling achieves three important things:

- It preserves your exposure in the direction of the breakout
- It decreases risk and takes "money off the table"
- By accomplishing the first two, it put you in a strong mental position and increases your "staying power".

Unsuccessful Position Risk Management

When the trade is unprofitable, you will have to aggressively manage the short call or short put component of the trade, while deciding what to do with the residual long put or long call component that is now far out of the money.

Whenever you enter a trade, it's always imperative to have a risk management strategy in place ahead of time. If, in fact, it becomes clear that one's forecast is mistaken, then it is time to get out the position. This is commonly achieved through the use of stop-loss orders. Stop-loss orders are buy or sell orders placed in the market that trigger if certain price conditions are met, turning them into market orders. Traders will usually use stop-loss orders to close losing positions if key price levels are violated–indicating an incorrect price forecast.

CHAPTER 16

Option Straddles

The straddle or strangle can, if initiated and managed properly during the right market conditions, prove to be a very profitable strategy. However, in order to successfully manage any strategy, one must first understand it thoroughly—what it is, when to put it on, how to use it, and when to modify it or exit. As you will soon find out, the straddle (and its cousin the strangle) can be deceptively simple.

Straddles and strangles are strategies that fall into the group of "non-directional" strategies. Both a call and a put are either purchased or sold, simultaneously. This means that one is not necessarily forecasting a path in the market, but rather a divergence from its current mean. Additionally, When you buy or sell a strangle or straddle, you are on one level stating that the market is mistaken, that the market is not correctly pricing the implied volatility of the options contracts involved.

The Straddle & Strangle: Basic Concepts

A straddle consists of the combination of both a long call and a long put, (or a short call and a short put when short the strategy) on the same underlying. Moreover, the strike price and expiration date must be the same. A strangle consists of the simultaneous purchase of a call and a put, but of different strikes. Typically, but not always, out of the money strikes, approximately equidistant from the current underlying price, are used when initiating a strangle.

Calls	Strike	Puts
	100	
+1	105	+1
	110	

Long Straddle

Figure 1

Calls	Strike	Puts
	100	+1
	105	
+1	110	

Long Strangle

Figure 2

Calls	Strike	Puts
	100	
-1	105	-1
	110	

Short Straddle

Figure 3

Calls	Strike	Puts
	100	-1
	105	
-1	110	

Short Strangle

Figure 4

- Hereafter I will use the term straddle synonymously with strangle.

The straddle falls under a category of strategies known as "volatility spreads". This name implies that the trader or investor who puts on (i.e. buys or sells) the straddle or strangle is speculating on the volatility, not necessarily the direction, of the underlying instrument. Now "volatility", as we all know, can be a hopelessly confusing concept. Thankfully, for our purposes, it is enough to define volatility as the degree of price fluctuation of the underlying over a given period of time.

The trader who establishes a volatility spread is much less concerned with the underlying's directional bias, than is, say, the trader who puts on a vertical spread, e.g. bull call, bear call, bull put or bear put. The volatility spreader, on the other hand, doesn't so much care if the underlying moves in a particular direction. Instead, he focuses on forecasting the degree of movement, if any, of the underlying instrument.

As with any options strategy, one can be either long the straddle or short the straddle. Whether one is long or short the straddle fundamentally alters one's perspective on the hoped-for degree of movement in the underlying. The investor who is long the straddle expects that the underlying will move substantially in one direction or the other, while the investor who is short the straddle anticipates little movement.

When the trader is long the call and the put, then he is said to be "long the straddle". When he is short the call and the put, he is said to be "short the straddle".

The "Greeks" of Straddles

The long straddle is comprised of a long call and a long put and carries the sensitivities that all long option positions carry: positive gamma, positive vega, and negative time decay (theta). The exact opposite holds true for the short straddle: short gamma, short vega, and positive time decay (theta). The straddle delta is dependent on the location of the underlying versus the strike. Because of the way it is structured, the straddle will have a positive delta when the underlying is above the strike price, a negative delta when the underlying is below the strike price, and be approximately delta neutral when the underlying is at the strike price.

	Long Straddle	Short Straddle	Long Strangle	Short Strangle
Delta	Dependent on strike price	Dependent on strike price	Dependent on strike price	Dependent on strike price
Gamma	Long	Short	Long	Short
Vega	Long	Short	Long	Short
Theta	Short	Long	Short	Long
Max Profit	No limit	Premium collected from both options	No limit	Premium collected from both options
Max Risk	Premium paid from both options	No limit	Premium paid from both options	No limit

Straddle/Strangle Greek Characteristics

Figure 5

Delta

The delta of a straddle/strangle is the aggregate of its components. For example the delta of a standard at the money straddle would be calculated as follows:

At-the-money put delta = (-.50)

At-the-money call delta = .50

Straddle delta = (- .50*1) + (.50*1) or 0.00 (delta neutral)

250

In this example, the at the money put has a negative delta, but a positive (long) position yielding a negative position adjusted delta. The at the money call has a positive delta and a positive (long) position, yielding a positive position adjusted delta. The position in this instance above has a delta of zero, commonly referred to as delta-neutral.

The net delta of a straddle/strangle can range between +1.00 and -1.00 contingent on the price of the underlying relative to the strike price involved, time left until expiration, implied volatility levels, and skew. The net delta will hover near zero when the underlying price is near the strike price. Since it is position that benefits from movement, the delta becomes gradually positive as the underlying moves above the strike, or increasingly negative as the underlying moves below the strike.

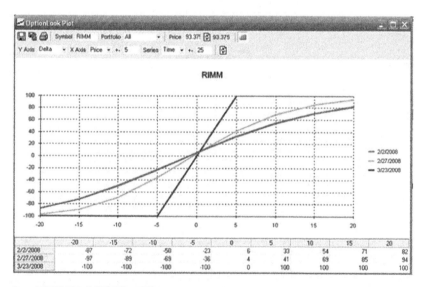

Long RIMM March 93.375 Straddle

Figure 6

Notice from Figure 6:

- The net delta of a long straddle moves favorably as the underlying moves, becoming gradually <u>more positive as the</u>

251

underlying moves higher and negative as the underlying moves lower.

- The delta of the long straddle is roughly zero when the underlying price is at the strike price. Eventually, if the underlying diverges far enough above or below the strike price the delta will reach + 1.00 or -1.00, when the long call or long put component goes deep in the money. (See Chapter 3: "Options Delta").

- Note that the rate at which the delta of the long straddle changes is highly dependent on the amount of time remaining until expiration. The sensitivity of the delta of the long straddle to changes in the underlying price increases dramatically as expiration approaches.

Gamma

The gamma of a straddle is the sum of the position-adjusted gammas of its options. For instance the gamma of the long XYZ 1500 straddle would be determined as follows:

1500 put gamma = .12

1500 call gamma = .12

Straddle gamma = (.12*1) + (.12*1) or .24

A gamma of .24 signifies that the net delta of the straddle would vary by roughly .24 for every 1 point move in the underlying. As viewed in Figure 7 below, a positive gamma suggests that the position delta will increase (become longer or less short) as the underlying trades higher, and decrease (become shorter or less long) as the underlying trades lower.

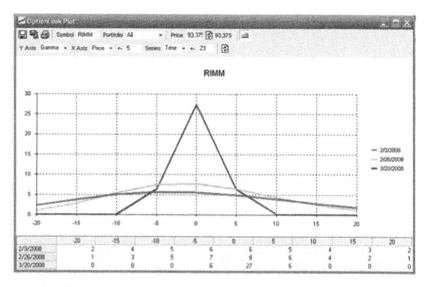

Long RIMM March 93.375 Straddle

Figure 7

Practical Gamma Considerations:

- Gamma is highly dependent on both the strike relative to the underlying and time to expiration.

- Gamma is also affected by relative implied volatility levels.

- An at-the-money option near expiration will have a greater gamma than an at the money option with greater time left until expiration. (See Chapter 4 "Options Gamma")

- Short-dated options gamma will evaporate more quickly than options with greater time until expiration.

- When there is more time until expiration the gamma curve is flatter. The position will still have the greatest amount of gamma when the underlying is at the strike, but the degree of change in the gamma of the position as the underlying moves away from the strike is less extreme.

253

Vega

The vega of a straddle/strangle is the aggregate of its component options. Case in point the vega of the long XYZ 1000 straddle would be calculated as follows:

1000 put vega = .12

1000 call vega = .12

Straddle vega = (.12*1) + (.12*1) or +.24

This signifies that for every 1% change in implied volatility the price of the straddle would change by approximately .24, rising when implied volatility rises, falling when implied volatility falls.

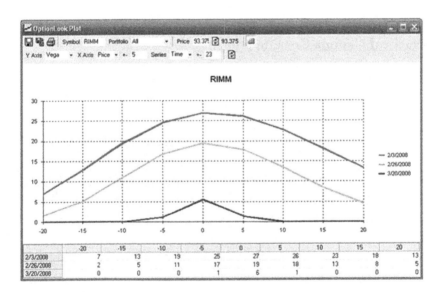

Long RIMM March 93.375 Straddle

Figure 8

Take note that the vega of the long straddle is larger when there is a larger amount of time left until expiration. (See Chapter 5: "Options Vega")

Theta

The theta of a long straddle is the sum of its component options. For instance, the theta of the long at the money 500 straddle would be calculated as follows:

500 put theta = -.10

500 call theta = -.10

Long Straddle theta = (-.10*1) + (-.10*1) or -.20

A long option position will erode with the passage of time. In the above example you see that the value of the long straddle would theoretically decrease by approximately .20 per day.

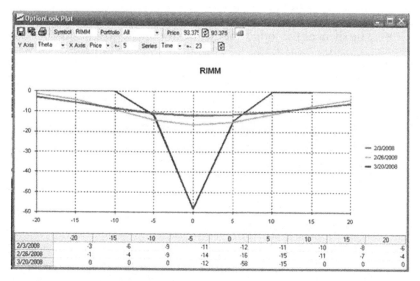

Long RIMM March 93.375 Straddle

Figure 9

Theta & Figure 9 Considerations

- Theta is reliant on the relationship between the straddle strike and underlying with at the money options having greater theta than in or out of the money options of the same expiration.

- Notice the theta of an at the money option <u>increases</u> as time to expiration <u>decreases</u> so, by extension, the theta of an at the money option with a lesser amount of time until expiration will be greater than the theta of an at the money option with a greater amount of time until expiration.

- Owning a long straddle – one that gets long when the underlying goes up, or gets short when the underlying goes down has a price tag associated (time decay) It is the potential effects of theta that one experiences as an offset to this position.

- The theta of the long straddle, in absolute terms, reaches its apex when the underlying is at the strike price, and increases with approach of expiration.

The Long Straddle – a practical example

Example:

- Buy 10 ITI Oct 80 Calls @ $2.50
- Buy 10 ITI Oct 80 Puts @ $1.50

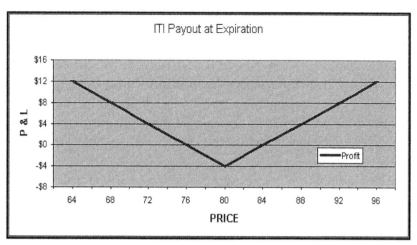

Figure 10

Price	Profit
64	12
68	8
72	4
76	0
80	-4
84	0
88	4
92	8
96	12

Straddle Break-even Chart

Figure 11

For investors encountering the long straddle for the first time, the strategy may appear rather counterintuitive. A question I frequently heard in my introductory level classes was this: "Tony, since a long call increases in value when the underlying goes up, and a long put increases in value when the underlying goes down why would a trader want to put both positions on simultaneously? Isn't this contradictory and self-defeating behavior?"

Well, let's think about it. To successfully answer this question, two points must be addressed:

First point, (regarding the direction of the market): as we now know the trader who buys the long straddle doesn't care if the market goes up or down, as long as the market moves considerably in either direction. If the price of the underlying changes substantially to the upside by the time of expiration, then his call may increase in value dramatically, while his put will trend towards worthless. Conversely, if the price of the underlying "tanks", then his put will increase in value while his call will lose its value.

The long straddle will become profitable at expiration for the trader if and only if the degree of movement of the now in the money option exceeds that (in dollar value) of the combined premiums paid for the both options. If the underlying does move substantially, the loss of the premium from the worthless option can be more than compensated for by the increase in value from the in the money option.

Second Point, (regarding the trader's motivation): The trader who buys the long straddle is assuming a high degree of risk. As one would guess, the straddle is a highly aggressive strategy that may result in significant profits. On the flip side, because it involves the outlaying of two premiums - (long the put & long the call). It can also be quite expensive. If the trader is wrong, and the market fails to move substantially in either direction, but instead just "sits there", both options may lose the entire premium paid!

The best way to grasp the rationale behind the long straddle is to provide a breakdown of its maximum risk, maximum reward and breakeven points.

First, familiarize yourself with Figure 10 and look at the call component (on the right), and trace out the increase in value as the underlying price moves higher. Next, do the same for the put side (on the left). Emblazon this graph in your mind now, and you will reap benefits in the future.

Maximum Loss: As mentioned above the maximum loss for the straddle is the sum of both premiums paid. Note that a total loss would occur only if the underlying closed at the straddle strike price.

Example: On Figure 10 above, the sum of both premiums paid is $4. This is your maximum loss, or risk. You would lose the entire $4 if and only if the stock closed right at $80.

Maximum Profit on Call: in theory, infinite. (Recall that the holder of a call profits when the price of the underlying spikes higher). Once the value of the underlying has increased enough to compensate for the combined premiums laid down the trader begins to profit.

Example: On Figure 11 above, the total debit incurred for the straddle was $4. Thus once stock climbs higher than $84, you begin to make money.

Maximum Profit on Put: Dollar for dollar down to zero, minus the combined premium.

Example: Again, because you paid $4 for the straddle, you would begin to make money at any point below $76.

Break-evens: As Figure 10 illustrates, lines break the X-axis at two points: $84 and $76. These values are the two breakeven points for the straddle: $84 represents the upside breakeven point, while $76 represents the downside breakeven point.

Upside = Strike Price + (call premium + put premium)
Example: 80 + 4 = 84

Downside = Strike Price − (call premium + put premium)
Example: 80 − 4 = 76

Figure 12

259

In other words, in order to break even, the in the money leg of the straddle must move far enough away from the strike price to cover the total premium paid.

The Long Straddle: Real World Example

American Express (AXP): Purchase the Jan 60 Straddle at $6.45. After studying some charts on American Express (AXP), I noticed the following:

- Volatility is low in its range. The Implied Volatility index for 52 weeks shows a high of 79.25 and a low of 35.84. The current level is 26.40.

- The stock is currently in a wedge; it will most likely go above its downtrend line or consolidate to lower levels. Also, the stock has a history, such that when it drops, it drops hard and fast and when it goes up, it really jumps. So a $7.00 move is not unrealistic.

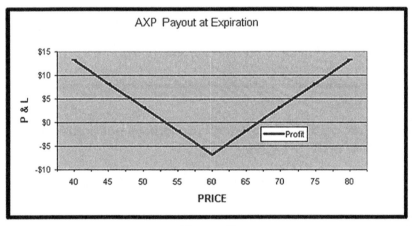

Figure 13

Price	Profit
40	13.2
45	8.2
50	3.2
55	-1.8
60	-6.8
65	-1.8
70	3.2
75	8.2
80	13.2

Straddle Break-even Chart

Figure 14

Managing the Straddle: Waiting vs. Working

<u>Initial position:</u> **Buy 20 AXP JAN 60 Calls @ $2.45 Buy 20 AXP JAN 60 Puts @ $4.00 = $6.45**

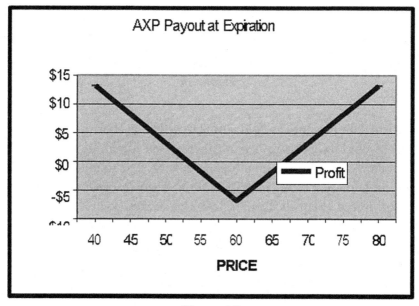

Figure 15

When I initiated the straddle at the open on December 3, AXP was at $58.91. I was looking for a reasonable move in either direction, either above $66.45 or below $53.55 by the JAN expiration. As I said, a 7-point move in AXP should not be unrealistic, especially in the seven weeks remaining until expiration. But as you can see in Figure 17 below this week saw a range with a high of $59.50 and a low of $56.50, and a few shorter moves in between, closing at $57.00 on Friday.

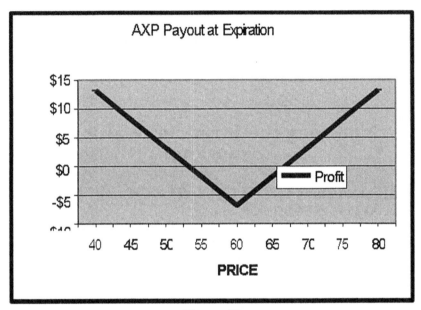

Figure 16

If I had done nothing, I would now have a position about the same price, but I would have lost a week of time without it making a significant move toward my breakeven price on the stock. The straddle closed with an inside market of 6.25 - 6.70 on Friday, which means the position is still priced about in the middle of the market.

I have two alternatives at this point:

One: I still have six weeks until expiration, the stock has moved to $57.00 (46.5% towards the breakeven on the downside), and therefore there is still plenty of time for me to see the move that I anticipate to make this straddle a big winner.

Two: My second choice is to manage the straddle by adjusting it with stock trades (i.e. positive gamma) as it moves around and therefore taking advantage of smaller price swings.

Here is what I did this week:

I established that I would neutralize this straddle every two points in the stock. I came to this decision because the position had a gamma of 150, thus every one-point move would change the position by 150 deltas, and if AXP went straight down, I would buy 200 shares every 2 points. I started with a negative delta of 100 for the 20 lot straddle, and we started $1 below the strike.

At that rate I would have two less straddles (in that direction) every two points and would be "flat" at $40 per share. I would have an average purchase price on the stock of $49 per share and thus a profit of $9,100 in the total position (remember our breakeven is $53.45 on the stock, thus I would have closed out the position $4.45 better than breakeven).

I also would have 20 calls remaining (real and synthetic calls) so that if this happened quickly the calls may still have some value increasing my profit potential. But I am looking at the worst-case scenario when I am strategizing.

The Trade

I bought 200 shares of stock on the 4th at $57.50. When the stock rallied back up on the 5th, I sold it back out at $58.75 (the position neutralized on the 4th got me long at $58.75 on the 5th, so I sold the stock back out). Now today I am back in the same position as we started, picked up an extra $250 and stand ready to buy a couple hundred shares on the open on Monday.

I. Taking Stock of My Position

Let's step back for a moment, and recap our actions and reactions to date:

I first outlined the basics of the long straddle, including the components of the strategy and its risk and reward profile. For illustrative purposes and to facilitate your moving up the learning curve, I purchased the AXP JAN 60 Straddle @ $6.45.

Initial position: **Buy 20 AXP JAN 60 Calls @ $2.45**

Buy 20 AXP JAN 60 Puts @ $4.00

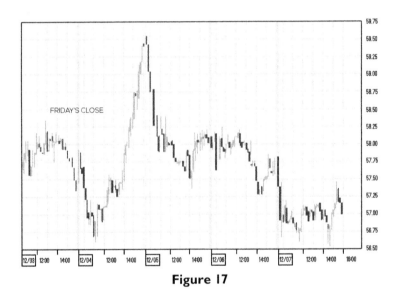

Figure 17

Upon initiation of the straddle at the open on December 3, AXP was at $58.91. At that time I was looking for a reasonable move in either direction, above or below breakeven points of $66.45 or $53.55 respectively, prior to the January expiration.

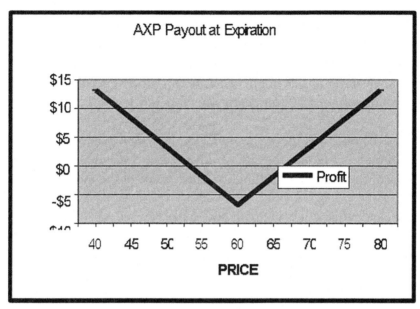

Figure 18

The above chart shows both the movement of AXP during the past two weeks, and the trades I made to modify our position since I put it on.

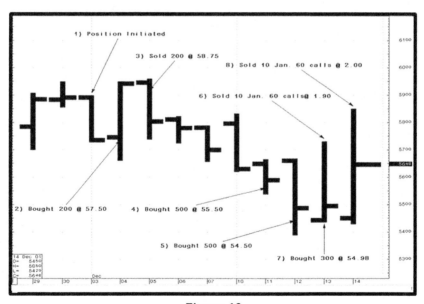

Figure 19

265

As you can see in Figure 19 above, there have been a lot of trades in the past two weeks. Had this stock gone straight south in the first week, I may not have made any adjusting trades. Since I was cautious about whatever upside might be left in this move, I decided to put in a trailing stop of $.50 from each new intra-day low or high.

Since the stock has moved around a lot, I've been able to make some good trades to reduce the cost of this straddle. I decided to close out some of the straddle by selling the calls on one of the moves up.

During the first week, I bought 200 shares of stock on December 4 at $57.50 and in affect scalped it when I sold it back out at $58.75 as the stock rallied back up on December 5th. On Friday December 7, I was back in the same position as I started, having picked up an extra $250.

I was looking to buy a couple hundred shares on the open on Monday, December 10. Since the market was so soft Monday, I placed my hedge order with a .50 stop (from retracement) and made the purchase near the low of the day on Tuesday, December 11, at $55.85. I waited until the position generated at least 300 short deltas, in this instance I waited until it was a bit over 500 deltas short and then bought the stock.

I scaled in (i.e. purchased) another 500 shares before AXP turned its head for a slight upside move. With $2.50 under my belt, I weighed selling out the stock or take advantage of a slight jump in the volatility. I decided to sell calls out, and did so twice, 10 lots each time, with a 300-share purchase in between.

Result:

Now I am "flat" the calls, still long the 20 puts and long 1,300 shares of stock. I am fairly close to neutral, and still have a similar risk reward profile as when I started.

BUT, I have taken in over $2,100 and the position nearly resembles the straddle with initiated. Note the graph below compared to the original.

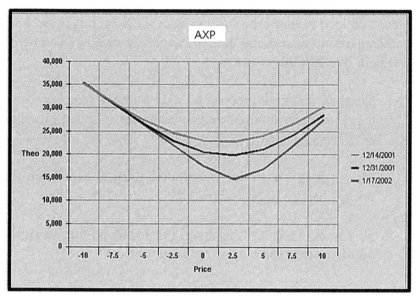

Figure 19

II. Formulating a Plan for Position Adjustment

Next, I present to you the decision-tree that I typically go through when deciding whether or not to adjust a position. I encourage you to try and internalize this thought process as a kind of "mental template".

- The first step is to assess the situation: where is the stock now? How is the position unfolding?

- The second step is to determine your market bias: how do you foresee the position moving from here?

- The third step involves the decision whether or not to adjust the position.

- The fourth step concerns the action you take (if any) to modify the position.

Since I decided to adjust the position from the start, I did so without outlining this to you at the beginning. I went right into the adjustments, and built the example set first.

1. <u>Situation:</u> stock has dropped $2 since Monday. I am beginning to get some of the movement I had expected as I put the straddle on. <u>Thus I have become short deltas.</u>

2. <u>Market Bias:</u> Determine if you are bullish or bearish on the stock. <u>I happen to neutral on AXP.</u>

3. <u>Do I want to adjust the position?</u> I do in fact want to adjust the position, and I will outline my actions below.

4. <u>Possible adjustments:</u> Recall that because stock dropped the position became net short deltas. I have a neutral bias in the stock; therefore I needed to get long deltas. So, I ask you, what actions could I have taken to make my position delta neutral?
   a) Adjust the position with stock: maintaining the current position.
   b) Adjust the position by trading options-decreasing the position.
   c) "Liquidate" the position

In the AXP position, I first opted for the first strategy, in which you would adjust your delta position by buying or selling underlying shares against the position (in fact, this is the route I take most of the time). You would, of course, sell shares as the stock moves up, and buy shares if the stock moves down. By delta hedging with stock, you maintain the size and number of options of your current position, but reduce the opportunity in the direction you are hedging.

One important caveat: whenever you purchase stock, you will convert an equal number of puts into calls, and whenever you sell stock you will convert an equal number of calls into puts. Thus, as I said, you reduce the opportunity in the direction you transact the stock.

In sum, the decision tree that I developed was as follows:

1. Assess the situation.
2. Determine your market bias.
3. Decide whether or not to adjust the position.
4. If warranted, take decisive action.

Formulating a Plan for Position Adjustment: Using Options to Modify the Initial Position

Adjusting by Selling Out Options: Reducing the Position

With this adjustment you modify the delta of the position by selling calls or selling puts against the position. The overall goal of the adjustment is to remain delta neutral.

So how do we put this theoretical verbiage to some practical use? In order to stay delta neutral you will sell calls as the market moves up, and sell puts as the market moves down. Because you are selling calls when the market is up (typically the calls are more expensive) and selling puts as the market moves down (typically the puts are more expensive), you are selling out straddles at better prices.

The table below shows option sale adjustments to a hypothetical position consisting of 50 long straddles:

Market Movement	Unchanged	Up	Down	Up	Down
Transaction	None	Sell 10 Calls	Sell 10 Puts	Sell 10 Calls	Sell 10 Puts
Call Position	50	40	40	30	30
Put Position	50	50	40	40	30

Figure 21

Adjusting by Buying Options: Increasing the Position

With this adjustment strategy you adjust the delta of your position by buying calls or by buying puts against the position. You will buy puts as the market moves up, and buy calls as the market moves down. This method slowly increases the size of the options position, typically at a better price.

Why? If you extend the reasoning from the above example this makes sense. Because you are buying calls when the market is down (and therefore the calls are typically cheaper), and buying puts when the market is up (and therefore puts are typically cheaper), you are adding additional options to the position at better prices.

The table below shows option purchase adjustments to a hypothetical position consisting of 50 long straddles:

Market Movement	Unchanged	Up	Down	Up	Down
Transaction	None	Buy 10 Puts	Buy 10 Calls	Buy 10 Puts	Buy 10 Calls
Call Position	50	50	6	60	70
Put Position	50	60	60	70	70

Figure 22

Adjusting by Trading Other Options: Rolling the Position

[Reminder: Step 2 of my decision tree mandates that I determine my market bias. As noted earlier, I am decidedly bearish. This bias will profoundly affect my decision concerning whether and how to "roll".]

Here are two ways to utilize a roll when trading a straddle:

- By "rolling out" the straddle (liquidating the position and buying a new at the money straddle in a deferred month).

- By "rolling up or down" (closing the position or a leg of a position at one strike and moving the position to a different strike price in the same month).

Rolling Out the Straddle

The long straddle is designed to profit from changes in volatility. If I purchase an at the money straddle I believe volatility is going to move higher. If the price of the underlying has been stable for some time, then it is highly probable that the implied volatility of the straddle has decreased. Moreover, time decay has begun to take its toll. If I have reassessed the market situation and still believe that a long straddle is warranted, then I would consider rolling the straddle to a month farther out. (To liquidate the position I would sell out both the put and the call in the current month).

Rolling Down the Put

I would consider rolling down the put if the price of the underlying has dropped. If I do roll the put down to a lower strike, I will lock in profit on my original position. My new strike will be determined by the degree of my bearishness and the volatility of the puts I am considering. If I do buy a put at a lower strike, I will no longer have a straddle on…I now have on a Strangle (because the strikes of the call and the put will no longer be the same).

Looking at AXP Position

We have been tracking the movement of the AXP JAN 60 straddle, which we initially purchased at $6.45. From the beginning of the trade, I made two additional delta adjustments to the position:

- 12/20 Sold 400 shares @ $60.38
- 12/21 Bought 200 shares @ $58.93

This brings the total number of my "gamma scalps" to nine over the past four weeks. Seven stock trades and two option trades. Naturally at any given point along the way I could have chosen to do things differently.

I could have traded at a shorter interval and thus traded more often for a smaller profit or I could have traded at a larger interval and traded less often, possibly for a larger profit. I could have chosen to make no trades at all and let the stock "run" in whatever direction it wished.

How you go about adjusting a position such as a straddle is very subjective and there is no right or wrong way. There is a little bit of science and art involved. Below is a table of the stock adjustments we have made to the straddle position:

Amount	Price	Settle	P/L
200	57.50	59.31	362.00
-200	58.75	59.31	-112.00
500	55.50	59.31	1905.00
500	54.50	59.31	2405.00
300	54.98	59.31	1299.00
-400	60.38	59.31	428.00
200	58.93	59.31	76.00
			6363.00

Figure 23

Below is a table of the option adjustments (selling January 60 calls) I have made to the straddle position:

Amount	Price	Settle	P/L
-10	1.90	2.70	-800
-10	2.00	2.70	-700
			-1500

Figure 24

Below are the adjustments graphically represented on a bar chart:

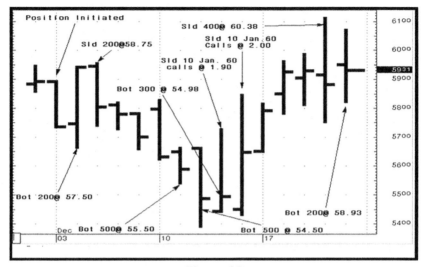

Figure 25

As we can see from the chart above, I have made many trades over the past three weeks. This requires a lot of time and effort. Was it worth the effort? Let's see...

Conclusion:

The original January 60 straddle was purchased at $6.45. For 20 contracts this is a net cost of $12,900. On Friday the straddle settled at $5.95 for a value of $11,900 for 20 contracts. Therefore, making no adjustments at all I would have a net loss of $1,000, but by aggressively trading against the position or "gamma scalping" I generated an additional $4,863 of profit, leaving me with a net profit of $3,863!

CHAPTER 17

Vertical Spreads

A vertical spread involves the purchase of a call (or put) of a certain strike, and the simultaneous sale of a call (or put) of a different strike, same month. It is the positioning of the strikes bought and sold that determines whether the spread has a bullish, bearish or subsequent volatility bias. There lies much confusion about vertical spreads as the terminology bullish, bearish, long, short, debit, and credit are tossed around without much concern to their meaning.

Credit vs. Debit Spreads

A *credit spread* is one in which the receipt of cash from the short option (the one sold) exceeds the amount of cash paid out for the long option (the one purchased). When a trader puts on a credit spread, money is received, or a credit is established. Examples of credit spreads are the **bull put spread** and the **bear call spread**.

Credit Spread	Premium	Delta
Bull Put	Collect	Long
Bear Call	Collect	Short

Figure I

With a *debit spread*, the amount of cash paid out for the long option exceeds the amount received for the short option. Thus, the trader who establishes this position ends up with a debit, or an outlay of cash. **Bull call spreads** and **bear put spreads** are debit spreads.

Debit Spread	Premium	Delta
Bull Call	Pay	Long
Bear Put	Pay	Short

Figure 2

Bull vs. Bear Spreads

A *bull spread* involves two or more options that will result in a profit from a rise in price of the underlying. A trader who is bullish on the underlying implements a bull spread.

Bull Spread	Premium	Spread Position	Market Position
Calls	Pay	Long	Long
Puts	Collect	Short	Long

Figure 3

A bear spread involves two or more options profiting from a decrease in the price of the underlying. The trader hopes to capitalize on an anticipated downward move.

Bear Spread	Premium	Spread Position	Market Position
Calls	Collect	Short	Short
Puts	Pay	Long	Short

Figure 4

- Both bull spreads and bear spreads come in two varieties. Bull spreads are either call bull spreads or put bull spreads, and bear spreads are either call bear spreads or put bear spreads.

- Beginners tend to equate bull spreads with call spreads and bear spreads with put spreads.

Bottom line: What determines whether a spread is bullish or bearish is not whether it is comprised of puts or calls. Rather, a good rule for determining the bias, i.e. bullishness or bearishness of a spread is whether you buy the lower strike option or the higher strike option that determines whether your spread is bullish or bearish. A bearish strategist would go long the higher strike, whereas a bullish trader would go long the lower strike.

Bull and Bear Spreads with Calls and Puts

Bull Spread Using Calls

A call bull spread consists of the purchase of one call option with a lower strike price and the sale of another call option with a higher strike price.

The bull call spreader is bullish towards the underlying in question, but perhaps is not bullish (certain) enough to buy the underlying or naked calls. When a trader hopes to gain from the anticipated increase in price of the underlying, on a risk-controlled basis, a hedged position is best. Establishing a bull call spread enables a trader to put on a bullish position with a bit of an insurance policy.

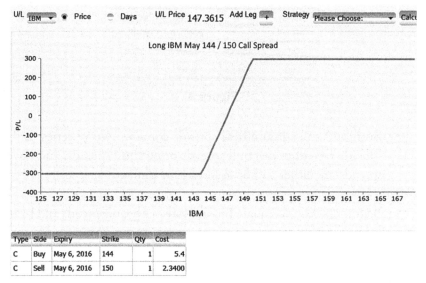

Long IBM May 144 / 150 Call Spread

Type	Side	Expiry	Strike	Qty	Cost
C	Buy	May 6, 2016	144	1	5.4
C	Sell	May 6, 2016	150	1	2.3400

Figure 5   Options Technology Solutions, UK

- **Maximum Loss:** The most the bull call spreader can lose in the above example is $3.06, ($306 per spread). As buying one May 144 call costs $5.40, but selling one May 150 call for $2.34 generates a $2.34 credit. Because the bull call spread is always a debit spread, the most a trader can lose when putting on a debit spread is amount paid out (the debit) to put on the spread. In this example it would be: $5.40 - $2.34 = $3.06.

- **Maximum Profit:** The big compromise in spreading is that the bull call spreader loses the potential for unlimited gain that is available with the naked long call, or by owning the underlying outright. The profit is limited to the difference between the strike prices (higher-lower) minus the difference between the premiums (premium 1 - premium 2), if and only if the underlying is above the second strike at expiration. Plugging in the numbers: (150 - 144) – (5.40-2.34) = (6.00)-(3.06) = $2.94.

- **Breakeven Point:** The breakeven point is equal to the lower strike price plus the difference in premiums. In our example:

278

(144) + (5.40 - 2.34) = (144.00) + (3.06) = $147.06. So, the breakeven on this vertical is $147.06 per share on the stock.

Bear Spread Using Calls

A call bear spread consists of the sale of one call option with a lower strike price and the purchase of another call with a higher strike price.

The bear spread offers potentially limited reward for limited risk. The trader establishing a bear spread has a view on the direction of the underlying, expecting it to decline. Additionally, the trader may enter this position considering the cost of entry of a naked long put position is too high. The trader might have a specific price target on the underlying.

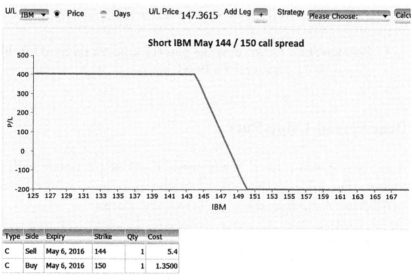

Figure 6   Options Technology Solutions, UK

Recall, if the trader buys the option with the lower exercise price and sells the option with the higher exercise price, the spread is bullish; conversely, when purchasing a higher exercise price and selling a lower exercise price the trader is bearish. Thus, a bear call spread is always a credit spread.

- **Maximum Gain:** Note that in Figure 6 if IBM is below $144 at expiration, both options expire worthless. Why? Because these are calls, and calls have intrinsic value only when the underlying is trading above the option's strike price. The two strike prices are $144 and $150, so anything under $144 means no intrinsic values for the calls. Remember, we already put on the spread and collected $4.05 for it. So if both options expire worthless, then we simply pocket the $4.05 credit. This $4.05 is our maximum gain.

- **Maximum Loss:** However, if IBM expires above $150, then both calls would be in-the-money. Let's take a look at what our maximum loss would be. (Difference in strikes) – Credit received = max loss. Or, (150 - 144) – ($4.05) = $1.95 net loss.

- **Breakeven:** is the lower strike plus the amount received for the spread. $144 + $4.05 = $ 148.05.

Bear Spread Using Puts

A put bear spread consists of the purchase of one put option with a higher strike price and the sale of another put option with a lower strike price. A put bear spread will always be a debit.

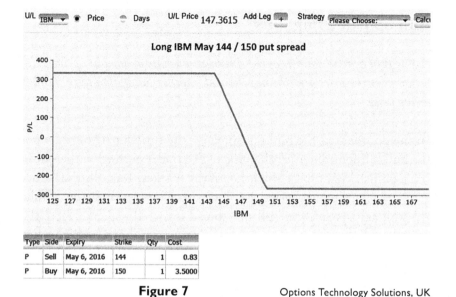

Long IBM May 144 / 150 put spread

Type	Side	Expiry	Strike	Qty	Cost
P	Sell	May 6, 2016	144	1	0.83
P	Buy	May 6, 2016	150	1	3.5000

Figure 7   Options Technology Solutions, UK

- **Max Loss:** The bear put spread is a debit spread, the maximum amount of loss is the amount paid for it. In this case Figure 7 the maximum loss is $2.67

- **Maximum Gain:** The maximum profit for a bear put spread is limited to the difference in strike prices. (higher strike – lower strike) MINUS the difference in the premiums when the underlying is below the lower strike at expiration (70 in this case).

Long 1 IBM May $150 put @ 3.50
Short 1 IBM May $144 put @ .83

Max gain: (150-144) less the money spent/received - (3.50 - .83)

($6) - ($2.67) = $3.33
The maximum gain on this spread is $3.33.

281

Bull Spread Using Puts

A Put Bull Spread consists of the simultaneous sale of one put option with a higher strike price and the purchase of another put option with a lower strike price.

In the put market, the bull put spread is the functional equivalent of the bull call spread in the call market. The trader putting on the spread has a bullish view on the direction of the market, and sells the higher strike put while purchasing the lower strike put. However, unlike the bull call spread, the bull put spread is a credit spread: Here the premium of the short put is greater than the premium of the long put.

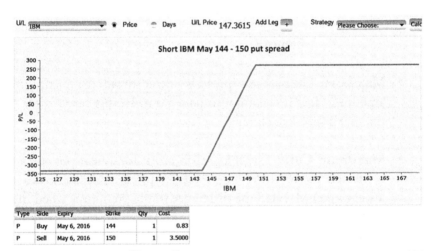

Figure 8   Options Technology Solutions, UK

- **Maximum Profit:** This is a credit spread.

SELL 1 IBM May 150 put @ $3.50
BUY 1 May 144 put @ $0.83
$2.67 credit

The sale of this IBM May 150/144 bull put spread nets the traders $2.67. This credit is the maximum potential profit.

282

- **Maximum Loss:** The worst-case scenario for the bull put spreader occurs if the underlying expires below the lower strike price less the premium collected at expiration. The seller of this spread loses the difference in the strike prices minus the initial credit.

(Difference between strikes) - (net credit) = max loss
(150 - 144) - $2.67 credit
6 – 2.67 = $3.33 loss

- **Breakeven:** The breakeven point of a bull put spread is always the strike price of the higher option minus the net credit.

150 – 2.67 = $147.33

So, the breakeven on this vertical is $147.33 per share on the stock.

The "Greeks" of the Vertical Spread

The "greeks" of a spread position are equal to the sum of the greeks of its component parts. Please review the definitions, characteristics, and sensitivities of the greeks (Chapters 3 through 6) and keep in mind the significance of the position (i.e., long or short) of the component options on the greeks of the overall spread position.

Delta

The delta of a bull spread is the difference in delta of the lower strike option and the higher strike option. For example the delta of the 100/105 bull call spread would be calculated as follows:

100 call delta = .75
105 call delta = .25
100/105 bull call spread delta = .75 - .25 or .50

Recall that puts have a negative delta, so the calculation of the delta of the 100/105 bull put spread would be as follows:

100 put delta = -.25
105 put delta = -.75
100/105 bull put spread delta = -.25 – (- .75) or .50

Your objective should dictate which strike prices to select. If your objective is gain absolute delta, select strike prices that are as close to at the money as possible. However, if your goal is to seek the greatest delta per dollars invested; pick strikes that are out of the money.

Call Spread Strikes	Net Delta
$95/$100	17
$100/$105	20
$105/$110	18
$110/$115	11
$115/$120	2

The Vertical Spread and Net Delta

Figure 9

The delta of a bull vertical spread can range between zero and 1.00 depending on location of the underlying relative to strike prices, time left until expiration, implied volatility levels, and other factors. Since it is bullish the delta will either be zero or a positive number, never negative.

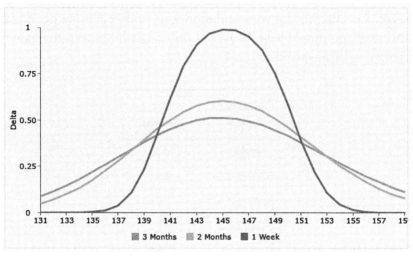

Figure 10   Options Technology Solutions, UK

As can be seen in Figure 10 above the delta of the bull spread is greatly dependent on location of the underlying and time until expiration. When expiration is near and the deltas of the component options are very sensitive to "money-ness" (whether they are in or out of the money) the delta of the bull spread is also sensitive to changes in underlying price, particularly when the underlying is between the upper and lower strikes and one option is in the money and one option is out of the money.

Observe that moving further away from expiration decreases the sensitivity of the bull vertical. It is also important to notice that the delta of the structure always returns to zero at the extremes, illustrating the limited risk/ limited reward characteristics of this type of position.

Gamma

Like options vega, an option's gamma is relative. A vertical spread has a gamma of zero when the strike price is at the equidistant mean. Vertical spread traders who want positive gamma should choose out of the money strike prices for debit spreads and in the money strikes for credit spreads. Also, if your ambition is to exploit gamma per dollar invested, you should have an even stronger bias for the out the money strikes on debit spreads.

Call Spread Strikes	Net Gamma
$95/$100	-0.02
$100/$105	0.02
$105/$110	0.02
$110/$115	0.01
$115/$120	0.005

The Vertical Spread and Net Gamma

Figure 11

The gamma (rate of change of the delta) of a bull spread is the <u>sum</u> of the gamma of the lower strike option and the higher strike option positions. Recall from chapter four that a long option position will have a positive gamma while a short option position will have a negative gamma, so in the case of the bull spread the lower strike option will generate positive gamma while the upper strike option will generate negative gamma.

For example the gamma of the 100/105 bull call spread would be calculated as follows:

100 call gamma = .15
105 call gamma = -.05
100/105 bull call spread gamma = .15 + (- .05) or +.10

Calls and puts of the same strike and expiration have the same gamma, so the calculation of the gamma of the 100/105 bull put spread would calculated as follows:

100 put gamma = .15

105 put gamma = -.05

100/105 bull put spread gamma = .15 + (- .05) or +.10

The gamma of a bull vertical spread can range between zero + 1.00 and -1.00 depending on location of the underlying relative to strike prices, time left until expiration, implied volatility levels, and other factors.

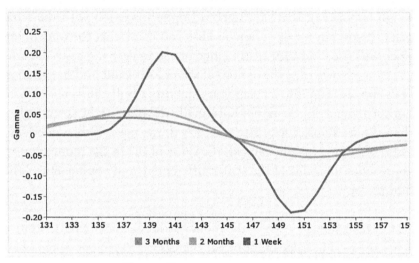

Figure 12   Options Technology Solutions, UK

As can be seen in Figure 12 above the gamma of the bull spread is greatly dependent on location of the underlying and time until expiration. When expiration is near and the gammas of the component options are very sensitive to "money-ness" (whether they are in or out of the money) the gamma of the bull spread is also sensitive to changes in underlying price, mostly when the underlying is near one of the strikes.

Notice that the gamma of the position is positive when the underlying is near the lower strike long option, negative when the underlying is near the upper strike short option, and neutral when the underlying is exactly between the strikes or on the extremes. Once again see that moving further away from expiration decreases the sensitivity of the

287

gamma of the bull vertical and that the gamma of the structure always returns to zero at the extremes.

Theta

One benefit of the vertical spread over a plain vanilla call or put position is that you can build the spread so that theta is small, or even with a sign opposite of that of a standard option position with the same delta. If you buy a call option because you think that the underlying price will rise, and instead the price of the underlying asset remains unchanged, over time the options contract loses value and the position loses money. Suppose instead you establish a bull call spread where both strikes are in the money. Originally the price of the spread is less than the strike price gap. But as expiry draws nigh, if the underlying asset value remains unchanged, the value of the in the money spread approaches the value of the strike differential, and you benefit as the bull trader.

- Debit spreads with in the money strikes generally have positive thetas. The value of the spread increases as expiration approaches.

- Debit spreads with out of the money strikes have negative thetas.

- Debit spreads with at the money strikes have small absolute thetas.

For credit spreads, the relation is upturned. If you want positive theta, select in the money options for debit spreads and out of the money options for credit spreads.

Call Spread Strikes	Positive	Negative
$23/$25	0.0291	
$24/$25	0.0173	
$24/$26	0	0
$25/$26		0.0173
$26/$27		0.0118

Long Bull Net Theta

Figure 13

The theta (sensitivity to the passage of time) of a bull spread is the <u>sum</u> of the theta of the lower strike option and the higher strike option positions. Recall from Chapter 6 that a long option position will have a negative theta while a short option position will have a positive theta, so in the case of the bull spread the lower strike option will generate negative theta while the upper strike option will generate positive theta. For example the theta of the 100/105 bull call spread would be calculated as follows:

100 call position theta = -.11
105 call position theta = +.03
100/105 bull call spread theta = -.11 + .03 or -.08

Calls and puts of the same strike and expiration have the same theta, so the theta of the 100/105 bull put spread would be calculated as follows:

100 put position theta = -.11
105 put position theta = +.03
100/105 bull put spread gamma = -.11 + .03 or -.08

The theta of the bull spread is also dependent on location of the underlying relative to strike prices, time left until expiration, implied volatility levels, and other factors.

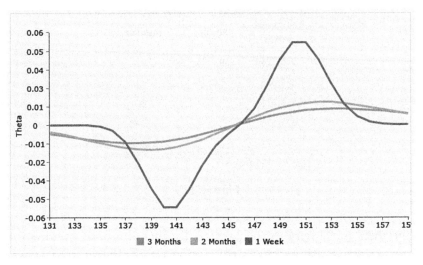

Figure 14   Options Technology Solutions, UK

As can be seen in Figure 14 above, like the other greeks, the theta of the bull spread is greatly dependent on location of the underlying and time until expiration. Notice that the theta of the position is negative when the underlying is near the lower strike long option, positive when the underlying is near the upper strike short option and neutral when the underlying is exactly between the strikes or on the extremes. Once again notice that moving further away from expiration decreases the sensitivity of the theta of the bull vertical position.

Vega

One of the advantages of vertical spreads is that they allow traders to shape positions that are delicate to some risk factors and not sensitive to others. Chapter 16 describes straddles and strangles, which are intended so that their deltas are near zero yet vega and gamma are high. In contrast, traders of vertical spreads prefer spreads with higher deltas while lowering exposure to vega risk. Vertical spread traders who seek to reduce their exposure to vega risk should choose at the money strikes, or strike prices that straddle the underlying asset price. That is, for the contracts bought and sold, the higher strike price is greater than the share price, and the lower strike price is less than the share price.

Call Strikes	Vega	Long Bull Call Spread Strikes	Net Positive	Vega Negative
$800	$0.16	$800/$850		($0.25)
$850	$0.41	$850/$900		($0.24)
$900	$0.65	$900/$950		($0.32)
$950	$0.97	$950/$1,000		($0.22)
$1,000	$1.19	$1,000/$1,050	$0.33	
$1,050	$0.86	$1,050/$1,100	$0.56	
$1,100	$0.30	$1,100/$1,150	$0.24	
$1,150	$0.06	$1,150/$1,200	$0.04	
$1,200	$0.02			

The Vertical Spread and Volatility

Figure 15

The vega (sensitivity to changes in implied volatility) of a bull spread is the sum of the vega of the lower strike option and the higher strike option positions. Recall from chapter one that a long option position will have a positive vega while a short option position will have a negative vega, so in the case of the bull spread the lower strike option will generate positive vega while the upper strike option will generate negative vega.

For example the Vega of the 100/105 bull call spread would be calculated as follows:

100 call position vega = .28
105 call position vega = -.12
100/105 bull call spread vega = .28 + (- .12) or +.16

Calls and puts of the same strike and expiration have the same vega, so the vega of the 100/105 bull put spread would be calculated as follows:

291

100 put position vega = .28
105 put position vega = -.05
100/105 bull put spread gamma = .15 + (- .05) or +.10

The range of the vega of a bull vertical spread cannot be defined. It is also dependent on location of the underlying relative to strike prices, time left until expiration, implied volatility levels, and other factors.

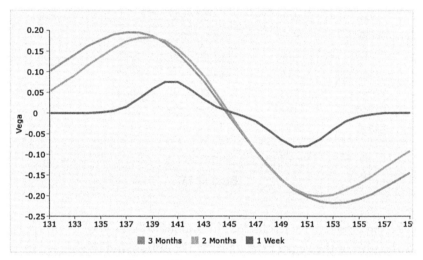

Figure 16   Options Technology Solutions, UK

As can be seen from Figure 16 above, like the other greeks, the vega of the bull spread is greatly reliant on location of the underlying and time until expiration. Notice that the vega of the position is positive when the underlying is near the lower strike long option, negative when the underlying is near the upper strike short option, and neutral when the underlying is exactly between the strikes or on the extremes.

However, since vega increases with time to expiration notice that moving further away from expiration increases the sensitivity of the vega of the bull vertical position as the vega of the individual options increases with greater time to expiration.

Vertical Spreads and Volatility

Apart from path dependency and time decay risk, volatility is another critical factor in deciding on whether to establish a vertical spread and – if so, which strikes to implement.

Generally speaking, when volatility increases, an at-the-money option will increase more than an in the money or out of the-money option. Conversely, the at the money option will lose value at a greater rate than an in the money or out of the money option if implied volatility decreases. The real question is how to use the vertical spread to take advantage of anticipated movements in implied volatility.

If you believe implied volatility will rise, you can establish a vertical spread by purchasing an at the money option and selling either the in the money or out of the money option against it. If you feel that implied volatility is too high, you can set up a vertical spread by selling an at the money option and buying either an out of the money or an in the money option against it.

To better understand how volatility affect vertical spreads, consider the next three examples. The examples use three different implied volatilities while keeping the underlying stock constant at $27.50.

	Implied	Theoretical	Implied Volatility	Implied Volatility
Call Strike	Volatility	Value	Up.05%	Up.10%
$17	36.20%	$6.26	$6.28	$6.29
$19	34.06%	$4.35	$4.37	$4.39
$21	33.31%	$2.64	$2.69	$2.74
$23	31.43%	$1.31	$1.37	$1.43
$25	30.20%	$0.51	$0.56	$0.61
$27	31.58%	$0.19	$0.23	$0.26
$29	31.58%	$0.06	$0.07	$0.09

		Value Up	Value Up
Call Spread	Spread Value	5% Volatility	10% Volatility
$17/$19	$1.91	$1.91	$1.90
$19/$21	$1.71	$1.68	$1.65
$21/$23	$1.33	$1.32	$1.31
$23/$25	$0.80	$0.81	$0.82
$25/$27	$0.32	$0.33	$0.35
$27/$29	$0.13	$0.16	$0.17
$17/$21	$3.62	$3.56	$3.55
$19/$23	$3.04	$3.00	$2.96
$21/$25	$2.13	$2.13	$2.13
$23/$27	$1.12	$1.14	$1.17
$25/$29	$0.45	$0.49	$0.52

Vertical Spread—Comparing Vertical Spreads with Varied Implied Volatilities

Figure 17

Example #1: XYZ 30-day $20/$25 call. For this in the money call spread, as volatility increases, the value of the spread decreases. This is because with the increased volatility, the underlying share price will tend to change, and that leads to a higher likelihood of the share price reaching a level where the $20/$25 call spread will no longer finish in the money. The rule of thumb is that as volatility increases, the value of in the money vertical spreads decrease. As volatility decreases, an in the money vertical spread's value increases.

Example #2: XYZ 30-day $25/$30 call. For this at the money call spread, we see little if any effect with changes in volatility. With the underlying asset price located equally distant from the strike prices of the two options contracts, the volatility component for each strike price will very similar. Thus, when volatility increases, both options will increase equally. With the spread set up so that the trader owns one contract and sells the other, the increase in values will offset each other so the value of the spreads will remain constant.

The rule of thumb with at the money spreads is that when volatility increases or decreases, the value of an at the money vertical spread will remain constant.

Example #3: XYZ 30-day $30/$35 call. For this out of the money spread, as volatility increases, the value of the out of the money call spread increases. This is simply because the increase in volatility assumes that the share price of the underlying stock will be more likely to move, and thus the out of the money vertical spread will have a greater chance of becoming in the money. The general rule is that when volatility increases, the value of an out of the money vertical spread also increases. When volatility decreases, the spread's value decreases.

Summary: Comparing Vertical Spreads and Implied Volatility

An in the money call spread has the same net implied volatility exposure as its corresponding out of the money put spread. With XYZ at $40, selling the thirty-day $25/$30 put spread will have the exact same implied volatility exposure as purchasing the thirty-day $25/$30 call spread.

An easy way to remember volatility's effect on a spread is to think in terms of the spread's median value. For example, the median value of a $5 vertical spread will be $2.50, whereas a $10 spread will have a median value of $5. An increase in volatility will cause vertical spreads to move toward their median value. The higher the volatility, the closer the spread will move toward its median.

In other words, if a $5 vertical spread has a value over $2.50, it will lose value and move toward its median price when volatility increases.

Meanwhile, the increased implied volatility will cause a spread with a value less than its median value to increase, moving up toward the median price. If implied volatility goes down, you can expect the opposite to occur. That is, the value of a $5 spread will move away from the median price of $2.50. With that, when implied volatility decreases, all the spreads valued above $2.50 will increase in value (toward maximum value), while spreads valued below $2.50 will lose value (see Figure 18 below).

Strikes	Volatility 26.05%	Volatility 28.65%	Volatility 31.26%
$98/$103	$2.34	$2.41	$2.47

Bull Call Spread Spread Values

Strikes	Volatility 23.73%	Volatility 26.1%	Volatility 28.47%
$98/$103	$2.62	$2.57	$2.52

Bull Put Spread Spread Values

Figure 18

A Trader's Logic for Trading a Vertical Spread

Reason #1: Lowering Your Net Cost, Qualifying Your Risk

You are bullish regarding the share price for XYZ, so you decide to convert your opinion from buying a call contract to creating a bull spread, where you would buy a set of call contracts at one strike price and sell an equal number of call contracts with a higher strike price but with the same expiration date.

This call spread will lower your net cost and therefore your maximum possible loss. It will also decrease your breakeven point, making profit more likely. The only problem in this strategy is that you have severely limited your profit if the underlying share price rises sharply. You should always think carefully when capping your potential profitability. To be profitable over the long haul, you must limit your losers while riding your winners.

Reason #2: Flexibility

You can implement a bullish strategy with puts or a bearish strategy with calls.

You can go long on the market by selling options and short the market by buying. Suppose you begin with a short put and convert it into a put bull spread by buying a second put at a lower strike price. In this case, you have reduced your risk exposure since possible losses (at expiration) are now limited to the difference in the two strike prices less the net price. Since possible losses are now defined, you also lower your margin requirement. The disadvantage of converting the sale of the put contracts to a bull spread is that you lower your maximum gain and raise the breakeven point, and therefore the likelihood of a loss.

For the same strikes, both call and put bull spreads have identical deltas, vegas, gammas, and payoff patterns. But the net cash flow differs. For the put contracts, the resulting vertical spread is a credit spread. You receive cash when setting up the spread, because the price you paid for the contracts you bought is less than what you received from the contracts you sold. The call bull spread, however, is a debit spread. Setting up the spread has a net cost, because the price of the options you bought exceeds the price of the options you sold. This is also true of bear spreads. A put bear spread is a debit spread (you receive net cash), whereas a call bear spread is a credit spread (you have a net loss of cash).

Figure 19 below demonstrates the parity between a bull spread with calls as opposed to a bull spread with puts with the same strike price.

Strike	Call	Delta	Gamma	Theta	Vega	Implied Volatility
$24.00	$0.77	50	0.21	0.014	0.028	26.75%
$25.00	$0.42	33	0.17	0.011	0.026	25.96%

Long 24/25 Bull Call Spread

Strike	Put	Delta	Gamma	Theta	Vega	Implied Volatility
$24.00	$0.77	50	0.21	0.014	0.028	26.75%
$25.00	$1.42	33	0.17	0.011	0.026	25.96%

Short 24/25 Bull Put Spread

Price	Delta	Gamma	Theta	Vega	Risk	Reward
$0.35	17	0.04	0.003	0.002	$0.35	$0.65

Long 24/25 Bull Call Spread

Price	Delta	Gamma	Theta	Vega	Risk	Reward
($0.65)	17	0.04	0.003	0.002	$0.35	$0.65

Short 24/25 Bull Put Spread

Figure 19

Reason #3: Taking Advantage of Direction and Greeks are contained by a Predefined Risk Profile.

A vertical spread can be implemented with the profile of being long the market while long theta, or long the market and short theta. A vertical spread can be short the market while being either long or short gamma. Furthermore, you can devise a vertical spread that captures both your directional conviction and volatility conviction—simultaneously!

Vertical spreads are great tools, especially when you understand that greeks can help supplement a bad directional decision or increase a good one. Unfortunately, there are two sides to that coin—a vertical spreader can win on his directional call yet lose horribly due to the spread's delinquent greek position. That said, a vertical spread could potentially afford the trader many distinct advantages in terms of contained greek exposure. It's of key importance that the investor both understands and appreciates the possible implications of the greek exposure of any vertical spread.

Reason #4: Moderate Directional Underlying Movement

In the "moderate move" scenario the investor is expecting a directional move, either up or down, of moderate magnitude. A vertical spread is well suited to this type of scenario because its structure allows it to participate in a directional move in the amount equal to the strike differential, so if the investor is looking for a rally to a certain point, or a sell off to a certain point, the bull or bear vertical spread will allow him/her to capture that type of move. One would not use a vertical spread, for example, if one were forecasting a large magnitude up or down move because a vertical spread would only capture a portion of such a move.

Reason #5: Income Generation in a Limited Risk Fashion

Selling out of the money options to collect premiums and generate income through time decay has always been a very desirable strategy. The problem with that strategy is that it is very risky as the naked selling of calls and puts leaves one open to unlimited risk should some sort of unforeseen event take place. Obviously this is highly undesirable and downright scary. Vertical spreads offer a way around this. By selling limited-risk out of the money credit spreads (bull or short put spreads, bear or short call spreads), investors can still sell premium and generate income through time decay. The advantage gained by using vertical spreads is that should the unforeseen event take place the investor's risk is limited rather than open-ended. The investor will lose money, but the amount of loss will be limited, hopefully allowing him to "stay in the ballgame".

Reason #6: Additional Key Takeaways:

- Staying spread is staying alive: Putting on a spread means trading the possibility of unlimited reward for the benefit of limited risk.

- Vertical spreads are strategies that are put on by the trader who has an opinion on the direction of the underlying. A bear spreader believes the underlying is going down, while a bull spreader feels it is going up.

- A vertical spread consists of at least one long option and one short option where both options are of the same type (puts or calls) and expiration, but have different strike prices. One-to-one verticals are typical, have limited risk/reward profiles and are all we have discussed.

- The maximum amount of profit in a debit spread (one that has been purchased) is the maximum value of the spread minus the net amount paid.

- The maximum loss of a debit spread is the amount paid for it.

- The maximum profit potential of a credit spread (one that is sold) is the amount of cash received.

Vertical Spread Trade Management

Even though vertical spreads are pretty tame from a risk standpoint – they are generally low cost and have limited risk- it is still a good idea to "have a plan" as to what you will do whether your market forecast is correct or incorrect. Good traders have their exits planned before they enter the trade.

- What is the most efficient way to take profits? Losses?
- What should I do if the underlying reaches my target ahead of schedule?
- What should I do if I am completely wrong on direction?
- What should I do if I underestimated the magnitude of the move?
- What if volatility behavior or any of the other assumptions that went into my forecast turn out to be incorrect?

These are all questions that need to be addressed before the trade. One mistake that is consistently made by options traders (probably because they tend to fancy themselves as "chess masters"), is staying too long in a position, or making too many modifications when their market view changes from the initial forecast. The simplest and most effective rule in risk management is this: **If you are wrong, get out!**

This means that if any of the assumptions that went into a market forecast turn out to be wrong you should get out of the position. Don't stick around hoping or praying for "diarrhea to turn into gold dust". It won't happen.

Sample Adjustments

When to Exit

There are two reasons to exit a trade: When one's market forecast has been met, or when one's market forecast has changed. The vertical spread is a directional strategy and should be applied when one is forecasting a moderate directional move. If one's market view suddenly shifts away from this view then the trade will need to be modified or liquidated, depending on the shift in market view. In the case of liquidation there are two ways to exit a vertical spread. One is to liquidate the original position; the other is to liquidate via the synthetic equivalent.

How to Exit

The decision whether to liquidate using the original position versus the synthetic equivalent depends on two factors: price and liquidity. Price is simple enough if one remembers to apply the pricing rules and use the most advantageously priced bull or bear spread to liquidate the position. The other factor is liquidity, and liquidity issues usually have to do with the "money-ness" of the individual options that compose the vertical spread. As options move "in the money" they acquire a larger delta, and this makes hedging them riskier for market makers.

Accordingly, market makers will widen the bid-ask spread of in the money options to compensate for this risk. Conversely, out of the money options have a lower delta, making hedging them less risky for market makers. This usually results in out of the money options having a narrower bid-ask spread than their in the money counterparts. The net effect on vertical spreads is that a spread consisting of in the money options will usually have a wider bid-ask spread than a vertical spread consisting of out of the money options. Since an in the money call vertical has a synthetically equivalent out of the money put vertical, and an in the money put vertical has a synthetically equivalent out of the money call vertical. This "money-ness" effect (especially on profitable trades) can make using synthetically equivalent positions to exit a trade even more appealing.

Modifying the Vertical Spread

"Rolling" Vertical Spreads

Occasionally the magnitude of a directional movement might be underestimated, and the trader may want to "roll" the spread into a different set of strikes so that it can continue to participate in the further price movement of the stock. When one's price target is reached prematurely, or when the underlying looks as though it might make a stronger move in the anticipated direction, "rolling" the spread up or down can allow one to continue to participate in the move. Rolling a vertical spread is accomplished by using another spread, the butterfly. Selling a butterfly that overlaps to the upside rolls a bull spread up:

Example 3: "Rolling-up" a Bull Call Spread

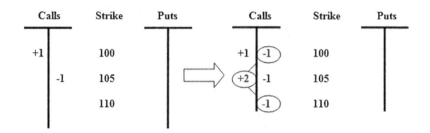

Bull Call Spread   Sell the Overlapping Call Butterfly

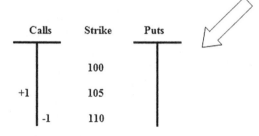

New Bull Call Spread at Higher Strikes

Figure 20

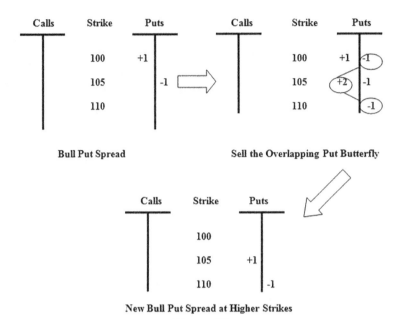

Figure 21

The great thing about rolling vertical spreads by selling butterflies is that it takes a little money off the table, and allows the trader to stick with the trade idea and participate on the extended directional move. Selling a butterfly that overlaps to the downside rolls a bear spread down:

Example 5: "Rolling-down" a Bear Call Spread

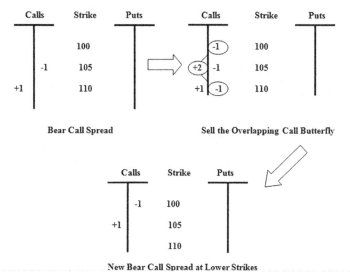

Figure 22

Example 6: "Rolling-down" a Bear Put Spread

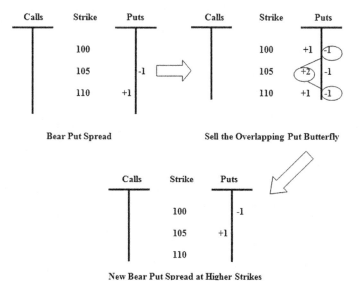

Figure 23

305

Using this technique the trader is able to buy time should the underlying reach the target price prematurely, or, participate in movement of a greater magnitude should it appear that the underlying is set to continue its directional move in a magnitude greater than originally forecast.

CHAPTER 18

Calendar Spreading

"If you do not have a sophisticated option risk management system, would you be able to properly assess the risk in your positions? Through position break-down, anyone can quickly ascertain their risk and always be ready for the next trade - the hallmark of a Saliba options education."

- Chris Hausman

The calendar spread or "time spread" can be used as an approach to use both theta and vega to your advantage. If applied correctly, the calendar spread can provide you with a market-neutral strategy without the predicaments that often turn up with other types of strategies.

Calendar spreading use options of the same class yet different expiration cycles with the intent of capturing specific market conditions. Calendar spreads are divided into two separate categories: "Horizontal" and "Diagonal" time spreads.

- Horizontal Spreads – options of the same class and strike prices but different expirations.

- Diagonal Spreads – options of the same class but different strike prices and expirations.

Horizontal Calendar Spreads (Time Spreads)

- Can involve either calls or puts

- Can be "long" or "short"

- Can have a bullish, bearish, or non-directional bias

Naming Standards

Calendar spread jargon can be unclear because they can be composed of calls or puts of a range of expiration cycles. To keep it simple, keep the image of buying and selling *time* in mind. If one buys a call or put of a longer-dated expiration compared with the call or put that is sold, one is buying *time* and is long the time spread, if one buys a call or put of a shorter-dated expiration than the call or put that is sold, one is selling time and is short the time spread.

The Basic Calendar Spread -Structure

Long Call Calendar:

- Purchase deferred call, sell the near term call, same strike price.

Long Put Calendar:

- Purchase deferred put, sell the near term put, same strike price.

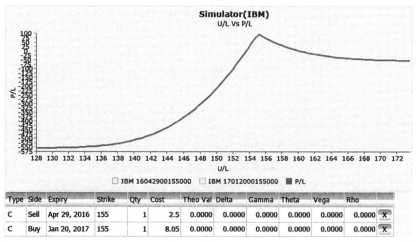

Figure 1   Options Technology Solutions, UK

Type	Side	Expiry	Strike	Qty	Cost	Theo Val	Delta	Gamma	Theta	Vega	Rho	
C	Sell	Apr 29, 2016	155	1	2.5	0.0000	0.0000	0.0000	0.0000	0.0000	0.0000	X
C	Buy	Jan 20, 2017	155	1	8.05	0.0000	0.0000	0.0000	0.0000	0.0000	0.0000	X

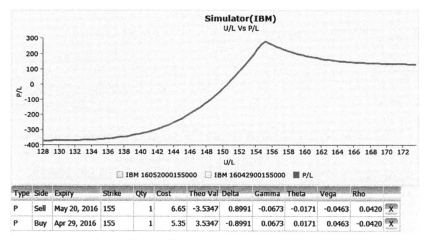

Figure 2   Options Technology Solutions, UK

Type	Side	Expiry	Strike	Qty	Cost	Theo Val	Delta	Gamma	Theta	Vega	Rho	
P	Sell	May 20, 2016	155	1	6.65	-3.5347	0.8991	-0.0673	-0.0171	-0.0463	0.0420	X
P	Buy	Apr 29, 2016	155	1	5.35	3.5347	-0.8991	0.0673	0.0171	0.0463	-0.0420	X

Short Call Calendar:

- Sell deferred call, purchase the near term call, same strike price.

Short Put Calendar:

- Sell deferred put, purchase the near term put, same strike price.

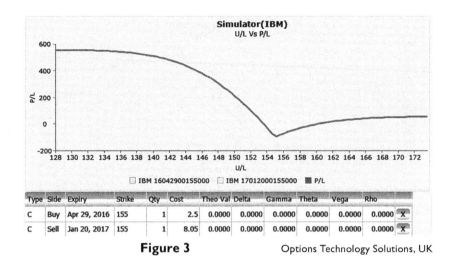

Type	Side	Expiry	Strike	Qty	Cost	Theo Val	Delta	Gamma	Theta	Vega	Rho	
C	Buy	Apr 29, 2016	155	1	2.5	0.0000	0.0000	0.0000	0.0000	0.0000	0.0000	X
C	Sell	Jan 20, 2017	155	1	8.05	0.0000	0.0000	0.0000	0.0000	0.0000	0.0000	X

Figure 3   Options Technology Solutions, UK

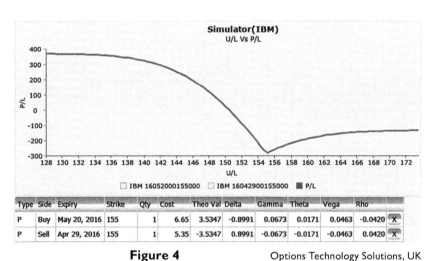

Type	Side	Expiry	Strike	Qty	Cost	Theo Val	Delta	Gamma	Theta	Vega	Rho	
P	Buy	May 20, 2016	155	1	6.65	3.5347	-0.8991	0.0673	0.0171	0.0463	-0.0420	X
P	Sell	Apr 29, 2016	155	1	5.35	-3.5347	0.8991	-0.0673	-0.0171	-0.0463	0.0420	X

Figure 4   Options Technology Solutions, UK

The Basic Calendar Spread Pricing

The very first thing the spread trader will notice when pricing calendar spreads is that the call calendar and the put calendar trade at different prices, with the call calendar generally being more expensive than the put calendar. This is because option prices are based on the forward price of the underlying, and generally, as one goes out in time, the forward price increases. This means that calls should usually trade at a premium to puts by the amount that the forward price trades at a premium to the spot price.

Does this mean that one should buy only put calendars because they are always cheaper, or sell only call calendars because they are always more expensive? No! This interest rate component of the calendar spreads is embedded, and remains a component of the spread. Buying the less expensive put calendar when one wishes to buy the calendar, or selling the more expensive call calendar when one wishes to sell the calendar, will gain no advantage.

Month	Strike	Call/Put	Value	Month	Strike	Call/Put	Value	Combo
May	640	Call	30.12	May	640	Put	9.63	660.49
May	660	Call	17.73	May	660	Put	17.12	660.61
May	680	Call	8.93	May	680	Put	28.57	660.36

Month	Strike	Call/Put	Value	Month	Strike	Call/Put	Value	Combo
June	640	Call	37.85	June	640	Put	16.97	660.88
June	660	Call	26.00	June	660	Put	25.10	660.90
June	680	Call	16.65	June	680	Put	35.60	661.05

Calendar Spread	Value
May/June 640 C	7.73
May/June 640 P	7.34
May/June 660 C	8.27
May/June 660 P	7.98
May/June 680 C	7.72
May/June 680 P	7.03

Underlying: AMZN= $660.42

Figure 5

The Basic Calendar Spread –Strategies

The Long Calendar Spread - Market view: Neutral or Market Stagnation

The long calendar spread is employed when one believes there will be little or no movement during the lifetime of the short near term option. When this is the case, the strikes chosen for the spread should be located where the trader expects the underlying to trade during the life of the near term option.

311

Near term options have a higher rate of time decay than deferred options and as time passes the spread will expand (Chapter 6: "Option Theta"). As expiration approaches, time decay for the near term option accelerates dramatically, causing the spread to widen further. Should the near term option expire worthless, the investor will be left with a naked long deferred option.

The point of maximum profit would occur if the underlying price were equal to the strike price at expiration. The near term option would expire worthless, leaving the investor with a long deferred option at its point of maximum extrinsic value. The amount of profit is impossible to quantify, because there is no way of knowing what the term structure of implied volatility will be at expiration.

The Risk, Reward, and Breakeven Points of the Long Calendar:

- **Risk:**   Premium paid (P).
- **Reward:**   Cannot be determined
- **Breakeven:**   Cannot be determined

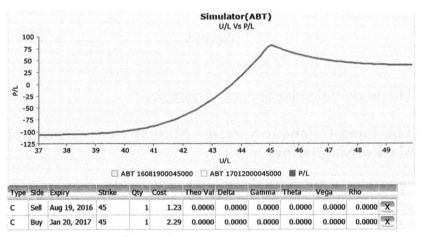

Type	Side	Expiry	Strike	Qty	Cost	Theo Val	Delta	Gamma	Theta	Vega	Rho	
C	Sell	Aug 19, 2016	45	1	1.23	0.0000	0.0000	0.0000	0.0000	0.0000	0.0000	X
C	Buy	Jan 20, 2017	45	1	2.29	0.0000	0.0000	0.0000	0.0000	0.0000	0.0000	X

Figure 6   Options Technology Solutions, UK

The Short Calendar Spread

Market view: Volatile, Strong Directional Move (Either Way) Expected

The short calendar spread is engaged when one believes there will be extreme market divergence during the lifetime of the long near term option. When this is the case, the strikes chosen for the spread should be located from where the investor expects the stock to move away from during the life of the near-term option.

Maximum profit occurs if the underlying makes a powerful move in either direction. The calendar spread will begin to collapse as both options become either far out of the money, and therefore worthless, or deep in the money, and trade at intrinsic value. Since intrinsic value is the same for both options, the spread will have collapsed. The investor would then pocket the premium collected when the spread was sold.

Maximum risk occurs if the underlying price stays near the strike price into expiration. The near term option would expire worthless, leaving the investor with a short deferred option at its point of maximum extrinsic value. The amount of risk is tough to quantify, because there is no way of knowing what the term structure of implied volatility will be at expiration. (Theoretically, if the long expires before the short the risk is unlimited for the short call and substantial for the short put).

The Risk, Reward, and Breakeven Points of the Short Calendar:

- **Risk:** Theoretically unlimited for the short call calendar and, substantial for the short put calendar
- **Reward:** Premium received (P).
- **Breakeven:** Cannot be determined.

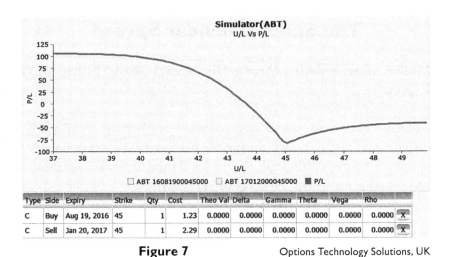

Type	Side	Expiry	Strike	Qty	Cost	Theo Val	Delta	Gamma	Theta	Vega	Rho	
C	Buy	Aug 19, 2016	45	1	1.23	0.0000	0.0000	0.0000	0.0000	0.0000	0.0000	X
C	Sell	Jan 20, 2017	45	1	2.29	0.0000	0.0000	0.0000	0.0000	0.0000	0.0000	X

Figure 7   Options Technology Solutions, UK

Calendar Spreads and Directional Bias

Trading directional calendar spreads can sometimes involve more art than science. The price of a calendar spread reacts to changes in underlying price, time until expiration, changes in implied volatility levels in both months, interest rate and dividend structures. It is sometimes difficult to visualize how changes in these variables will affect the price of the spread.

A firm understanding of the "greeks" and how they affect term structure can be very beneficial. A good alternative is to have access to a basic options calculator or options position analyzer, and walk through different circumstances to get a feel for the behavior of the calendar spread. As is the case with any options strategy, aberrations in implied volatility can have a dramatic impact on the price of the calendar spread.

The Calendar Spread – With a Directional Bias

The Long Calendar:

A calendar spread with a directional bias is a spread where the investor believes that the underlying will diverge in a beneficial direction between trade date and expiration date. As previously discussed, a long calendar spread reaches its point of maximum profitability when the underlying price is equal to the strike price of the spread exactly at expiration. Therefore, location of the strike price relative to the underlying price determines whether the spread is bullish or bearish. The unique thing is the long calendar spread can be both.

Strike price > Underlying price? Bullish Call Calendar

This makes sense on a perceptive level. If the long calendar spread reaches its point of maximum profitability when the underlying price is equal to the strike price, then, the investor would need the underlying to rally UP to the strike price (hopefully at expiration), making this a bull spread.

For the mathematically inclined, if you put a long calendar spread into a position analyzer, with the underlying price below the strike price of the spread, it will throw off a positive delta, indicating a position that would benefit from a bullish move.

Strike price < Underlying price? Bearish Call Calendar

This also makes sense on an instinctive level. If the long calendar spread reaches its point of maximum profitability when the underlying price is equal to the strike price, then, the investor would need the underlying to move DOWN to the strike price (hopefully at expiration), making this a bear spread.

Again, if you put a long calendar spread into a position analyzer, with the underlying price above the strike price of the spread, it will throw off a negative delta, indicating a position that would benefit from a bearish move.

Strike price = Underlying price? Neutral, No Movement

In this case the investor is hoping for no movement.

A long calendar spread put into a position analyzer, with the underlying price equal to the strike price of the spread, it will throw off a neutral delta, indicating a position with no bias. However, taking the analysis a step further, this spread will also generate a negative gamma and a positive theta, indicating that little or no movement is desirable.

The Short Calendar

A short calendar spread reaches its point of maximum profitability when the underlying price moves sharply away from the strike price of the spread (in either direction). Therefore, location of the strike price relative to the underlying price determines whether the spread is bullish or bearish. The short calendar spread can also be both.

Strike price > Underlying price? Bearish

If the short calendar spread reaches its point of maximum profitability when the underlying price is far from the strike price, then, the investor would want the underlying to keep moving away from the strike price (the further, the better). In this case the underlying is already below the strike price, the investor would want the underlying to keep moving DOWN, making this a bear spread.

Again, for the mathematically inclined, if you put a short calendar spread into an analyzer, with the underlying price below the strike price of the spread, it will throw off a negative delta, indicating a position that would benefit from a bearish move.

Strike price < Underlying price? Bullish

Once again, the short calendar spread reaches its point of maximum profitability when the underlying price is far from the strike price. In this case the underlying is already above the strike price, the investor would want the underlying to keep moving UP away from the strike price, making this a bull spread.

316

If you put a short calendar spread into an analyzer, with the underlying price above the strike price of the spread, it will throw off a positive delta, indicating a position that would benefit from a bullish move.

Strike price = Underlying price? Volatile Movement, Either Direction

In this case the investor is hoping for extremely volatile price movement, hopefully taking the underlying price a great distance from the strike price of the spread.

A short calendar spread put into a position analyzer, with the underlying price equal to the strike price of the spread, it will also throw off a neutral delta, indicating no bias. This spread generates a positive gamma and a negative theta, indicating that a sharp move would be desirable.

Calendar Spreading and the Greeks – Long Time Spread

Delta

The delta of a long calendar spread is the net difference (in delta) between the longer-dated and the shorter-dated option. For example the delta of the ABC 50 call calendar spread would be calculated as follows:

ABC (t+n) 50 call delta = .55

ABC t 50 call delta = .50

ABC (t+n, t) 50 call time spread delta = .55 -.50 or .05

Recall that puts have a negative delta, so the calculation of the delta of the ABC (t+n, t) 50 put time spread would be calculated as follows:

$$\text{XYZ } (t+n) \text{ 50 put delta} = -.45$$

$$\text{XYZ } t \text{ 50 put delta} = -.50$$

$$\text{XYZ } (t+n, t) \text{ 100 put time spread delta} = -.45 - (-.50) \text{ or } (-.05)$$

Be aware that the long calendar spreads apex of profitability is when the underlying price is sitting AT the strike price, at expiry. Therefore, it makes sense that the delta of a long calendar spread is positive when the underlying price is below the strike price, and negative when the underlying price is above the strike price. This is apparent in Figures 8 and 9 below.

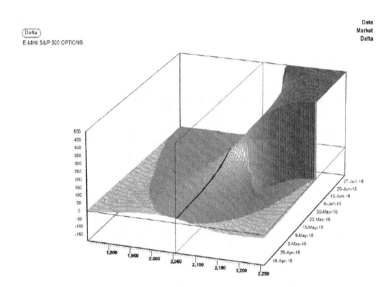

Figure 8   Option Scape

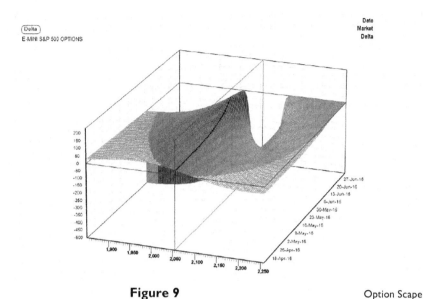

Figure 9   Option Scape

Synthetic Equivalency of Long Call Calendar Spread and Long Put Calendar Spread

Take note of the delta similarity between Figures 8 and 9. Recall the discussion in Chapter 2, "Rules of Options Equivalency," and how it applies to the same strike and same expiration call and put calendar spreads. Call and put calendar spreads are connected by their strike and expiry sameness. Suffice to say that the delta, gamma, theta, and vega of call and put time spreads (same underlying, same strike, same set of expirations) are identical.

Gamma

We know from Chapter 4, "Options Gamma" that a long option will contain long gamma while a short option will contain short gamma. With long calendar spreads in mind, the deferred option will generate positive gamma while the short-dated option will contain short gamma. Thus the net gamma of the long calendar spread will "generally" be negative however; the net negativity depends on how close the short option is till expiration.

319

It's crucial to be aware that the gamma of a long calendar spread is negative when the underlying price is nearest to the strike price due to the disparity of gamma between the short-dated and deferred options. However, due to the great amount of convexity in the shorter-dated option, the net gamma could well flip from negative-to-flat-to-positive if the underlying diverges far enough away from the strike price.

In Figure 10, notice how the net gamma negativity changes as the underlying diverges from the strike price.

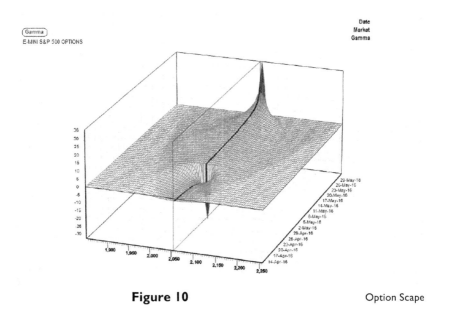

Figure 10   Option Scape

Vega

Recall from chapter five, "Options Vega" that a long option position will have a positive vega while a short option position will have a negative vega. Additionally, a long-dated option will have a larger vega than a shorter-dated option of the same strike. The net vega of a long calendar spread is the sum of the long call (deferred option) subtracted by the vega of the short (short-dated) option.

Reviewing Figure 11 you will notice that the net vega of this spread begins to rise as expiry draws near as the vega of the short-dated option begins to drop compared to the vega of the longer-dated option.

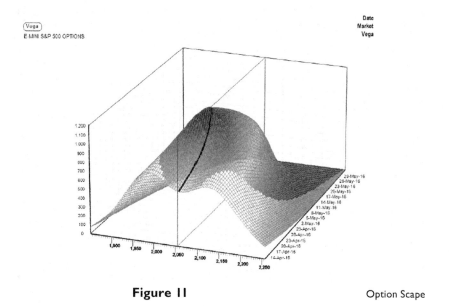

Figure 11   Option Scape

Theta

In Chapter 6, "Options Theta" we learned that short-dated options (assuming they are near or around-the-money) have a larger theta compared to longer-dated options of the same strike and month. That said, a long calendar spread will generally have positive theta – it will rise in value with the passage of time.

The net theta of a long calendar spread is highly dependent on its time till expiry and its location relative to the underlying. The theta of the long calendar spread is positive when the underlying price is near the strike price, but if the underlying price diverges far enough away from the strike price in either direction, the theta can become negative. Like gamma, the theta of an at the money option increases hurriedly as expiration approaches and the theta of a long time spread will generally increase as well.

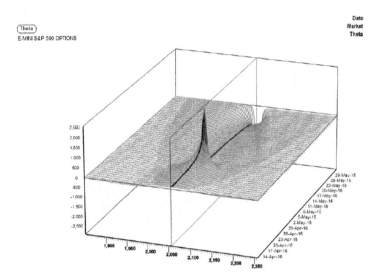

Figure 12   Option Scape

Spread Type	Delta		Gamma	Vega	Theta
Long Time Spread	Up	-	Negative	Positive	Positive
	Dn	+			
Short Term Spread	Up	-	Positive	Negative	Negative
	Dn	+			

Figure 13

Long Time Spreads

- Negative gamma, positive vega, positive theta
  - o Sideways trade, rising implied volatility
  - o Directional move toward a target price

322

Short Time Spreads

- Positive gamma, negative vega, negative theta
    - o Sharp movement away from the strike, falling implied volatility

Calendar Spread Strategy and Risk Management

A prudent calendar spreader needs to have deep convictions on both time and space!

- <u>Bullish outlook</u> – one should buy a time spread currently out of the money – the more bullish the more out of the money you can go. Remember your short option (short-dated) must end up at or near the underlying price by expiration.

- <u>Neutral market prognosis</u> - calls for a long time spread at a strike that parallels to the current market price.

- <u>Market breakout</u> - lean towards selling a current at-the-money call calendar spread.

Example: Long Call Calendar with Bullish Prediction

Suppose you believe that XYZ, currently trading at $100, is going to rise gradually over the next 30 days. With that confidence, you review data such as that in the table below, which gives you the various (call) fair values of the XYZ index.

Call Strike	Three Days till Expiry Value	Thirty-One Days till Expiry Value	Fifty-Nine Days till Expiry Value
$95.00	$5.05	$5.88	$6.78
$100.00	$1.30	$3.17	$4.34
$105.00	$0.01	$1.00	$1.95

XYZ = $100

Figure 14

You review data such as that in the table below and decide to buy the $105 call calendar spread for a net price of $.95. In this case you would buy the 59-day call for $1.95 and write a call contract for 31 days for $1.

Strike	Calendar	Index	Spread Value	Spread Delta
$95.00	Call	XYZ	$0.90	-0.05
$100.00	Call	XYZ	$1.17	0.01
$105.00	Call	XYZ	$0.95	0.07

XYZ = $100. Long option, fifty-nine days until expiration, at-the-money volatility = 24.5%. Short option, thirty-one days until expiration, at-the-money volatility = 24.1%.

Figure 15

Twenty-eight days go by. Your $105 long calendar spread now has 31 days for the long contract and 3 days remaining for the short. But you were incorrect on your outlook of XYZ. The share price has remained largely unchanged (at $100) over the course of the past 28 days. The table below demonstrates what happens to the price of the calendar spread with time decay but no movement in the underlying share price.

Strike	Calendar	Index	Spread Value	Spread Delta	Spread P/L
$95.00	Call	XYZ	$0.83	-0.24	-$0.07
$100.00	Call	XYZ	$1.87	0.01	$0.70
$105.00	Call	XYZ	$0.95	0.25	$0.00

XYZ = $100. Long option, thirty-one days until expiration, at-the-money volatility = 24.21%. Short option, three days until expiration, at-the-money volatility = 27.59%.

Figure 16

Now consider the table below, which shows a typical outcome of the effect on the price of various calendar spreads with time decay and with the stock price climbing from $100 to $105 a share.

324

Strike	Calendar	Index	Spread Value	Spread Delta	Spread P/L
$95.00	Call	XYZ	$0.45	-0.07	($0.45)
$100.00	Call	XYZ	$1.10	-0.25	($0.07)
$105.00	Call	XYZ	$1.91	0.01	$0.96

XYZ = $105. Long option, thirty-one days until expiration, at-the-money volatility = 22.25%. Short option, three days until expiration, at-the-money volatility = 27.03%.

Figure 17

Risk Management Considerations:

- <u>Time value and volatility are not necessarily interconnected.</u> The relation between time value and volatility is not as clear and precise as it seems. Buying a calendar spread is not the same as buying volatility.

- <u>Avoid supposing too much about front-month versus back-month vega differentials.</u> A calendar spread is normally long vega. Generally, an increase in implied volatility will help the position, and an overall decrease in implied volatility will hurt the position. It's that simple.

- <u>At extreme prices, differences in parity may appear.</u> If an underlying price falls to $0, all of the put strikes will be at parity. But no matter how high the underlying goes, it can theoretically go higher still. So call contracts can still carry a value.

- <u>Don't over-think implied volatility.</u> Awareness that a calendar spread has positive vega is pointless without accounting for how the implied volatility might change for the two months included in the calendar spread. There is no rule regarding how implied volatility may differ between the options contracts in a calendar spread.

- <u>Don't over-think greek values.</u> The greeks are both fascinating and useful calculations. But in the end, they are simply theoretical risk-measurement tools. Over the long haul, they won't necessarily help you find good risk-adjusted trades.

- <u>Good forecast – bad timing</u> OR <u>late arrival</u>. Getting the direction right and the timing wrong, correctly forecasting a directional move, but making very little profit on a long time spread happens much more often than publicized. Know what you will do BEFORE it happens to you.

CHAPTER 19

Diagonal Spread

"If there is one thing I learned about trading, it is how important emotions play a role in how a person trades. I am privileged to have been able to start my career on the floor of the CBOT and witnessed firsthand the different types of personalities and characters trading attracts. The one common character trait of all the successful ones was their ability to remain calm and confident no matter how volatile the market got. With that said, I started my trading career in the summer of 2008 as a clerk in the 10-yr treasury options pit, so you can imagine how volatile some days got...

When I left the floor to start my career as an upstairs trader at Tony Saliba's Hedge Fund, one of the first character traits I saw in Tony and the team he assembled around him was the level headed nature of everyone. Even as an upstairs trader, the market swings create emotions. Tony's ability to always be poised and confident no matter how good or bad of a day we were having is in my opinion the key driver to his many years of success in the Options Market. The traders that are sporadic and emotional are the ones that will see their P&L act in such a way as well.

Those who have a rock solid state of mind will have a rock solid trading career."

- Joe Z. Guediguian

The diagonal calendar spread is a complex variation of the basic calendar spread. The diagonal calendar spread or simply "the diagonal" should be studied and analyzed under different time, volatility, and underlying price scenarios before it is implemented. Changes in these parameters can affect the outcome of a diagonal strategy.

Generally a diagonal is utilized for multi-dimensional market views. Up, down, or unchanged in terms of underlying price are generally blended with velocity, magnitude, timing, or implied volatility views. The trader must be able to visualize the different ways in which such a spread responds to changes in the above. Once again, a strong understanding of the "greeks" or access to a sophisticated position analyzer is almost essential.

The Diagonal Spread Structure

The basic calendar spread involved the purchase (sale) of a deferred call (put), and the sale (purchase) a near term call (put), same exercise price. The diagonal spread uses different exercise prices. The different exercise prices used depend on the market view of the spreader.

Because using different strikes can change the amount of premium paid or collected when initiating the diagonal, the terms "long" and "short" become blurred. It is necessary to spell out exactly which month and strike is the long, and which month and strike is the short.

There are many permutations of the diagonal spread, and many market views can be expressed (too many to cover here). We will examine some of the most common diagonals. Many of you will immediately notice that the diagonal is actually a combination of two spreads, a calendar spread, and a vertical bull or bear spread. Again, the reason for combining these two strategies is to express a multi-dimensional market view, or take advantage of some serious mispricing. Dissecting the diagonal spread to reveal these embedded sub-spreads will usually reveal the strategy behind the diagonal.

The "Up and Out" Spread

The "Up and Out" diagonal spread is a spread where one purchases a near term lower strike call option and sells a higher strike deferred call option. It gets its name from the fact that it is a spread commonly used by buy-writers to move their written calls "up and out". This spread can be initiated for a debit, a credit or even money, depending on the strikes involved, the time until expiration, and the implied volatilities of both months.

This spread is a combination of a short calendar spread and a bull call spread in the deferred month:

Strike Price	Calendar Spread		Vertical Spread	Diagonal Spread	
	Near Option	Deferred Option	Bull Spread-Deferred	Near Option	Deferred Option
Low Strike	+	-	+	+	
High Strike			-		-

Figure I

The short calendar spread component indicates that the trader would like a sharp move. The vertical spread component in the deferred month indicates that the trader would like a move up. Combining the two yields a strategy geared for a sharp move up.

329

The Implied Volatility Component

To understand how this spread would be affected by shifts in implied volatility, one must examine the vega of the individual component options. Vega is the greek letter used to denote an option's exposure to changes in implied volatility. Expressed in monetary terms, vega indicates the amount one can expect the price of an option to change per 1% change in implied volatility. When implied volatility rises, option prices rise, when implied volatility falls, option prices fall. Longer-dated options have greater exposure to fluctuations in implied volatility than shorted dated options; therefore they have a higher vega. At the money options have a higher vega than in the money or out of the money options.

In the above case the trader is short the deferred option which will have a higher vega than the near term option. Therefore, in this case, the trader may also be looking for implied volatilities to decline as well.

The "Down and Out" Spread

The "Down and Out" diagonal spread is a spread where one purchases a near term higher strike put option and sells a lower strike deferred put option. It gets its name from the fact that it is a spread commonly used by cash covered put writers to move their written puts "down and out". This spread can also be initiated for a debit, a credit or even money, depending on the strikes involved, the time until expiration, and the implied volatilities of both months.

The vega exposure of a diagonal spread is a very complex issue. It can flip-flop with underlying movement, choice of expiry months, strike location, time passing, etc. I STRONGLY encourage any would-be diagonal traders to get a position analyzer and go through some different scenarios with any spread under consideration.

This spread is a combination of a short calendar spread and a bear put spread in the deferred month:

Strike Price	Calendar Spread		Vertical Spread	Diagonal Spread	
	Near Option	Deferred Option	Bear Spread-Deferred	Near Option	Deferred Option
Low Strike			-		-
High Strike	+	-	+	+	

Figure 2

The short calendar spread component indicates that the trader would like a sharp move. The vertical bear spread component in the deferred month indicates that the trader would like a move down. Combining the two yields a strategy geared for a sharp move down.

The "Reverse Up and Out" Spread

I'll be honest, the "Reverse Up and Out" is a name I just made up. It doesn't have a name (that I know of). It is simply the opposite of the "Up and Out". This diagonal spread is a spread where one sells a near term lower strike call option and purchases a higher strike deferred call option. This spread can be initiated for a debit, a credit or even money, depending on the strikes involved, the time until expiration, and the implied volatilities of both months.

This spread is a combination of a long calendar spread and a bear call spread in the deferred month:

Strike Price	Calendar Spread		Vertical Spread	Diagonal Spread	
	Near Option	Deferred Option	Bear Spread-Deferred	Near Option	Deferred Option
Low Strike			-		-
High Strike	+	-	+	+	

Figure 3

The long calendar spread component indicates that the trader would like the underlying to move toward the short near term strike. The vertical bear spread component in the deferred month indicates that the trader would like a move down. Combining the two yields a strategy geared for a slow move down to the short near term strike.

The Implied Volatility Component

In the above case the trader is short the near term option which will have a lower vega than the deferred option. Therefore, in this case, the trader may also be looking for implied volatilities to rise. This seems incompatible with the desire for a market moving slowly to the short near term strike but, remember, diagonal spreads are all about scenarios. Consider the scenario where the market moves slowly before an important event (earnings, government report, etc.), yet implied volatility rises.

The "Reverse Down and Out" Spread

Yes, I made this up too. It the opposite of the "Down and Out". This diagonal spread is a spread where one sells a near term higher strike put option and purchases a lower strike deferred put option. This spread can be initiated for a debit, a credit or even money, depending on the strikes involved, the time until expiration, and the implied volatilities of both months.

This spread is a combination of a long calendar spread and a bull put spread in the deferred month:

Strike Price	Calendar Spread		Vertical Spread	Diagonal Spread	
	Near Option	Deferred Option	Bear Spread-Deferred	Near Option	Deferred Option
Low Strike			-		-
High Strike	+	-	+	+	

Figure 4

The long calendar spread component indicates that the trader would like the underlying to move toward the short near term strike. The vertical bull spread component in the deferred month indicates that the trader would like a move up. Combining the two yields a strategy geared for a slow move up to the short near term strike.

The "Up and Out" Spread

You will recall that the "Up and Out" diagonal is a spread where one purchases a near term lower strike call option and sells a higher strike deferred call option. The market view for this type of spread is a quick move up. The implied volatility view, if any, would be for a decline in implied volatility.

Now we will take a theoretical diagonal spread and analyze the performance (P/L) with respect to underlying price, time to expiration, and implied volatility. We will also examine risk in terms of the "Greeks."

For the sake of simplicity we assume the spot price is equal to the forward price (interest rates = 0.00, no dividend), implied volatilities will be identical for both months, and use no implied volatility skew.

	30 day 100 Call	90 day 110 Call	Spread Total
Price	5.71	6.12	.41credit
Delta	.529	.398	.131
Gamma	.028	.016	.012
Vega	.114	.192	-.078
Theta	.095	.053	-.042

Figure 5

The "Greeks" of the 100/110 up and out diagonal spread (Long the 100 strike 30 day call, short the 110 strike 90 day call).

Stock = 100, implied volatility = 50%

If we were to buy the 30-day 100 calls and sell the 90-day 110 calls using the above parameters, we would realize a $0.41 credit.

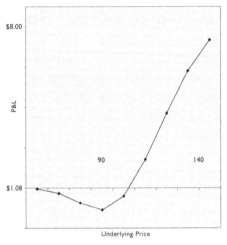

Figure 6

Looking at Figure 6 above, this looks like an attractive spread. It has a maximum risk is about $1.08 at $90, and it could make up to $8.00 at $140.

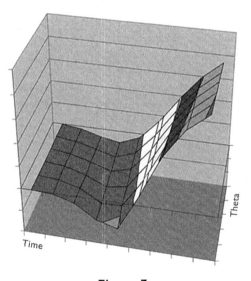

Figure 7

Now we can see the risk in this spread a little bit better. The short-dated option has a greater rate of time decay (theta) than a long dated

334

option when it is at the money. We can see that if the underlying stays near $100, as time passes the short-dated call decays much more rapidly than the deferred call. With 5 days left to expiration this spread would show approximately a $2.5 loss.

Here we can see the implied volatility component very clearly. An increase in implied volatility, particularly with the stock hovering around the $100 area, would be very painful for the owner of the up and out. However, a rally with declining implied volatility would produce positive results.

This is just an example of the complexity of the diagonal spread. They are truly multi-dimensional, and not to be taken lightly due to the risk involved. However, if you are the type of trader who has complex market opinions, the diagonal may be for you.

The "Down and Out" Spread

The "Down and Out" diagonal is a spread where one purchases a near term higher strike put option and sells a lower strike deferred put option. The market view for this type of spread is a quick move down. The implied volatility view, if any, would be for a decline in implied volatility.

Now we will take a theoretical down and out diagonal spread and analyze the performance (P/L) with respect to underlying price, time to expiration, and implied volatility. We will also examine risk in terms of the partial derivative "greeks."

For the sake of simplicity we assume the spot price is equal to the forward price (interest rates = 0.00, no dividend), that implied volatilities will be identical for both months, and we use no implied volatility skew.

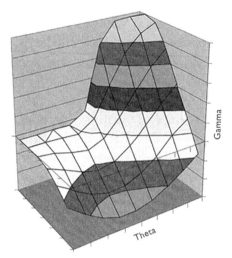

Figure 8

Stock = $100, implied volatility = 50%

If one were to buy the 30-day 100 puts, and sell the 90-day 90 puts using the above parameters, we would have to pay approximately $0.50. Initially, the spread is short delta, long gamma, short vega, and has a negative theta.

Here is how the spread would perform over an array of underlying prices:

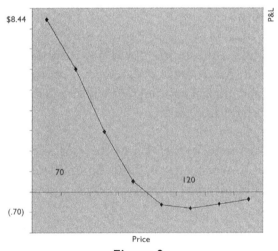

Figure 9

Looking in only two dimensions, this appears to be a very attractive spread. It seems to have a maximum risk of about $0.80 at $120, and it makes about $8.44 at $70. However, analyzing the performance of a diagonal in only two dimensions can be very misleading. Let's look at the spread vs. underlying price and time:

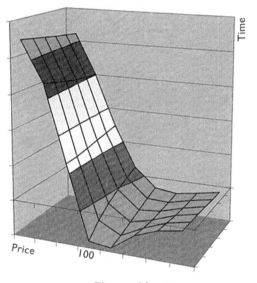

Figure 10

The time decay aspect of the spread is now evident. The short-dated option has a greater rate of time decay (theta) than a long dated option when it is at the money. We can see that if the underlying stays near $100, as time passes the short-dated put decays much more rapidly than the deferred put. With 5 days left to expiration this spread would show approximately a $1.60 loss.

You may recall from our discussion earlier that the dissection of the down and out revealed a short calendar spread combined with a bear put spread in the deferred month, indicating that a quick move down was desirable. This is also evident from the above chart. You may also recall that the down and out will have a negative vega, meaning it will benefit from a decline in implied volatility:

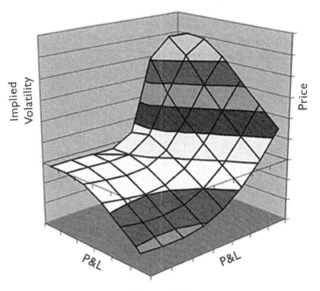

Figure 11

Here we can see the implied volatility component very clearly. An increase in implied volatility, particularly with the stock rallying, would be very painful for the owner of a down and out. His short-dated puts would continue to decay at a faster rate than his long dated puts, and they would react to a rise in implied volatility less than the long dated puts. However a sell off with declining implied volatility would produce better results.

Now that we've seen that the diagonal is a spread that benefits from a quick move to the short strike, but also benefits from a decline in implied volatility, you may be wondering when such a scenario would occur, after all, doesn't implied volatility rise when the underlying makes a sharp move? Aren't the two market views "quick move" and "declining implied volatility" mutually exclusive?

How about the behavior of markets following earnings reports, government reports, Federal Reserve announcements, or any other important market-impacting announcement? Usually there is a sharp move as the earnings or the report is announced (benefiting a position long gamma) and then, as the markets find equilibrium, a sharp decline in implied volatility (benefiting a position short vega).

Up to this point we have analyzed these positions with implied volatility being at the same level for both months. Obviously, that is seldom the case.

Valuation of Calendar Spreads

When is a calendar cheap? When is a calendar expensive? The answer to these questions is very subjective and depends upon your market view. However, common sense along with some statistical analysis can help with the decision making process.

Volatility: Past, Present, and Future

- **Historical volatility** is the annualized standard deviation of the returns of a particular stock. It describes how the price of a stock has moved in the past.

- **Implied volatility** is the level of volatility implied by current options pricing. It reflects the current market consensus as to what volatility is likely to be between the present date and the expiration date of the option. Obviously, this can change rapidly as volatility expectations change.

- **Realized volatility** is the volatility that will be realized between the present date and a certain time in the future (expiration date). It is essentially future volatility, and is un-known.

Volatility is mean-reverting, meaning that short-term fluctuations (or lack thereof) in the market may move volatility, but eventually it will revert to historical levels. In the case of options, this means that short-dated options are much more sensitive to short-term market volatility, while longer dated options reflect longer-term volatility:

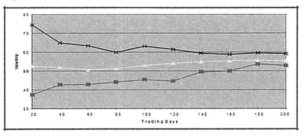

Figure 1. A Volatility Cone

Note: Options trading involves substantial risk and is not suitable for all investors. Also note that spreading strategies involve multiple commissions and are not risk-free.

Figure 12

The volatility cone above in Figure 12 graphically displays the range of implied volatilities versus time to expiration. Note how shorter dated option volatilities react to short-term events, while longer dated option volatilities are more indicative of the long-term mean. Since the implied volatility level of an option series is simply a reflection of the market consensus of what volatility will be between the present date and expiration of that series, options of different expiration cycles will trade at different implied volatilities. This volatility structure is referred to as the "term structure" of implied volatility.

As order flow pushes implied volatility levels up and down in different months, sometimes the term structure can get distorted, leaving an opportunity for the calendar spreader. These distortions can be revealed by forward volatility analysis.

Forward Volatility Analysis

Forward volatility analysis is the analysis of term structure and the volatilities implied by the differences in implied volatilities between months. Consider a 30-day option and a 90-day option:

Since the expiration dates overlap and both trade at a different implied volatility, there is a volatility implied for the period between the two dates. This is the implied forward volatility. This makes sense intuitively, since

340

the volatility that takes place during the life of the 30-day option must also affect the 90-day option, then the difference in implied volatilities must be explained by the expected volatility between day 30 and day 90.

Computing Forward Implied Volatility[*]

Computing Forward Implied Volatility[1]

$$Vola_{m_2 - m_1} = \sqrt{\frac{(Vola_2)^2 * days_2 - (Vola_1)^2 * days_1}{(days_2 - days_1)}}$$

Where:

$Vola_2$ = Implied volatility of the longer dated option

$Vola_1$ = Implied volatility of the shorter dated option

$Days_2$ = Days to expiration of the longer dated option

$Days_1$ = Days to expiration of the shorter dated option

Figure 13

For example:

$Vola_2$ = .54

$Vola_1$ = .36

$Days_2$ = 90

$Days_1$ = 30

Figure 14

This means that by pricing 90-day volatility at 54% and the 30-day volatility at 36%, the market is pricing 61% volatility for the period between 30 and 90 days.

---

* Nassim Taleb "Dynamic Hedging", (John Wiley and Sons, 1996), 155

How do we use this information to trade calendar spreads? We simply use this as a part of our decision making process. Common sense must be involved as well. There may be a perfectly good reason that forward volatility is at a substantial discount or premium to the long-term mean. What if the 30-day option includes a holiday weekend or a seasonally slow period (August, for example)? It makes sense that it would trade at a discount to the other longer dated options. What about the October (crash) options or options covering earnings periods? They usually trade at a premium, and for good reason.

Let's take a look at a decision making process for a calendar trade:

Market View: You expect the market to continue to move sideways through the end of the year, however, with implied volatilities at these low levels, you am reluctant to sell volatility outright. You would like to put on a calendar spread instead.

Forward Volatility Analysis: ABC stock has a 2-year historical volatility of 40%. The options are priced as follows:

Forward Volatility Analysis: ABC stock has a 2-year historical volatility of 40%. The options are priced as follows:

Month	Implied Volatility	Days to Expiry	Fwd. Implied Vola.
Sept.	35%	38	NA
Oct.	41%	66	48%
Jan.	36%	157	32%

Figure 15

This analysis reveals that the volatility implied for the period between September expiration and October expiration is 48%, 20% higher than the long term mean. The September/ October calendar might be considered a sell candidate. The volatility implied for the period between October expiration and January expiration is 32%, 20% lower than the long term mean. The January/October calendar might be

342

considered a buy candidate. Given the above market view, the logical choice would be to buy the January/October calendar spread.

There are many other considerations that go in to the selection of a calendar spread, and buying cheap or selling expensive implied forward volatility is no guarantee that you will make money, but it can be of great help if one is "on the fence" regarding strategy selection.

CHAPTER 20

Ratio & Backspreading

Ratio spreads involve buying one options contract and selling two or more options contracts with a strike price that is further out of the money than the contracts you buy. The options are either both calls or both puts. The ratio of the spread is the quantity of short options divided by the quantity of long options. Ratio spreads strategies are often used when one has a complicated forecast involving market direction and implied volatility or timing.

Technically speaking, any spread in which the number of long contracts does not equal the number of short contracts is referred to as a ratio spread. Given this definition, the most common types of ratio spreads are the backspread and the ratio vertical spread. While both the backspread and the ratio spread are volatility spreads, they are mirror images of one another in terms of their risk and reward profiles.

The backspread is designed to potentially profit in a very volatile market, while the ratio spread potentially profits in a quiet, range bound market. (By "range-bound market" I am referring to a situation or time-period during which the underlying security establishes a certain set of values with fairly well-defined high and low prices and proceeds to trade within those bounds).

345

The Strategy behind a Call Ratio Spread

The decomposition of a call ratio spread will reveal the motivation behind it. A call ratio spread is basically a bull call spread that is financed by the sale of additional out of the money calls. The sale of the additional out of the money calls leaves open-ended risk, but only to the upside. Therefore, the desirable outcome for a call ratio spread is for the market to move slowly to the upside, with maximum profit occurring if the underlying reaches the short strike at expiration. Declining implied volatility, declining actual volatility, and the passage of time are all very beneficial to the call ratio spread as it causes the away-from-the-money options to decline in value and lose sensitivity to market movement and the movement of implied volatility.

The Structure of a Call Ratio Spread

Purchasing at, or near-the-money options, and selling two or more away- from- the- money options constructs a ratio spread. Depending on market variables such as time until expiration, implied volatility, underlying price, and of course the strikes selected, this can result in the spread being a debit spread, a credit spread, or a zero cost spread.

You create the call ratio spread by purchasing an at-or near-the-money call, and selling two or more away-from-the-money calls of a higher strike price. An example of a call ratio spread would be the purchase of a 50 call and the sale two 55 calls. As I mentioned above, this could be done for a debit, a credit, or zero cost, depending on market conditions.

Theoretical Payout Diagrams

Below is a diagram of the payout of a call ratio spread at expiration. In this case a 50 call was purchased for 4.00 and two 55 calls were sold for 2.00 each. The spread was therefore initiated for "even money" (zero cost).

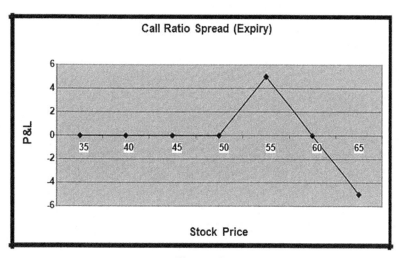

Figure I

As we can see from the diagram above, the loss on the downside is equal to the cost of the spread, if you paid nothing, you lose nothing, and if you received a credit when executing the spread, you would retain the credit. On the upside we have a ten-point zone of profitability before the additional short call begins to cause losses. If an extremely large upside move were to take place, losses are theoretically unlimited.

Payout diagrams of option strategies at expiration can sometimes be misleading, and I must caution you that any time before expiration it can be a very different picture. For example, the diagram below is the same spread executed with 30 days until expiration and implied volatility of 50%:

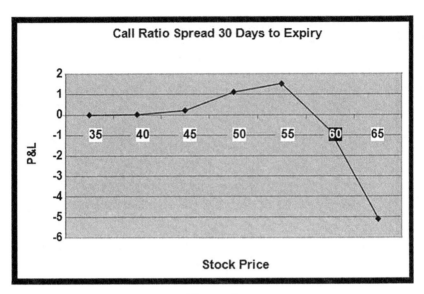

Figure 2

Now the P&L shifts to a lower payout and a quicker loss. This is because with 30 days left until expiration the short 55 calls still have a great deal of sensitivity the movement of the underlying, and to the movement of implied volatility.

- **Risk / Reward Breakdown (at Expiration)** With a call ratio spread risk and reward must be broken down in terms of upside risk and downside risk.
- **Downside Risk** There is only downside risk if the spread was done for a debit. In this case the risk is equal to the debit.
- **Upside Risk** Unlimited beyond breakeven
- **Reward** Upper Strike (K u) – Lower Strike (K l)
- **Breakeven**

{(# of short calls * short call breakeven) – (# of long calls * long call breakeven)}
(# of short calls - # of long calls)

348

Application of the Call Ratio Spread

When is it best to apply a call ratio spread? The call ratio spread benefits from a slowly rising market with declining implied volatilities. Therefore a stock or index with a somewhat limited upside, or the potential for a large volatility decline would be an attractive candidate for a call ratio spread.

- The risk and reward profile resembles that of a butterfly, with two exceptions. On the downside, if the spread was put on for a credit, the spread will always yield a credit. On the upside, the risk is always unlimited beyond the breakeven point (the trader has the possibility of an unlimited loss should the market make a substantial rally).

- Both declining implied volatility and the passage of time are a beneficial to the call ratio spread. This is because they cause the out of the money options to decline in value and lose sensitivity to the movement of implied volatility.

The Ratio Spread as an Escape or Repair Strategy

I never like to discuss strategies with open-ended risk without discussing escape strategies. As I mentioned above, the call ratio spread is designed for a slowly rising market with steady or declining implied volatility. If something goes wrong and the market starts to accelerate upward, there is one easy escape strategy. Purchasing an appropriate amount of calls at a higher strike can instantly turn the call ratio spread-with unlimited upside risk, into a call butterfly with limited risk.

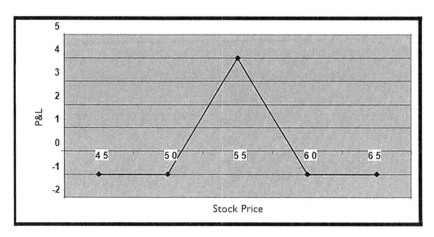

Figure 3

The keys to choosing the right ratio spread as a repair or escape, is timeframe and strike location. With a reasonable amount of time, you can create a ratio spread that returns a credit, without giving away too much of the upside opportunity.

Option	Premium	Quantity	P/L
Long September 17.50 Call	$3.40	1	($340.00)
Short September 20.00 Call	$2.35	2	$470.00
			$130.00

Ratio Call Spread at Expiration ; XYZ = $ 17.00

Figure 4

	Stock Price	$10.00	$12.50	$15.00	$17.50	$20.00	$21.00	$22.00	$25.00	$26.00	$27.00	$28.00	$29.00
XYZ	P/L	-700	-450	-200	50	300	400	500	800	900	1000	1100	1200
$17.5 Call	P/L	-340	-340	-340	-340	-90	10	110	410	510	610	710	810
$20.0 Call	P/L	470	470	470	470	470	270	70	-530	-730	-930	-1130	-1330
Total	P/L	-570	-320	-70	180	680	680	680	680	680	680	680	680

Figure 5

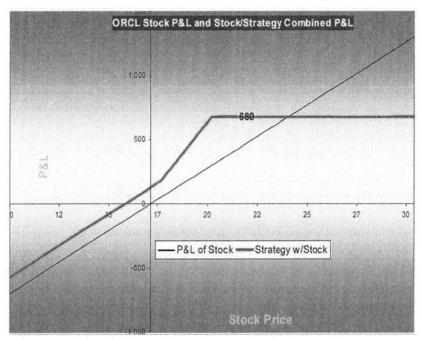

Figure 6

As you can see, all of the examples generate a credit and the payout is equal to or better than the payout of the stock alone, to a certain price. A few of the examples have the long call just out of the money, one is at the money and one of them has the long way out of the money.

This last example, the ratio spread, has us purchasing a call that is almost 20% out of the money and selling two at a strike that is almost 40% out of the money. This is possible because of the implied volatility that the options are experiencing. By going out six months we can pick up over 5% in credit with this ratio spread and the upside in this stock is unscathed until it is up almost 58%! This would allow a great number of holders 'get healthy', considering the stock spent most of the past year above $100 per share.

But it only gives you three points of downside protection. So if you think that a 58% move in the next six months is an impossible target

351

on QCOM, you can lower your strikes. This would enable you to pick up even more in credit, thus giving a greater downside cushion.

Let's walk through the four possible outcomes that we have:

- Stock lower

- Stock unchanged

- Stock rallies to the short strike of our strategy

- Stock rallies beyond the short strike of our strategy

If the stock goes lower, you will keep the credit you collected upon entering the strategy, which will offset the losses sustained in the stock to the degree of the credit received. Since you were going to hold the underlying position in any respect, this outcome is better than the holdings without the strategy. But don't do this strategy in lieu of blowing out of your long position altogether. If you're queasy, let 'em out easy. This does not give you much downside protection, if any.

If the stock is unchanged, the same credit is retained and becomes income against the backdrop of the static stock price, reducing the cost of that position. Your holdings are the same as those with which you began.

If the stock rallies, there is a zone that you make a profit that is somewhat larger than if you were only long the stock. This zone rewards you for a slight move up in your stock.

Stock rallies to the short strike. The zone of improved returns begins at the price that is the difference of the current price and the credit received from the strategy. This zone proceeds up through the strike at which you have the long leg of the repair strategy and to the strike where you have the extra short calls. At the strike with the shorts, you attain your maximum payout with this strategy.

If the stock rallies past the strike where you have the short leg. Assuming your strikes are equidistance from each other your breakeven, vis-à-vis just holding the naked stock, is the next higher strike above the calls that you are short plus the credit you received per share initially. This point may be called your point of indifference. Beyond this point your strategy with underlying stops making you money. (You stop making money at your upper strike price).

Another way to look at this strategy is that we are buying a vertical spread and selling a covered call against our stock position. Depending upon the premium levels in the calls you are looking to sell, this strategy can lower the cost basis in a holding while allowing for continued upside participation in that stock (up to the short call strike). It's a good strategy to initiate on top of a stock, in and of itself, if you like the stock. You're always going to own some or all of the downside exposure of the stock.

The Put Ratio Spread

The trader notes that the stock IVT has traded within the range of $45-$55 over the past few months. Presently, the stock is at $54.50. He has followed IVT for years and strongly believes that it is currently overbought. After extended analysis, he concludes that the stock is forming a rounding top and will begin a protracted sell-off in the near future. Given this evaluation of this market scenario, what strategies might he select to potentially profit? One viable option is to initiate a put ratio spread.

The first point we wish to stress is that a trader establishes the put ratio spread when he expects that the market will sit still, or move slowly to the downside. As we will make clear below, the optimal case for the put ratio spreader occurs when the underlying closes exactly at the strike price of the short options. After we examine its composition, we will better understand why this is so.

The Put Ratio Spread: Basic Concepts

The put ratio spread is similar to the call ratio spread in that the trader is short more option contracts than he is long. However in the case of the put ratio spread, the trader buys a certain number of puts at a higher strike and sells a greater number of puts at a lower strike (the inverse of the situation is the case, you will recall, in the call ratio spread, where the trader bought a number of calls at a lower strike price and sold a greater number of calls at a higher strike). Therefore an example of a put ratio spread would be as follows: With the stock trading at $54.50, the trader purchases a 50 put at $6 and sells two 45 puts at $4 each.

There is another way that the put ratio spread is conspicuously different than the call ratio spread: The market directionality that constitutes the spread's "worst case scenario." You will recall that the worst-case scenario for the call ratio spread occurred when the stock rallied substantially and suddenly higher. Conversely, the worst-case scenario for the put ratio spread is when the market moves sharply and substantially lower.

After our lessons on the dynamics of the call ratio spread, the reason behind this risk profile should be readily apparent. Recall that we said a call ratio spread was simply a long bull call spread with extra contracts sold against the long side, and that the sale of the additional out-of-the-money calls leaves the trader with open-ended risk on the upside. I suggest you view the put ratio spread as a long bear put spread with extra contracts sold against the long side. In this case the extra short puts are uncovered, and therefore carry with them substantial risk (because the risk on a "naked" or uncovered short puts are limited only by the fact that the stock can't drop below zero).

The Put Ratio Spread: Profit and Loss Scenarios (at Expiration)

So now for the big question: How does the trader potentially make money with a put ratio spread? I will discuss three scenarios in which you can.

1. As we have already noted, the trader potentially makes money if the stock sits still. In this market scenario, the two short puts would not be exercised, and so the trader would keep the total credit received. However, his long put would expire worthless, meaning that he would lose the total amount of the premium paid.

Buy one 50 put @ $6	**$ 6 debit**
Sell two 45 puts @ $4	**$ 8 credit**
Total	**$ 2 credit**

2. He potentially makes money if the stock moves slowly and moderately to the downside. At any point down to $45, the short puts would expire worthless, and the trader would keep the full credit received. Moreover, at any point below $50 his long put would be in the money. For example, if the stock closes at $47, the long 50 put would be 3 points in the money. Doing the math, the trader comes out ahead:

Buy one 50 put @ $6	**$ 6 debit**
Sell two 45 puts @ $4	**$ 8 credit**
One 50 put (3 points ITM)	**$ 3 credit**
Total	**$ 5 credit**

3. In fact, if the trader initiates the spread for credit (as in this example) the trader would even make money if the stock rallied substantially. If the stock closes above $50, the long put would expire worthless and he keeps the credit received from his short puts.

Buy one 50 put @ $6	**$ 6 debit**
Sell two 45 puts @ $4	**$ 8 credit**
Total	**$ 2 credit**

Just as was the case in the call ratio spread, the trader achieves the greatest profit if the underlying closes at the strikes of his short options. In this case, he would not be assigned on either short puts, and would keep the credit received. Moreover, his long put would be in the money by 5 points.

Buy one 50 put @ $6	**$ 6 debit**
Sell two 45 puts @ $4	**$ 8 credit**
50 put (5 points ITM)	**$ 5 credit**
Total	**$ 7 credit**

The trader's worst-case scenario, as we mentioned above, occurs when the stock drops substantially below the strike price of his short puts. In this case, he would be assigned on these puts, and his risk exposure here is virtually unlimited. Why? Because one (or more) of the short puts is "uncovered," and the potential risk on an uncovered short put is unlimited, bounded only by the fact that the stock can't trade below zero! If he is assigned on that uncovered short put, the trader must buy the stock at the short strike price.

I always like to spread out my risk— I never leave myself open to unlimited loss. So, when I initiate a put ratio spread, I always have a viable "escape strategy." Looking at the trader's position, I note the following: Even in this worst-case scenario, the trader still has some fairly painless ways to hedge his risk. The first would be the most logical: buy back the extra 45 put and leave yourself simply long the 45/50 put bear spread. The other would be to buy the equidistant lower strike put, in this case the 40 put. He has now limited his risk by turning his put ratio spread into (my favorite) a butterfly.

The Put Ratio Spread: Risk and Reward Scenarios (at Expiration)

Let's look at a diagram to clarify the risk/reward profile of the put ratio spread:

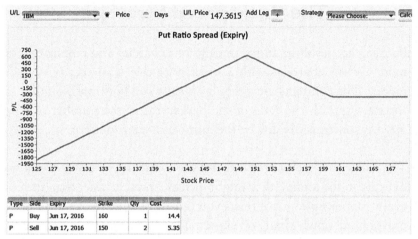

Figure 7

Options Technology Solutions, UK

- **Market Outlook:**   Neutral to Bullish

- **Composition:**   Long 1 put at K2
  Short 2 puts at K1

- **Max profit:**   (k2-k1) +/- Credit/ Debit

- **Max Loss:**   Unlimited to the downside

- **Breakeven Points:** K2-debit (on upside) or if credit received, the credit is the amount of profit at/above K2; and: K1 – [(K2-K1 +/- credit/debit x Extra # of puts sold}

The extended downward slope of the line indicates that the trader has substantial risk to the downside. This makes sense since one of the short puts is "naked" or uncovered. He is liable to incur a loss at any point past his breakeven point down to zero. (As you will recall, because a stock cannot fall below zero, the maximum risk of a short put is the strike price minus the credit received).

The Backspread Strategy

Backspreads result in selling one options contract and buying two or more options contracts with a strike price that is further out of the money. The contracts are either both calls and both puts. Similar to the ratio spread, the ratio of the backspread is the number of long options contracts divided by the number of short options.

The risk with a backspread is that if the contracts you sell move closer to being in the money, they might increase in value faster than the out of the money options contracts you buy if the underlying share price moves more slowly than you expect. This happens even more rapidly as expiration draws near.

Types of Backspreads

First, let us note that the backspread comes in two varieties: the call backspread and the put backspread. A call backspread is composed of a short at-the-money call and a greater number of long out-of-the-money calls, i.e. at higher strike price. A put backspread is composed of a short at-the-money put and a greater number of long out of the money puts, i.e., at a lower strike price.

Regardless of the classification, (call backspread or a put backspread), the trader should attempt to initiate a backspread for a net credit or at least for even money. This may not always be possible, and the trader must decide for himself whether the market scenario warrants putting on the spread for a debit. The point to remember is that if the spread is put on for a credit, the trader can utilize the credit as a "buffer zone" or a partial hedge in the event that the direction of his market prediction fails to materialize.

The Backspread is a Volatility Spread

The backspread is, primarily, a type of volatility spread. Recall that a trader who initiates a volatility spread is speculating on the volatility or degree of price fluctuation rather than the direction of the underlying.

In general, a backspread takes advantage of an underlying that is about to make a fast and substantial move or one that is beginning to trend in a particular direction. The crucial point is this: the trader who establishes a backspread is looking for a substantial increase in volatility. I will elaborate on these points below.

However, unlike the trader who establishes other types of volatility strategies, for example the straddle or the strangle, the backspreader is concerned with the direction of the underlying. If the trader foresees a market with strong upside potential, he will most likely implement a call backspread. On the other hand, if he foresees a market with strong downside potential, he will most likely select a put backspread.

Any trader who takes on volatility exposure must find a way to reduce the risk that the purchase or sale of options could seriously harm him in the short-term. One way to do this is to engage in Delta Neutral spreading. This strategy takes the risk out of his position by balancing the long deltas with the short deltas.

The trader who initiates a backspread is vulnerable to this type of volatility exposure and he therefore attempts to remain delta neutral. In order to achieve delta neutral status, options with smaller deltas will be purchased, and options with larger deltas will be sold where all options expire at the same time. It follows that the backspreader would sell an option that is closer to the at the money strike, and buys a greater amount of out of the money options at another strike.

Backspreads and the Volatility "Skew"

Ok, so we have established that the backspread is a volatility spread. How exactly does the trader harness the moves in volatility? The trader who implements the backspread attempts to take advantage of the volatility "skew" between the strike prices of the options. In order to exploit the skew, the trader must carefully select his strike prices.

Remember that high implied volatility entails high option prices and lower implied volatility entails lower option prices. The fact that an option is "expensive," means that the market place has built a high volatility estimate into its current price. In other words, the market is forecasting a lot of movement in the underlying before expiration.

The volatility "skew" or "smile" is the graphic representation of the implied volatilities of an option (plotted on the y-axis) as a function of its strike price (x-axis). Skews are a result of the fact that the assumptions behind a theoretical pricing model are not 100% accurate.

If all the assumptions were accurate, then the implied volatilities of all the options on the same underlying contract with the same maturity would have the same value. In the real world, this is not the case: Some options on the same underlying contract with the same expiration trade at repeatedly higher volatilities, and some trade at repeatedly lower volatilities.

Risk/Reward Profile of the Backspread

What about the risk profile for backspreads? Thinking of them in terms of "the other side" of the ratio spread will help us here. You will recall that the ratio spreader faced an unlimited risk component for calls, and a significant risk component for puts should there be a large move in the opposite direction—to the upside for the ratio call spread and to the downside for the ratio put spread. Imagine being the trader on the opposite side of these ratio spreads—he can make money in the event of a large move in a favorable direction, and can lose money should the stock remain neutral. In fact, the worst-case scenario for the backspreader (unlike the ratio spreader) occurs when the stock closes directly at the strike price of his long options.

The Call Backspread

Recall that we established the following points about backspreads. First, in terms of their risk and reward profiles they can be thought of as the 'flip-side' of the ratio spread. Second, the trader who puts on a backspread is looking for a substantial increase in volatility. Third, in terms of composition, the backspread can be thought of as a short vertical spread with extra units on the long side. Fourth, the backspread should be put on for a credit or at least for even money.

The Call Backspread: Composition

Most often a call backspread is composed of a short at the money call (lower strike), and a greater number of long out of the money calls (higher strike). Like the ratio spread, the trader can use just about any ratio of contracts at any strike, so long as the number of long contracts exceeds the number of short contracts.

If the trader establishes a call backspread, he is forecasting a large upside movement in the stock (in fact, the backspread has a potentially unlimited profit potential to the upside). He is both bullish on the direction of the underlying, and he is expecting a sudden and substantial rally. The crucial point is that he is looking for a significant increase in volatility.

361

The Call Backspread: Utilizing the Volatility Skew

In the "normal" equity volatility skew, the lower strike options trade at a higher implied volatility than the higher strike options. Given this type of skew, it makes sense that in order to be long volatility (i.e. profit from a rise in volatility) a trader would purchase higher strike options, and in order to be short volatility (i.e. profit from a decline in vol) he would sell lower strike options. In the case of the call backspread, the trader hopes to exploit this type of skew.

The Call Backspread: Risk and Reward Profile

A glance at a diagram of a hypothetical call backspread clearly illustrates its risk and reward potential. For illustrative purposes, let us use the following prices:

Example:
XYZ stock trading at $90
Long 2 XYZ Oct 100 Calls at $4.00
Short 1 XYZ Oct 90 Call at $10.50
= XYZ Oct 90/100 Call Backspread at $2.50 (credit)

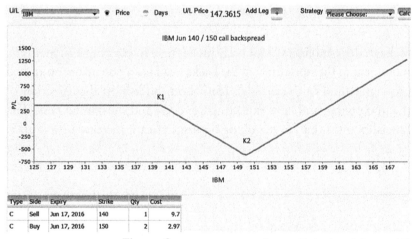

Figure 8   Options Technology Solutions, UK

362

We mentioned above that the call backspread can be thought of as a type of vertical spread, and now we can demonstrate why this is so. We can clearly see the short call component at K1, and the long call components at K2 (the components of a bear call spread with extra units on the long side).

Summary of Risk/Reward Profile

Composition: Short 1 ATM call @ K1
Long 2 OTM calls @ K2

Max Profit: Unlimited above the breakeven on the upside.

Max Loss: (K2-K1) - Credit.

In our example: (100-90) – (2.50) = $7.50.

The worst-case scenario would occur if the stock closed exactly at the strike of the long calls. Here the trader loses the maximum value of the vertical spread minus the credit received.

Breakeven points:

Downside: K1 + Credit x (# extra options purchased). In our example: (90) + (2.50) x (1) = $92.50

Upside: K2 + (K2-K1) + Credit.

In our example: (100) + (100-90) + (2.50) = $112.50

The Call Backspread: Real World Example

The only way to truly learn how to properly implement the call backspread is to practice.

Scenario: Stock XYZ is currently trading at $75. You have been carefully watching XYZ for several months and tracking its volatility. Earnings are coming out very soon, and you expect them to be excellent, far exceeding those of other stocks in its sector. What might you do? One viable strategy might be to initiate the call backspread.

Your Trade: You just the traded the 75/90 call backspread. You sold one 75 call at $8.50 and simultaneously bought two 90 calls for $3.00 each.

Q: Describe your maximum loss, maximum gain and breakeven points.

A: The backspread is traded for a $2.50 credit. The maximum loss is at the long strike, 90. The loss would be 90-75-2.50 = 12.5. The maximum gain is unlimited to the upside. The downside breakeven point is 75 + 2.50 = 77.50 and 90 + 15- 2.5 = 102.5 on the upside.

The Put Backspread

Let us begin with a review of some similarities between the call and put backspread. First, both spreads attempt to potentially harness a rise in implied volatility. In order to achieve this end, both spreads potentially take advantage of a sharp and substantial movement in the underlying. Moreover, both spreads are composed of one short option together with two or more long options. In fact, the put backspread can be thought of as a mirror image of the call backspread and the opposite side of the trade for a ratio put spread.

There is, of course, one crucial difference between the call backspread and the put backspread; namely, the desired direction of that sharp and substantial movement. Whereas the call backspread potentially makes money when the underlying moves substantially to the upside, the put backspread potentially makes money when the underlying moves substantially to the downside. We will elaborate on these points below.

The Put Backspread and the Volatility Skew

I noted above that when a trader establishes a put backspread he is predicting a large downside movement in the stock, and therefore a rise in implied volatility during the lifetime of the spread. Does this mean that the trader is looking for the exact same type of volatility "skew" here as he did with the call backspread?

No, it does not. In fact, he looks for a skew that is an inversion of the one he employed with the call backspread. Recall that when a trader initiated a call backspread, he utilized a skew wherein the implied volatility of the lower strikes traded at a higher implied volatility than those of the higher strikes.

The trader implementing a put backspread is long two or more out of the money contracts at a lower strike and short one at the money contract at a higher strike. He utilizes a "forward" type of skew where the higher strikes trade at a higher implied volatility than the lower strikes. The trader sells the more expensive option at the higher strike and buys the less expensive options at the lower strikes.

Both the call backspreader and the put backspreader hope for a substantial rise in implied volatility during the lifetime of the spread.

Risk and Reward Profile

A glance at the diagram below clearly illustrates the risk and reward profile of the put backspread. Note that the trader's maximum profit can be potentially significant when the underlying price falls below the breakeven. The potential profit is finite, of course, since the underlying cannot drop below zero. On the upside (above the higher strike), the trader's risk is limited to the debit paid for the spread. Often, however, the spread is established on for a credit. In this case, the trader simply keeps the credit should the stock spike higher.

Just as in the case of the call backspread, the trader's worst-case scenario (i.e. maximum loss) occurs if the underlying closes exactly at the strike price of the long puts at expiration. In this case the trader would lose the maximum value of the spread plus the debit or minus the credit received

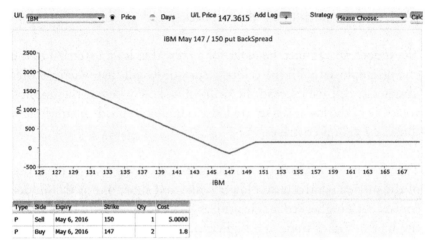

Figure 9   Options Technology Solutions, UK

Composition: Short 1 put at K2
Long 2 puts at K1

Maximum profit: Can be significant from the lower breakeven down to a stock price of zero. Above the higher strike, the trader simply loses what he paid to put on the position. If the trade is put on for a credit, he keeps the credit.

Maximum loss: (K2-K1) +/- Debit/Credit (in other words, the Maximum value of vertical spread +/- the debit/credit).

Breakeven:

- Upside: K2-credit, none if debit
- Downside: K1 – (K2-K1) -/+ Debit/Credit

In the example above:

Composition: Long 2 XYZ Jan 70 Puts at 1.00
Short 1 XYZ Jan 80 Put at 2.50
= XYZ 70/80 Put Backspread at .50 (credit)

Maximum profit: After the stock breaks the lower breakeven point, the profit is potentially unlimited to down to zero.

Maximum loss: (K2-K1)- Credit {10 - .50 = 9.50}. This occurs if stock closes at 70.

Breakeven:

Upside: K2-credit. {80 - .50= 79.50}
Downside: K1 − (K2-K1) + Credit {70 −10 + .50 = 60.5}

One final point to note about backspreads: The trader will want to exit the trade when there are at least 30 days left in its life. If the underlying stock or index does not move in the appropriate direction, the trader begins to lose money quickly. By exiting the trade with a month remaining, the trader's long options will potentially retain some value. He can close out hopefully, for not too large a loss.

CHAPTER 21

Butterfly Spread

"One of the most versatile positions is the butterfly spread...no doubt, one of Tony's favorite 'plays.' Early on in my career Tony harped on the value of this strategy and it ultimately lead to my own spreading of my 'wings'."

- Chris Hausman

I would like to discuss with you the concept of butterfly spreads. Those of you, who know anything about me, are probably not too surprised. After all, this has been a pet strategy of mine for over 30 years. It has helped me learn the art of relative pricing - that method of knowing what to pay for an option (or collect for it if I am selling) without having sophisticated modeling techniques at hand.

My passion stems from the flexibility in methods of construction and the versatility as a trading vehicle. Once you add this to your arsenal of "investment vehicles", you will have a powerful advantage over the average investor. You will be able to benefit from stagnant markets, for one. You will also have the ability to turn certain strategies around and adjust exposure to the market.

Butterflies fit into the class of "non-directional" strategies. In terms of market opinion they are similar to straddles and strangles in that one is not primarily guessing a particular *direction* in the market, but rather the *size of that movement.*

- *Long* butterflies should be used when one is predicting little or no directional movement or a "trading range" in the underlying, and the trader seeks to profit from an increase in the value of the position due to time decay or falling implied volatility.

- *Short* butterflies should be used when one is predicting a large magnitude move in either direction, and the trader pursues profit from a decrease in the value of the overall position due to an increase in implied volatility or a move away from your long strikes.

The classic long butterfly consists of two longs and two shorts. Typically a long at one strike, two shorts at a strike greater than the long and then another long at a strike greater yet than your short strike. These three strikes are usually equidistant from each other and they are usually all calls or all puts in the same expiry (of course on the same underlying).

Example: Long Butterfly

IBM January 95 calls   +1
IBM January 100 calls   -2
IBM January 105 calls   +1

This gives you, a long vertical spread and a short vertical spread.

Depending whether you sold the middle strike (the body) or sold the lowest and highest strikes (the wings), determines whether you are long the butterfly or short it. Whatever you do with the wings is what you have done with the spread. Long butterfly spreads are safer when you construct them with a lot of time left until expiry (they are usually very inexpensive) and get more expensive as one gets closer to expiry with the spread still near the money.

Below is a payout graph at expiration for an S&P 500 5-point butterfly:

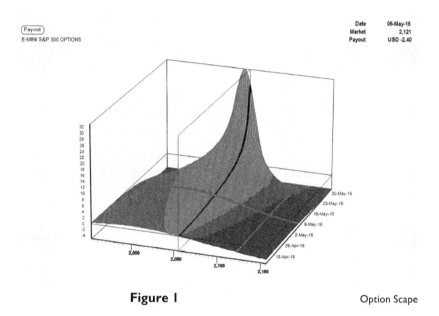

Figure I   Option Scape

Since you are selling the center and buying wings, you have a chance of making a maximum of the difference between the two strikes, less your cost of the butterfly.

The most you can lose is the amount you paid for the butterfly, giving most typical butterflies a 5:1 up to a 10:1 risk/reward ratio. Expanding out to skip a strike and do butterflies with a larger span, to say 10-point butterflies, increases the cost, but also increases the range of payout and the risk/reward stays high.

I want you to think of these now, because they are a safer way to sell premium than just selling premium naked. As the volatilities climb, butterfly spreads should get "cheaper" and this is a fine time to put some elongated butterflies or butterflies that skip strikes in the middle (called Condors) on in the May through August expirations.

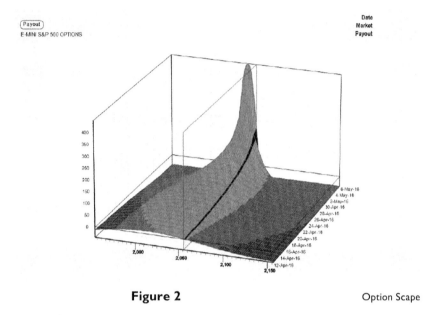

Figure 2   Option Scape

The Long Butterfly

Think of a long butterfly as containing an embedded short straddle wrapped within a synthetic long strangle. This type of structure allows the properly positioned long butterfly to capitalize from time decay and/or falling implied volatility just as a short straddle would. The big difference is that the long strangle "wrap" of the long butterfly severely limits the risk in the position, making it an appealing "directionless" strategy for risk-adjusted return traders.

Composition

The classic long Butterfly consists of four options positioned in a 1:2:1 ratio spanning three consecutive strikes. The positioning is as follows:

One long option at the lowest strike, two short options at the middle strike, and long one option at the highest strike.

The strike prices of the options are always:

- Equidistant from one another.
- Of the same type (either all calls or all puts).
- In the same expiration month.

For example:

Composition:

- Long 1 call at K1
- Short 2 calls at K2
- Long 1 call at K3

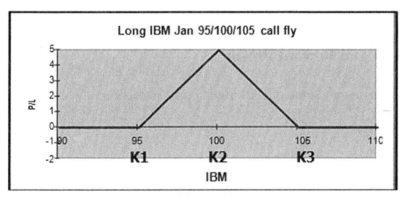

Figure 3

A glance at the graph above reveals how the strategy derived its name: the outline somewhat resembles a butterfly in flight (we options traders are creative folk!). The two short options in the middle of the graph (100 strike) correspond to the "body" of the creature, while the two flanking long options (95 & 105 strikes) constitute its "wings." So we say that in the long butterfly, we are "long the wings and short the body."

When to use long Butterflies: Directionless Markets

Butterflies are ideally suited for trading in directionless markets: The foundational reason to put on a butterfly is to target a well-defined price range within which the stock will trade at expiration.

This statement begs the question, "What is a directionless market?" A directionless, or "sideways" market is one that shows no definite or sustained direction in price movement. Although the price of the underlying may fluctuate, it tends to trade within a certain well-defined range, i.e. it doesn't penetrate either the defined support level or the defined resistance level.

It should be noted that directionless markets are the most common markets a trader encounters; more so than either a bull or a bear market! The adept trader will develop the ability to identify such a market by recognizing when a stock is consolidating. An adept studying of charts (technical analysis) is important here

Risk and Reward Profile

Butterflies are limited risk/limited profit strategies.

Profile:

Max Profit: (K3-K1)/2 –debit.

Max Loss: Debit paid.

Breakeven Points: K1 + debit; K3 – debit.

Why do we say that the long Butterfly is a "limited risk" strategy? That's simple: if you put on a long Butterfly, you can never lose more than the initial debit paid out. The Butterfly is constituted so that it is "exposed" to losses on either side of its "body", but this exposure is hedged by the location of the "wings".

Why do we say that the Butterfly is a "limited reward" strategy? Well, at expiration the long Butterfly will always have a value between zero and the width between each strike price (5 points here). In other words, the price of a 5-point Butterfly will never exceed $5.

Note that the spread will be worth its maximum value if it closes right at the strike of the shorts. If this happens, the long OTM (out of the money) option as well as the two shorts will expire worthless. The long ITM (in the money) option, however, will expire worth its full value of $5. So we know that the greater the chance of it closing at the middle strike on expiration, the more expensive it will be.

Any movement away from the middle strike will cause the spread to lose value. The worst-case scenario occurs if it closes either below the lowest strike long option, or above the highest strike long option. In our example above, the call Butterfly will lose value below $100, because as stock drops below $100 the ITM 95 call will begin to lose value. The call Butterfly loses value above $105 because the loss from the two short 100 calls will be twice as much as the gain from the 95 call.

Pricing Butterflies

Because Butterflies consist of four options, calculating the P/L can be a bit tricky at first. However, if we look at the Butterfly from a different perspective, we can simplify matters considerably. *I suggest thinking of the Butterfly as the combination of two adjacent vertical spreads (one long and one short) that share the short options at the middle strike.* In the example above, we can regard the 95/100/105 Butterfly as a combination of a 95/100 call spread and a 100/105 call spread.

- You should establish a long butterfly spread if you believe that the underlying is likely to remain within a narrow range until the contracts expire.

- The long butterfly position reaches its highest possible value if the market is quiet and the share price remains stable.

- A long butterfly spread compares well to a ratio spread – it's a risk-adjusted ratio spread.

The Short Butterfly

Now consider the opposite strategy. If you sell a butterfly spread, you have a lot in common with a trader setting up a backspread because you want the underlying share price to move as far from the inside exercise price as possible.

Think of the short butterfly as containing an embedded synthetic long straddle wrapped by a synthetic short strangle. This type of makeup allows the well-positioned short butterfly to benefit from sharp movement just as a long straddle would. The important difference is that the short strangle "wrap" of the short butterfly limits the profit possibility, making it a much less attractive "big move" strategy.

When the butterfly expires, you want the underlying price to be either below the lowest strike price (less than $50) or above the highest strike price (above $60). A short butterfly acts like a backspread in that it tends to increase in value if the market is moving.

To return to the original example, assume a trader sells a $50/$55/$60 call butterfly (sells a $50 call, buys two $55 calls, and sells a $60 call). If the share price of the underlying asset falls below $50 when the contracts expire, none of the contracts will be exercised but will expire as worthless.

The butterfly will be worth $0, but the trader will profit in that he gets to keep the net premium from selling the contracts. If the share price rises above $60, all of the contracts will be exercised, but the amount earned from the $50 and $60 contracts together will offset the cost to satisfy the $55 contracts when they are assigned. So the short butterfly works the same way as the long butterfly if the share price climbs—the net value of the butterfly is $0, but the trader keeps the net premium earned.

Now suppose the share price of the underlying asset is $55 at expiration, between the strike prices of the two outside contracts—$50 and $60— and matching the strike price of the inside contracts. The $50 call contract will be worth $5 a share, whereas the $55 and $60 calls will expire as worthless.

The $50 call contract would be exercised against you, so you would lose $5 a share, minus the amount of premium earned when completing the trades to set up the spread. If the underlying moves away from $55, the value of the butterfly will decline, but its value can never fall below zero.

As with a backspread, you would set up a short butterfly if you feel that the share price of the underlying stock will change significantly before the contracts expire so you can record the net premium earned in the trade as a profit.

Short Butterfly—Expiry Break-Even

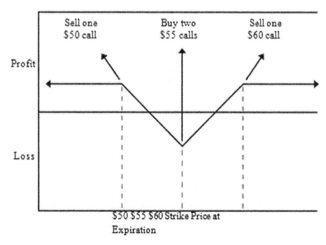

Figure 4

377

Butterfly Spreads Time to Expiry

Like the vertical spread the closer a butterfly is its expiration, the more sensitive its price will be to a change in the price of the underlying. Far from the expiration date, if the underlying price changes, it doesn't necessarily affect the value of the butterfly spread.

- This may suggest that trading butterfly spreads is not optimal if you want to exploit long-term changes in an underlying asset value.

- A butterfly spread can be long volatility or short volatility, and either a bull or bear strategy. But these depictions don't mean much unless you are fairly close to the expiration date.

Butterfly	Expiry 5-Days	Expiry 50-Days	Expiry 100-Days
$61/$62/$63	$0.30	$0.18	$0.12
$57/$62/$67	$3.30	$1.50	$1.10

Theoretical Value of XYZ Butterfly with Regard to Time

Figure 5

Call and Put Butterflies and Synthetic Equivalency

All butterflies are worth their maximum amount when the underlying matches the strike price of the inside (short) contracts. Therefore, you could achieve the same result using either a call or a put butterfly as long as the expiration date and strike prices are the same.

Both the thirty-day $130/$135/$140 call butterfly and the thirty-day $130/$135/$140 put butterfly will be worth no more than $5 if the share price of the underlying asset reaches $135 at expiration. The butterfly has a minimum value of $0 if the share price falls below $130 or climbs above $140. The table below demonstrates the likeness—or parity—of a call or put butterfly given three different price scenarios at expiration (see Figures 6 and 7).

| XYZ @ $130 Expiry Values | | | XYZ @ $135 Expiry Values | | | XYZ @ $140 Expiry Values | | |
Call	Strike	Put	Call	Strike	Put	Call	Strike	Put
$0.00	$130	$0.00	$5.00	$130	$0.00	$10.00	$130	$0.00
$0.00	$135	$5.00	$0.00	$135	$0.00	$5.00	$135	$0.00
$0.00	$140	$10.00	$0.00	$140	$5.00	$0.00	$140	$0.00

Butterfly—Intrinsic Value of Various Strike Prices at Expiration

Figure 6

$130/$135/$40 Call Butterfly Value	$130/$135/$140 Call Butterfly Value	$130/$135/$140 Call Butterfly Value
$0.00	$5.00	$0.00

$130/$135/$40 Put Butterfly Value	$130/$135/$140 Put Butterfly Value	$130/$135/$140 Put Butterfly Value
$0.00	$5.00	$0.00

Parity between Call and Put Butterfly with the Same Strikes

Figure 7

Greek Values and the Butterfly

The price of the butterfly spread becomes increasingly more sensitive to changes in the underlying with thirty days or less to go until expiration. The greeks of the butterfly respond the same way, in that they can also change dramatically and exponentially with less time to expiration.

But for all of the greek values, keep in mind that the delta, gamma, theta, or vega is not of much interest if the contracts in the spread are ninety days or more away from expiration. Far away from expiration, the greek values are minor factors; they become noteworthy only when the contracts are within thirty days of expiring.

Delta

For a long butterfly, such as the $150/$155/$160 spread in the example, the delta will be as follows:

- Positive when the underlying share price falls below the inside strike price ($155)
- Neutral when it matches the inside strike price
- Negative when it climbs above the inside strike price

The butterfly reaches its greatest value when the price of the underlying equals the inside strike price. Therefore, if the share price falls below the middle strike, that share price must rise for the butterfly to make money—hence the positive deltas. If the price of the underlying asset is above the middle strike price, it must fall for the butterfly to make money. That leads to a negative delta value.

XYZ Price	$150.00	$155.00	$160.00
50 Days	0.19	0	0.19
20 Days	0.38	0	0.38
10 Days	0.51	0	0.51

Net Delta of $150/$155/$160 Call Butterfly with Varied Days till Expiration and Varied

Figure 8

Gamma

The gamma value of a long butterfly flows from positive to negative, or vice versa. When the underlying price reaches the outer strike prices of the butterfly, the gamma is positive. This shows that the butterfly would produce positive deltas if the underlying share price rises, and negative deltas if that share price falls, albeit to the extent that the underlying is close to a long strike. This matches the behavior of the delta of the long butterfly as shown in Figure 9.

Meanwhile, the gamma of the long butterfly is negative when the underlying share price matches the inside strike price (see Figure 9). This shows that the butterfly will create negative deltas if the underlying share price rises and positive deltas if the share price falls. But you want your delta to be neutral; you want the share price to match the inside strike price and stay there.

XYZ Price	$150.00	$155.00	$160.00
50 Days	0	0.07	0
20 Days	0.06	0.2	0.06
10 Days	0.17	0.36	0.17

Net Gamma of XYZ $150/$155/$160 Call Butterfly with Various Closing Prices and Days till Expiration

Figure 9

Theta

Think of theta as the opposite of gamma. If a long butterfly is negative gamma, the theta will be positive; if a short butterfly is positive gamma, it will have a negative theta. For any butterfly, the theta will be positive if the stock price approaches the inside strike price. As the expiration date approaches, a positive theta is good for a long butterfly and bad for a short butterfly. If, however, the underlying price trades either high or low, and thus near one of the outer strike prices, the theta is positive for a short butterfly and negative for a long butterfly (see Figure 10).

That is, if the underlying price is close to one of the outer strike prices, it benefits the holder of the short butterfly, because the theta will be positive, but the theta will be negative for the long butterfly. With the short butterfly, remember, you sold the contracts with the outside strike prices (say, $60 and $50), bought two contracts with inside strike prices ($55 each), and earned a net premium in the transaction. With a short butterfly, you make a profit if the share prices climb toward the highest strike price ($60) or fall toward the lowest strike price ($50). The short butterfly profits if the market is active, and the theta tends to reflect that.

XYZ Price	$150.00	$155.00	$160.00
50 Days	0	0.013	0
20 Days	0.014	0.047	0.014
10 Days	0.036	0.086	0.036

Net Theta of XYZ Long $150/$155/$160 Call Butterfly with Various Closing Prices and Days till Expiration

Figure 10

Vega

When the underlying price matches the inside strike price, the vega of a long butterfly is negative (see Figure 11), and it is positive for a short butterfly. That means that any increase in the implied volatility of the underlying share price decreases the value of the long butterfly. This should make sense. The long butterfly's value depends on the likelihood that the share price will approach the inside strike price when the contracts expire.

The lower the implied volatility, the more likely it is that the share price will stay close to the inside strike price. Therefore, in this situation, the price of the butterfly falls if the implied volatility increases. On the other hand, if the share price is high or low and closer to one of the outside strike prices, an increase in the implied volatility increases the value of the butterfly.

If the implied volatility is high, it suggests that the share price is going to move somewhere, either up or down. So if the share price is likely to move at all, it is more likely that the share price will move back toward the middle— closer to matching the inside strike price—before the expiration date. In this event, vega will be positive for a long butterfly.

XYZ Price	$150.00	$155.00	$160.00
50 Days	0.02	0.054	0.02
20 Days	0.022	0.069	0.022
10 Days	0.028	0.061	0.028

Net Vega of Long XYZ $150/$155/$160 Call Butterfly with Various Closing Prices and Days till Expiration

Figure 11

Butterfly Trade Management:

One of the reasons butterflies are popular professional strategies is that they are limited risk positions. Recall that a long butterfly is synthetically a short straddle with a long strangle wrap while the short butterfly is synthetically a long straddle with a short strangle wrap.

The fact that butterflies have limited risk makes things a little easier from the risk management standpoint, but the position must still be managed. Points to consider:

- What is the most effective way to take profits?

- What if the trading range begins to diverge?

- What if the trading range reduces?

- How should I handle risk/take losses?

Trade Management:

Take Fractional Profits

If you are lucky enough to have a profitable butterfly, consider taking partial profits occasionally by scaling out of the trade. For example, if your position consists of 20 butterflies, don't be afraid to take profits on 3 or 4 here and 3 or 4 there. Slowly scale out of the position as it goes in your favor. This action takes profits and limits remaining risk.

Be Vigilant with your Market

Recall the reason you got into this trade in the first place. If the underlying in which you have your position starts to behave as though this trend may end – get out!

Use Common Sense

Don't be foolish and take a butterfly into a situation that might lead to a breakout or a drastic change in volatility – unless it is part of your game plan.

Use Synthetics to Exit

Butterflies have synthetic components - a long butterfly is synthetically a short straddle with a long strangle wrap, a short butterfly is synthetically a long straddle with a short strangle wrap. You can use this knowledge to exit the trade in a clever fashion.

CHAPTER 22

Condor Strategy

Two rules and adages I have lived by for what they are worth:

    1. In trading, often what you make is much less important than what you avoid losing.

    2. Whatever bad happens to you in the markets today, you must still retain enough capital to be in business tomorrow. Always have a firm grasp of your maximum possible loss. Risk management is everything!

- William Floersch

Former CBOE Market Maker

As we shall see, the condor is nothing more than a butterfly spread with an "elongated wingspan". As we might suspect, the structure and risk/reward profile of the condor is quite similar to that of the butterfly. To be clear-cut, the condor's expiry date risk/reward resemblance to something that flies does serve to offer clues on both how and when they should be traded. And, by the end of this chapter, this seemingly difficult subject will—with any fortune —become somewhat intuitive to you.

The condor is composed of four options of the same type (all calls or all puts) in a 1:1:1:1 ratio. Whereas the Butterfly had a 1:2:1 ratio, in the condor, the two "shorts" that compose the body are split. In other words, the two short options (in the case of a long condor) are spread out over two strikes, instead of sharing the same strike as with the butterfly, hence the 1:1:1:1 ratio. Note that the distances between the strikes are all equal.

Technically, a condor cannot skip strikes—they must be consecutive and equidistant. When a trader elongates the strategy even further by varying the distances between the strikes, he has put on what is called an "albatross."

The composition of the long condor can be looked at from two perspectives:

- A modified butterfly spread with an elongated or disjointed body that spans two or more strikes.

- A combination of a bull vertical spread and a bear vertical spread of the same class (all calls or all puts).

Long Call Condor Structure

CALLS	STRIKE	PUTS
+1	90	
-1	95	
-1	100	
+1	105	

Figure I

Long Put Condor Structure

CALLS	STRIKE	PUTS
	90	+1
	95	-1
	100	-1
	105	+1

Figure 2

Long Call Condor Structure

CALLS	STRIKE	PUTS
+1	90	
-1	95	
-1	100	
+1	105	

Figure 3

Long Put Condor Structure

CALLS	STRIKE	PUTS
	90	+1
	95	-1
	100	-1
	105	+1

Figure 4

Condors: When to consider using them

Long Condor:

The long condor is, like the butterfly, a spread designed for use in non-directional markets. Recall that by a non-directional market I mean one that shows no definite or sustained price movement.

Instead, it trades within a well-defined range. Therefore, the motivation behind a condor trade is the idea that the stock will trade in a given range.

Long condors are usually safer when you construct them with a great deal of time to expiration, because they are usually less expensive at that time. They get more expensive as they approach expiration.

Also, a good time to establish a condor is when volatilities are relatively high. As volatilities climb, condors tend to get cheaper. Because of this tendency, condors may be a safer way to sell premium rather than selling premium naked.

As you have all undoubtedly noticed, we are continually noting that the characteristics pointed out concerning the condor also hold true for the butterfly. So why would a trader put on a condor instead of a butterfly? Are they identical in all respects? No they are not. With a condor, the trader exchanges a smaller level of profitability for a larger window, or range, of profitability.

Short Condor:

The short condor is, like the butterfly, a spread designed for use in directional markets. Recall that by a directional market I mean one that shows a definite or sustained price movement. Short condors are usually safer when you construct them with less time to expiration, because they are usually more expensive at that time.

Another good time to establish a condor is when volatilities start to fall. As volatilities fall, condors tend to get more expensive. Because of this tendency, condors may be a safer way to purchase premium rather than buying premium naked.

Condor Risk/Reward

Like the butterfly, the condor is a "limited risk" strategy. When long, you can never lose more than the initial debit paid out. When short, you can never lose more than the difference between two strikes involved.

Upon expiration, the condor will always have a P&L number between zero and the width between each short strike, less the debit or credit. In other words, if the distance between the shorts is 10 points, then the condor will never exceed $10.

Whereas the butterfly will achieve its maximum profit potential at expiration at one point only (the strike price of the two short options). The condor will achieve its maximum profit potential over a wider range (at or between the two short options). This "extra range" usually translates into a greater value than the butterfly of approximately the same strike prices. In other words, condors tend to be more expensive than butterflies because they have a wider profit zone.

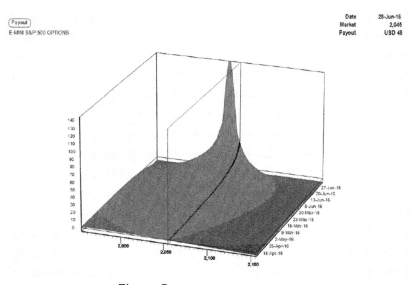

Figure 5   Option Scape

389

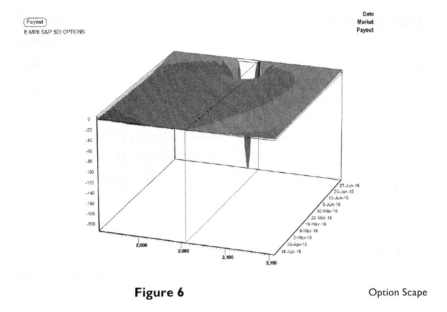

Figure 6   Option Scape

Condor and Sensitivity

Condor's pricing effect to change in the underlying price is related precisely to the time left to expiration. For example, the closer a condor is to expiry, the more sensitive its price is to an alteration in the price of the underlying security. What this suggests is that condors that are far off from expiration don't always change in value very much when the underlying price moves. This could imply that far-term condors aren't necessarily the best strategy for profiting from changes in the underlying price. Condors may be bullish or bearish, long or short volatility, or positive or negative one of the greeks. The bottom line is that the nearer a condor is to expiration, the more pronounced that effect can/will be.

Condors achieve their greatest value when the underlying price is between the middle or body strike(s) at expiration. Condors are at their lowest value when the underlying price is either at or above the higher wing strike or at or below the lower wing strike at expiry. Consequently, condors can be efficient tools when you think that the underlying price will settle inside a particular range and within a precise time frame.

Let's assume you are certain that the underlying price will swing somewhere between two defined prices, long condors with middle body strikes at the low and high prices of the underlying price range might work best. Let me encourage you to consider it this way: Long condors are likened to short straddles and strangles—without the unlimited risk. Glance at the graph in Figure 7 showing the value of a long condor at expiration. You should notice that the middle of the spread resembles that of a short straddle.

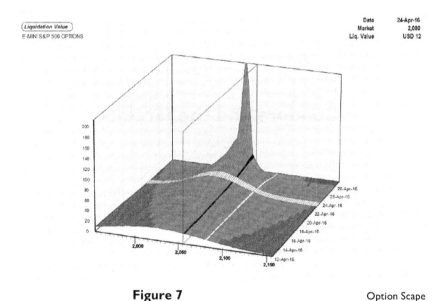

Figure 7 Option Scape

Alternatively, if you should sense the underlying price is ready to move away from a particular point or beyond a specific range of prices, short condors may well be a respectable option. They perform in the vein of long straddles and strangles, but without the unlimited profit/loss potential. They are also normally much less expensive. Look at Figure 8, which show the value of a short condor at expiration, and you'll notice the middle of the butterfly looks a lot like a long straddle.

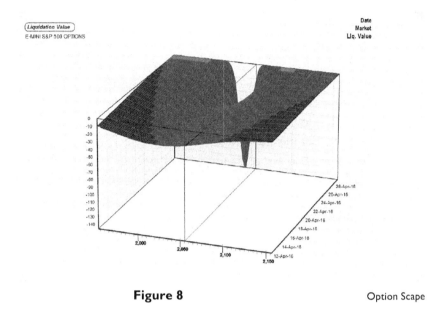

Liquidation Value
E-MINI S&P 500 OPTIONS

Date
Market
Liq. Value

Figure 8   Option Scape

Condors and the Greeks

Delta

The delta associated with a condor is not necessarily intuitive and is somewhat of an interesting concept once grasped. A long condor's delta is positive when the underlying price is below the middle strike of the butterfly, neutral when the underlying price is at the middle strike, and negative when it's above the middle strike. In addition, the delta will go away once the underlying price has gone beyond the upper and lower limits of the spread.

The insight behind this is that the long condor gets the most out of its value when the underlying price is at the middle strike. Therefore, if the underlying price is below the middle strike, it has to rise for the long condor to make money, thus the positive deltas. If the underlying price is above the middle strike, it has to fall for the condor to make money— therefore the negative deltas. The reverse would be true for a short condor.

The delta of a condor is the sum of the *position-adjusted* deltas of its component options. For example the delta of the long 500/510/520/530 call condor would be calculated as follows:

500 call delta = .60

510 call delta = .50

520 call delta = .40

530 call delta = .25

Long call condor delta = (.60*1) + (.50*-1) + (.40*-1) + (.25*1) or -.05

The delta of the long 500/510/520/530 put condor would be calculated as follows:

500 put delta = -.40

510 put delta = -.50

520 put delta = -.60

530 put delta = -.75

Long put condor delta = (-.40*1) + (-.50*-1) + (-.60*-1) + (-.75*1) or -.05

Similar to the long butterfly, the delta of the long condor is positive when the underlying is below the midpoint between the two inside strikes, negative when the underlying is above the midpoint between the two inside strikes, and approximately neutral at the midpoint between the two inside strikes. Since the point of maximum profitability of a long condor is anywhere between the middle strikes this makes sense.

Once again, note the sensitivity of the delta of the long condor to the amount of time left until expiration. As expiration approaches the delta of the long butterfly becomes much more sensitive to changes in the underlying price.

NEM

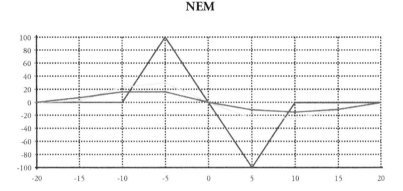

Long NEM April 42.50/47.50/52.50/57.50 Condor

Figure 9

Gamma

On an academic level, gamma is what's causing the condor's delta to potentially change direction from positive to neutral to negative as the gamma of a condor flows from positive to negative. For example, in the external strikes of the long condor, gamma is positive, indicating that the long condor would produce positive deltas if the underlying price rises, and negative deltas if the underlying price falls. This consistently matches with the means in which the delta of the long condor operates as described above.

The gamma of the long condor is negative when the underlying price is at the middle strike. This is a pointer to the reality that the long condor will, in fact, generate negative deltas if the underlying price rises and positive deltas if the underlying price falls. This is precisely what you don't want to happen!

The gamma of a long condor is the sum of the position-adjusted gammas of its component options. For example the gamma of the long 500/510/520/530 call condor is calculated as follows:

500 call gamma = .05

510 call gamma = .10

520 call gamma = .06

530 call gamma = .02

Long call condor gamma = (.05*1) + (.10*-1) + (.06*-1) + (.02*1) or -.09

A gamma of -.09 means that the delta of the overall position would change against the trader by approximately .09 for every 1 point the underlying moved. In other words, if the underlying moved up by 1 point, the position would become .09 deltas shorter, and if the underlying moved down by 1 point, the position would become .09 deltas longer.

Negative gamma positions always move against the trader. Gamma is greatly dependent on the money-ness and time to expiration. All things being equivalent, an at the money option near expiration will have a greater gamma than an at the money option with greater time left until expiration.

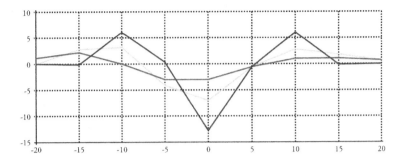

Long NEM April 42.50/47.50/52.50/57.50 Condor
Figure 10

Figure 10 clearly shows the dependency of the gamma of the long condor on location of the underlying and time until expiration. When expiration is near and the underlying price is near the strikes of the short options of the "body" of the long condor, the position will have a large negative gamma. This reverses quickly as the underlying moves away from the middle strike price into the area of the long "wings" of the outer strikes. Once again when there is greater time until expiration the gamma curve softens.

Theta

The theta of the condor is the mirror reflection of the gamma. Alongside negative gamma comes positive theta and vice versa. For the long condor, theta is positive when the underlying price is at the middle strike, indicative of the passage of time helping the long condor reach its highest value. At the outer strikes theta is negative, demonstrating that the condor is losing value as time moves on.

The opposite holds true for the short condor in that theta is negative when the underlying is at the middle strike, also indicative of the passage of time hurting the short condor. At the outer (short) strikes theta is positive, demonstrating that the condor is losing value as time passes.

Looking at the long condor, the theta is the sum of the position-adjusted thetas of its component options. For example, the theta of the long 500/510/520/530 call condor would be calculated as follows:

500 call theta = -.02

510 call theta = -.06

520 call theta = -.03

530 call theta = -.01

Long call condor theta = (-.02*1) + (-.06*-1) + (-.03*-1) + (-.01*1) or .06

This means that the value of an at the money long condor would increase by approximately .06 per calendar day. Because an at the money long condor has positive theta, the value of the at the money condor will rise as time passes and option values decay. Figure 11 below illustrates the theta of a long condor:

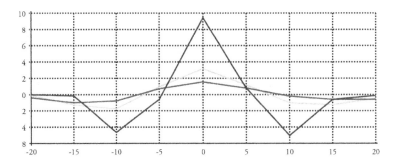

Long NEM April 42.50/47.50/52.50/57.50 Condor

Figure 11

Like the long butterfly, the long condor will have positive theta when the underlying price is near the short middle strikes, and will reverse to having negative theta when the underlying price is near the long "wing" strikes. The opposite holds true for the short condor. Recall the theta of an at the money option increases as time to expiration decreases so that, all things being equal, the theta of an at the money option with a lesser amount of time until expiration will be greater than the theta of an at the money option with a greater amount of time until expiration. This means that the theta of an at the money long condor will increase over time. This is apparent in Figure 11.

Vega

Like the other greeks, the vega of a condor varies depending on where the price of the underlying is relative to the strike price of the condor. When the underlying price is at the middle strike, the vega of the long condor is negative and positive for the short condor. That suggests that any increased implied volatility in the underlying price will decrease the value of the condor. This should make particular sense, since a condor's value depends on the probability that the underlying price will be at its middle strike at expiry. Higher implied volatility diminishes the possibility and perception that the underlying price will remain at the middle strike price; consequently the value of the condor would decrease with an increase in implied volatility. Vega is positive for the long condor at the outer strikes. Hence, an increase in the implied volatility of the underlying increases the value of the condor because of the greater likelihood that the condor will move toward the middle strike by expiry.

The vega of a condor is the sum of the *position adjusted* vegas of its component options. For example the vega of the long 500/510/520/530 call condor is calculated as follows:

500 call vega = .15

510 call vega = .20

520 call vega = .17

530 call vega = .14

Long call condor vega = (.15*1) + (.20*-1) + (.17*-1) + (.14*1) or -.08

This means that for every 1% change in implied volatility the price of the long condor would change by approximately .08. Because an at the money long condor is *short* vega the value of the condor will fall when implied volatility rises, and rise when implied volatility falls. Figure 12 below illustrates the vega of a long condor:

NEM

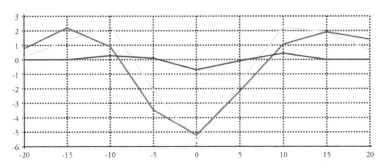

Long NEM April 42.50/47.50/52.50/57.50 Condor

Because of the +1/-1/+1/-1 structure of the long condor the position will be short vega
when the underlying price is near the short middle strikes, and will reverse to being long

Figure 12

Because of the +1/-1/-1/+1 structure of the long condor the position will be short vega when the underlying price is near the short middle strikes, and will reverse to being long vega when the underlying price is near the long "wing" strikes. Figure 13 shows the dependency of the vega of the long condor on location of the underlying price and time until expiration.

The Condor Spread – real life situation

Think of the condor spread as an ever so slightly stretched out butterfly. The condor is similar to a butterfly, except that the contracts in the middle (whether long or short) do not have matching strike prices as they would in a butterfly. With a long call condor, the trader might buy a $40 call, sell a $45 call, sell a $50 call, and purchase a $55 call—implementing equally spaced strikes with the same expiration date. This would be a debit transaction. A short condor would be the reverse where you would sell a $40 call, buy a $45 call, buy a $50 call, and sell a $55 call.

It is often helpful to think of a condor in terms of two consecutive vertical spreads: one bullish, the other bearish. This may help you to calculate both your risk and price faster. When long a call condor, think of yourself buying a bull vertical spread and subsidizing its cost by selling a bear vertical spread directly on top of it. On the other hand, when selling a condor, think of it in terms of selling a bear vertical spread and buying a bull vertical spread on top of it. Bear in mind that a true condor always uses equally spaced strike prices sharing the same expiration date.

Limited Risk/Reward Profile

Maximum profit for the long condor options strategy is achieved when the underlying price falls between the two middle strikes (your short strikes) at expiration. In other words, the most you can make on a long condor is the difference between the strikes in the spread minus the debit paid. If you paid $1.00 for the $40/$45/$50/$55 call condor, the most you can make is $4.00 ($5.0 – $1.00 = $4.00). Maximum loss for the long condor is the original premium paid. That would occur if, at expiration, the underlying price settled at or below $40.00 or at or above $55.00. The short condor would be the exact opposite. Refer to Figure 13 to see an exact expiration profit/loss break down of the long condor spread.

Underlying Expiration Price	$140/$145/$150/$155 Call Condor Expiration Value	$140/$145/$150/$155 Put Condor Expiration Value
$200.00	$0.00	$0.00
$160.00	$0.00	$0.00
$155.00	$0.00	$0.00
$154.00	$1.00	$1.00
$153.00	$2.00	$2.00
$152.00	$3.00	$3.00
$151.00	$4.00	$4.00
$150.00	$5.00	$5.00
$149.00	$5.00	$5.00
$148.00	$5.00	$5.00
$147.00	$5.00	$5.00
$146.00	$5.00	$5.00
$145.00	$5.00	$5.00
$144.00	$4.00	$4.00
$143.00	$3.00	$3.00
$142.00	$2.00	$2.00
$141.00	$1.00	$1.00
$140.00	$0.00	$0.00
$135.00	$0.00	$0.00
$0.00	$0.00	$0.00

Figure 13

At expiration, if the underlying price should settle below $40.00, all of your options will expire as worthless—the original premium paid will be lost. Similarly—but not exactly—if at expiration, the underlying price should settle above $55, all your options will be in-the-money; your long strikes ($40 and $55) would be exercised while your short strikes ($45 and $50) would be assigned. However, the net result would be the same—your long condor would expire as worthless as your two long calls would match in value with your short calls. Recall, you in effect purchased the $40/$45 call bull spread and subsidized it by selling the $50/$55 call bull spread—both your long and short spread settled at parity: $5.00.

The Condor and Term Structure

In Figure 14 notice the convergence—the similarity—of prices the further you go out along the time horizon. In contrast, observe how quickly the prices diverge—especially within the last month of the contracts life. Do understand that the speed of the condor's price convergence is also influenced by the implied volatility of the options.

Condor	1 day till Expiry	8 days till Expiry	15 days till expiry	57 days till expiry	134 days till expiry
130/131/132/133	0.02	0.11	0.14	0.08	0.05
131/132/133/134	0.05	0.28	0.17	0.09	0.05
132/133/134/135	0.52	0.32	0.19	0.11	0.06
133/134/135/136	0.95	0.38	0.26	0.11	0.08
134/135/136/137	0.44	0.26	0.21	0.11	0.07
135/136/137/138	0.02	0.11	0.16	0.12	0.06

Condor Pricing with Regard to Time till Expiration ; Underlying = $134.50

Figure 14

PART V

Practical Options Risk Management

CHAPTER 23

Practical Position Management Solutions

"The best education you will ever get in trading is taking your first major loss. It is the most painful "tuition" payment you will ever make, but the pain felt is something that either makes you quit or lights a fire in your belly to learn from that mistake and make a losing trading into a learning trade. One of my mentors once told me "If you're not pissed, you're not paying attention." It is that attitude, drive and competitiveness that separate the great ones from the quitters."

- Joe Z. Guediguian

Saliba Portfolio Management, LLC

One of the reasons options are an attractive trading vehicle is their flexibility. Positions can be built to express complex views of the market place rather than simply "up" or "down". Positions can be constantly modified to fit the trader's current market view, and positions can be applied and removed in stages allowing for sub-optimal timing on the part of the trader. It is this flexibility that is the key to continued success for many options traders. The first strategy – one that has many applications – is known as "rolling positions with vertical spreads."

Once a trade is established, regardless of how the decision-making process takes place, risk and money management begin. We all have been taught countless times that the key to trading success is to "let the winners run, and cut the losers." This is far easier said than done, and it is psychologically difficult sometimes to hold on to a winning position for fear of giving back profits. Rolling options positions allows the trader to hold a conviction longer while continuously taking profits.

What is rolling?

"Rolling" is, in its broadest definition, a way to adjust your position in response to changes in the market, such as stock price fluctuation or time until expiration. Specifically, rolling involves the liquidation of your existing position and the establishment of a similar position to replace it. "Liquidation" here is synonymous with "closing-out" a position. For example, in order to liquidate a long position you would sell it out, and to liquidate a short position you would buy it back.

Types of Rolling

Let's now explore the basic types of rolling - assuming that (for simplicity's sake) in each case we are dealing with a single option position.

An option can be rolled with respect to strike price, time until expiration or both strike price and time until expiration. The following terms describe the various types of rolling:

Rolling Up: Rolling Up is the liquidation of an existing position and the substitution of another with an option of the same class and date of expiration, but with a higher strike price.

Rolling up generally occurs when you have a short call position, and the underlying has made a move higher that places you at risk of additional losses or potential assignment. In the best of situations, the premium received (from the sold calls at both the original strike and the "rolled up" strike) will be sufficient to offset your buy-to-close costs. Sadly, this is rarely the case.

There are other scenarios where rolling up may make sense. For example, if you're short puts and the underlying has risen significantly above your short strike, you might roll up to collect a higher premium.

Rolling Down: Rolling Down is the liquidation of an existing position and the substitution of another with an option of the same class and date of expiration, but with a lower strike price.

A trader may decide to roll down if they've purchased put options that returned significant gains. By selling to close the in the money options and exchanging them for cheaper puts at a lower strike, you can capitalize on a continued move lower. Alternately, you might roll down a short call position if the underlying is trading lower, or roll down a short put if the underlying is dropping and you hope to avoid assignment.

Rolling Out: Rolling Out is the liquidation of an existing position and the substitution of another with an option of the same class and strike price, but with an expiration date that is further out in time.

There are two situations where it makes sense to roll out.

First, you've found or have a winning options trade, and you feel confident the directional move will continue to play out favorably. By taking profits on the shorter-term trade and simultaneously initiating the longer-term trade, you are now positioned to keep gaining from a prolonged move in your favor.

Second, you still feel confident in your original conviction -- but you've decided that more time is necessary. In this instance, you're essentially buying more time for the underlying to live up to your expectations.

With any trade, rolling out should be approached with attention. Under the first scenario, be certain that you're not simply getting greedy after a healthy winner. Also, reexamine your motivation for the trade. Does the underlying simply need more time to move favorably, or is it time to admit that your initial analysis is wrong?

Rolling Up and Out: Rolling "up and out" is the liquidation of an existing position and the substitution of another with an option of the same class that has both a later expiration date and a higher strike price.

Rolling up generally occurs when you have a short call position, and the underlying has made a move higher that places you at risk of additional losses or potential assignment. Instead of replacing it with just a higher strike price, the trader sells an option with a different expiration date.

Rolling Down and Out: Rolling Down and Out is the liquidation of an existing position and the substitution of another with an option of the same class that has both a later expiration date and a lower strike price.

A trader may decide to roll down if they've purchased put options that returned significant gains. By selling to close the in-the-money options and exchanging them for cheaper puts at a lower strike and a further out expiry date, you can potentially capitalize on a continued move lower.

Reasons to Roll

Rolling, as stated above, is a position adjustment strategy. A strategy always retains a subjective component, and therefore there are no hard-and-fast rules concerning when a trader should initiate a roll. However, there are certain market scenarios that lend themselves more favorably to rolling.

Let's take a look at two hypothetical market scenarios. In the first, our trader is long a call in a rising market. In the second, he is short a call in a stable market.

Rolling a Long Call

In this case, let us imagine that the stock has significantly appreciated in value shortly after the purchase of the call. What can the trader do? Well, a number of things, actually.

Obviously, he could sell the call and pocket the profit (a very conservative move which eliminates any possibility of participating in further gain). Alternately, he could hold the call until expiration, with the hope that it will continue to gain value (a risky move, because he runs the risk of the stock reversing direction, and therefore giving up his profit). Another strategy might be to sell a higher strike call against his long call and create a bull spread (a conservative move that puts a cap on the amount of profit potential). So what else might he do?

By "rolling up" the call, he has the chance of participating in future upward movement in the stock with less risk than holding the original call outright. Think about it: he can use the profit from the liquidation of the long call to finance the purchase of the higher strike call. The higher strike call should be considerably cheaper than the original call. In effect, he will be putting on a new position while pocketing some cash from the sale of the original position. If the market continues to move higher, he can participate in its movement via the new position.

Rolling a Short Call

The trader might consider rolling the short call for a number of reasons. He may want to roll if it has moved in the money; if he wants to avoid assignment; if the option is rapidly losing theta (time value); or if he simply wants to take a chance on increasing his profits.

Example: rolling a short call – Short XYZ January 30 Calls

- Imagine that 3 months ago, the trader sold an XYZ January 30 call, collecting $3.50. If XYZ has not moved much, then the call would have depreciated in value to only $0.75. At this point, the trader might consider buying back the call for $0.75, thus netting $2.75.

- However, if the trader felt that XYZ was going to continue to trade in a narrow range in the future? One possibility would be to "roll out" (see above) and sell the XYZ June 30 call. By selling this call, he would collect an additional premium of $1.25.

- In summary, the benefit of "rolling out" here is that the trader has pocketed $400.00, netting $275 on the January call and $125 on the sale of the June call.

Example: Rolling a long put - Purchase IBM October 110 puts for $7.50.

- Suppose you bought the IBM October 110 puts for $7.50, and you are quickly profitable. Now what do you do? You are of the conviction that IBM (and the market in general) is going lower. Do you take a quick profit and call it a day, or do you take a portion off the table and go for more?

- There is nothing wrong with taking a quick profit, but if you have a strong conviction that IBM is going much lower, you would hate to cash in here and then be sitting on the sidelines as the stock broke down. It would be better to take some money off the table, yet maintain short exposure.

- A trader with this type of bearish view should roll his position by using vertical put spreads. As IBM trades lower and the long put position became increasingly profitable, the trader would sell put spreads, "rolling" his long put position to a lower strike, and collecting money every time he sold a spread.

Rolling Trade Evolution Example: Long put trade with falling underlying price

- **IBM = 111.00 Trader** buys 10 October 110 puts @ $7.50. Net cost = $7500.

- **IBM = 105.00** Trader still bearish, but wants to take some profit. He sells the October 100/ 110 put spread @$ 5.00, collect $5000.

- <u>Result:</u> **Trader is now long the October 100 puts.**

- **IBM= 95.00** Trader still bearish, but wants to take some more profit. Trader sells the October 90/100 put spread at $5.00 and collect $5,000.

- <u>Result:</u> **Trader is now long the October 90 puts, and has $2500 profits "in his pocket."**

- **IBM = 85.00** Trader is satisfied that IBM has reached his downside target, and sells his October 90 puts @$9.00, collecting $9000 for a total profit of $11,500.

These are hypothetical prices and examples, but this is precisely the way practitioners roll positions. If the trader had simply held the original position, he would have made more money, but would he have held the position? The point of rolling is that it gives you greater staying power by putting you in a more powerful psychological position. Taking money off the table raises the trader's comfort level and allows him to stay with a trade much longer.

- Roll a long call position = sell vertical call spread.
- Roll a short call position = buy vertical call spread.
- Roll a long put position = sell vertical put spread.
- Roll a short put position = buy vertical put spread.
- Roll a long call vertical spread = sell call butterfly spread.
- Roll a short call vertical spread = buy call butterfly spread.
- Roll a long put vertical spread = sell put butterfly spread.
- Roll a short put vertical spread = buy put butterfly spread.

Adjusting/Rolling with Spreads

With this adjustment strategy the trader adjusts his position by buying or selling vertical spreads against the position. The trader will sell call spreads or buy put spreads as the market moves up, and buy call spreads or sell put spreads when the market moves down. This method allows the trader to take profits on short-term swings while maintaining the number of net units (calls and/or puts) of the position.

This type of adjustment strategy is somewhat complicated, and is illustrated with the following example :

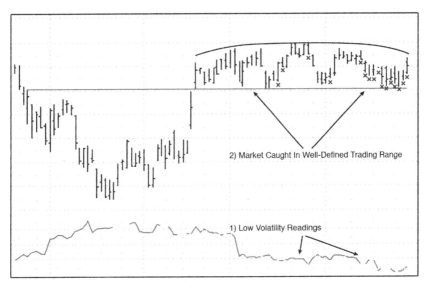

2) Market Caught In Well-Defined Trading Range

1) Low Volatility Readings

Figure 1

- Trader analyzes implied volatility structure of IBM (Figure 1) and finds that 60-day implied volatility is trading for less than 50% of 100-day historical volatility.

- Trader perceives that IBM is caught in a well-defined trading range.

- Because the support and resistance levels are well defined at $110.00 (support), and $120.00 (resistance), trader purchases 25 of the 110 put / 120 call strangle for $5.00, with the intention of going with the breakout.

- **Trader's position:** long 25 of the 110 puts at $2.50 and 25 of the 120 calls at $2.50. The trader is long the 110 put / 120 call strangle for $5.00.

Subsequently, the breakout occurs to the downside

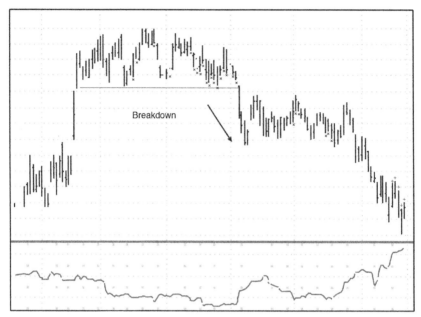

Breakdown

Figure 2

Trader must now decide which adjustment method to use. In order to do this the trader has to decide what type of movement to expect:

- A large directional move with no retracements?

- A choppy non-directional move with a lot of retracements (whipsaw)?

- A fast breakdown followed by consolidation before another breakdown?

- A mix of many different scenarios.

Trader's decision: Trader decides that there will be a large directional move, and decides to hedge his delta with vertical spreads in order to maintain his net call and put position.

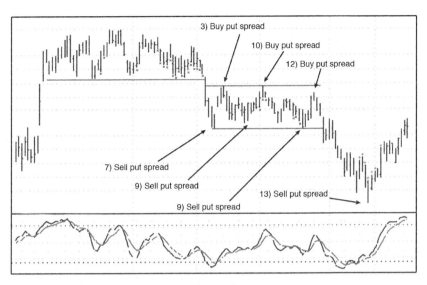

Figure 3

- **On the stock breakdown**, the strangle generates a short delta position. The trader balances his delta and sells the 100/110 put spread for $5.00, taking all of his original investment off of the table, and leaving him long the 100/120 strangle.

- **On the stock bounce**, the strangle generates long deltas, and leaning on the $120.00 resistance, the trader repurchases the 100/110 put spread for $3.00, re-entering the 110/120 strangle, now at a net cost of $3.00.

- **On the stock selloff**, the strangle generates short deltas. The trader balances his delta again and sells the 100/110 put spread for $4.00, this rolls him back into the 100/120 strangle at a $1.00 credit.

- **On the bounce**, the strangle generates long deltas, and once again the trader repurchases the 100/110 put spread for $2.50, re-entering the 110/120 strangle, now at a net cost of $1.50.

- **On the selloff**, the strangle generates short deltas. The trader balances his delta again and sells the 100/110 put spread for

$4.00, this rolls him back into the 100/120 strangle at a $2.50 credit.

- **On the bounce**, the strangle generates long deltas, and once again the trader repurchases the 100/110 put spread for $2.50, re-entering the 110/120 strangle, now at a net cost of $0.00.

- **This time the stock really tanks**, breaking through support at $101.50 and rocketing lower. The strangle generates short deltas. The trader balances his delta by selling the 90/110 put spread for $15.00, this rolls him into the 90/120 strangle at a $15.00 credit.

<u>Note:</u> **that the net call and put exposure remains constant throughout the entire process (25 calls and 25 puts), only the strikes change.**

To roll or not to roll?

The successful trader must constantly reevaluate the risk and reward profiles of his positions. As stocks approach important support or resistance levels, he must be ready to act quickly and decisively to take partial profits or cut losses. While the old saying "Let the winners run and cut the losers" is a sound piece of advice, it is (as every trader knows) psychologically and emotionally difficult to implement. When our positions are profitable, we are afraid of staying in too long and giving back money. And when our position moves against us, we are continually hoping for a reversal of fortune.

By rolling a vertical spread against our position, we may be able to alleviate the pain behind these choices. This is because rolling a position with vertical spreads allows the trader to stay in his position for a longer time and also to take profits off the table.

CHAPTER 24

Strategic Gamma Management

"Don't ever say I am long, short, or flat gamma! Rather, communicate gamma with regards to time, range, and implied volatility – gamma is not EVER static!"

- Larry Shover

Former CBOE & CME Market Maker

The Gamma Scalper's Toolbox

Statistical Tools

Volatility (standard deviations)

Converting annualized volatility to a daily time horizon can aid in location of hedges as well as indicating whether or not a strategy is working. In order to convert annualized volatility to another time horizon, simply divide the annualized volatility by the square root of the number of desired time units in a year.

For example:

Annualized volatility is 35%, meaning that one can expect the underlying to trade in a range of +/-35% over the course of a year, 68% of the time. In what range should it trade in one day?

Daily volatility = Annualized volatility / √252
(252 business days in a year), = 35% /15.87 = 2.21%.

We can expect the underlying to trade in arrange of +/- 2.21% 68% of the time.

Therefore, if the underlying was trading at $100, you could expect a range of $102.21 to $97.89 68% of the time. This is a one daily standard deviation move or a "sigma". Traders will usually execute gamma hedges at the one and two standard deviation levels, and let the market run beyond there.

The Rent

Traders (when long gamma) will refer to their theta as "the rent" because they have to pay it each and every day regardless of what happens in the marketplace. They have to pay "the rent" with the proceeds from their delta rebalancing. Short gamma traders collect "the rent", but have to deduct the costs of their delta rebalancing. Therefore it is useful to both long and short gamma players to be able to calculate how much the underlying must move in order to "pay the rent".

The gamma decay formula (for equities) allows traders to calculate the approximate breakeven points for long and short gamma positions in terms of underlying movement:

$$\text{Gamma Decay Value} = \left| \sqrt{\left(\frac{2\Theta}{\Gamma} \right)} \right|$$

Figure 1

For example, with the stock at 100- and 30-days to expiration, implied volatility of 35% and interest costs of zero, our gamma decay number is:

$$\left| \sqrt{\left(\frac{2*1338}{794} \right)} \right| = \sim 1.84 \text{ points}$$

Figure 2

This means the stock will have to travel 1.84 points in order to "pay the rent". This number will change along with time to expiration, implied volatility, and underlying price. There are a plethora of statistical measures that can be utilized to assist the gamma scalper.

What is Gamma Scalping?

"**Gamma scalping**" is a rather misleading industry term (originating on the exchange floor) referring to the periodic rebalancing (neutralizing) of the delta exposure of an option position, or "book" of multiple positions.

In layman's terms, gamma scalping is a tactic where one uses options to create, or "simulate" actual stock positions in order to benefit from favorable discrepancies between the "synthetic" position" and the "real stock position". Before we investigate the how's and why's of this strategy, I think we should nail down some terminology.

Recall that "gamma" is one of the "greeks". It is a measure of the rate of change of an option's delta for a $1 change in the price of the underlying instrument.

"Synthetics": Two or more trading vehicles packaged together to emulate another trading vehicle. Because the package involves different components, the price may differ, but the risk exposure is nearly always the same.

"Scalping" refers to a type of trading also typical for pit locals. Pit locals will take very short-term positions and attempt to capture small profits repeatedly. Just as is the case with the ticket scalper outside the stadium, the "Scalper" plies his trade by "buying low and selling high" as frequently as he can. If we extend this logic, the term "gamma scalping" would then imply that it is a process of constant profit taking.

The delta rebalancing of an option position is a risk management function. Any changes in any parameters used to evaluate option risk (underlying price, interest rate, implied volatility, time until expiration, etc.) will result in changes in the other parameters. This requires continual adjustment and fine-tuning. This is referred to as "dynamic hedging", and is usually more reactive than proactive.

Why Gamma Scalp?

Ok, so now we know something about the "what" of gamma scalping. More important, however, is the why. So why would a trader "Gamma scalp"? In theory, at least, gamma scalping affords the trader numerous potential benefits.

- First, the "simulated" stock position with options can be put on for a potentially cheaper cost than that of the "real" stock position.

- Second, the trader gains greater "staying power" i.e. the ability to withstand adverse price movements for a greater length of time.

- Third, the trader obtains greater leverage with options than with an actual stock position over his position.

Strategic Gamma Positioning

In this chapter, I make the case that familiarity with the partial derivatives (the greeks) is essential for gamma scalping. This is because as market price structure changes (i.e., breakout, breakdown, failure, etc.) market conditions in terms of volatility and option pricing will change as well.

Strategic gamma positioning is the placement of a long gamma position into a specific situation to take advantage of the long gamma properties of the position in order to maximize gains. These types of gamma trades are scenario trades based on expected directional movement in the underlying, not necessarily volatility movement. Naturally it is helpful if implied volatility is low when one implements this kind of position...as low volatility can mean inexpensive options. Depending on the magnitude, direction, and duration of the expected move, it is not always necessary.

Strategic gamma positioning is particularly suited to technical analysis because the pinpointing of key levels such as breakout, breakdown, support, resistance, or Fibonacci levels, etc. can give the trader an idea as to where and when volatility is likely to occur. Not to say that the fundamentalist can't use strategic gamma positioning—he can. Placing gamma positions around important fundamental developments such as earnings reports, new product launches, and government reports etc. may be lucrative. Indeed, one will often find that the market will approach important technical levels as important fundamental news dates approach.

We will explore different types of strategic gamma positioning and importantly, the adjustments made to these positions with a series of case studies. In these case studies, we will develop a strategy suited to a particular market view. The market views for these case studies will be generated with the aid of basic technical analysis tools but can apply to fundamental analysis views as well.

One of the keys to "running" a successful strategic gamma position is the adjustments you make to the position as the market moves. The adjustments made to a position must be compatible with one's goals!

Strategies

Although this list is by no means comprehensive (there are endless scenarios and variations), these are some of the strategies commonly used for long gamma positioning:

Non-Directional (at least in the beginning) **Moves**

The BIG move: In this scenario the trader expects a very large move in the underlying in either direction, and purchases straddles. He will profit by a large increase in the intrinsic value of his option position. When hedging the deltas in this situation it is important to MAINTAIN EXPOSURE.

Support and Resistance trades: In this type of scenario the trader looks to implement a long gamma strategy at a key support or resistance level. The thought process in this situation is that the support or resistance price will act as a repellent; the market will usually either penetrate the key level and accelerate or fail and retreat. Rarely does the underlying stick to these levels. The trader will seek to capture the volatility around these levels with a long gamma position.

Consolidation trades: In this type of scenario the market has entered into a consolidation pattern that indicates a breakout may be imminent. An example of this could be symmetrical triangle, ascending or descending wedges or triangles, or the handle portion of a "cup and handle" formation and many others. The trader looking forward to a possible breakout in the near future can use the "corkscrewing" movement of the consolidation phase to build his position at superior prices for the impending breakout.

Mean reversion (low volatility) trades: These can be utilized to identify markets that have breakout potential. Long gamma positions such as strangles are placed at key trigger points where market acceleration is likely to occur.

Directional Moves

If/Then explosion trades: In this type of scenario the trader is looking to place long gamma positions that will explode if the market makes a highly unexpected (long shot) move, but is benign if the move does not occur. Traders commonly refer these to as "lottery tickets".

Adjustments

As mentioned previously, it is paramount that any adjustment strategy utilized be compatible with the traders' market view and goals. Here are some adjustment strategies and the situations in which they might be used:

Buying or selling the underlying shares against the position. The trader will sell shares as the market moves up, and repurchase them as the market (hopefully) moves back down. This maintains the size and "optionality" of the current position. Remember, whenever you sell stock against calls, they become puts and whenever you buy stock against puts they become calls. Therefore, this hedging strategy may not be appropriate for a BIG MOVE type of scenario.

Buying options against the position. The trader will buy puts as the market moves up, and buy calls as the market swings back down. This method slowly increases the size of the options position at a superior price.

Selling options against the position. The trader will sell calls as the market moves up, and sell puts as the market swings back down. This method allows the trader to take profits and slowly decrease the size of the option position, at a superior price.

Buying or selling vertical spreads against the position. The trader will sell call spreads or buy put spreads as the market moves up, and buy the same call spreads or sell the put spreads when the market moves down (vice versa if the market starts lower first). This method allows the trader to take profits on short-term swings while maintaining the call or put exposure of the position. This type of hedging strategy is appropriate for the BIG MOVE type of scenario.

We will now turn to a specific example to help clarify these issues. We will examine the thought process, market view, the trade and subsequent adjustments used.

The Big Move

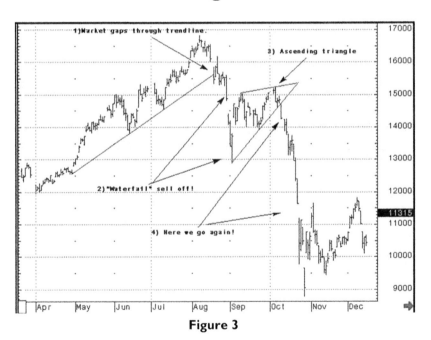

Figure 3

The thought process: A gap down off of a possible head and shoulders top penetrates an important trend line. The trader believes a big move may be imminent.

The trade: The trader must buy volatility, and therefore has to buy options. The trader is still unsure as to whether or not the market will collapse immediately (after having been stopped out repeatedly in the previous month), so he decides to play it safe and buy straddles.

The position: As his opening trade, the trader purchases 25 of the XYZ 15500 straddles. The strike price of the straddles is located near the trend line for maximum gamma power.

The adjustment method: In the above case, the trader felt that a very large move was coming, and wanted to maintain his option leverage. Therefore, he chose to hedge his delta with vertical spreads. Buying call spreads or selling put spreads on sell offs, and then selling call spreads and buying put spreads on rallies. This allowed him to maintain a constant option exposure to the market.

The result: As you can see, not only did a big move occur, an unbelievable move occurred. In fact, the biggest part of the move came on the second leg down. Adjusting with spreads allowed the trader to capture this move. Had he adjusted with underlying, he would have run out of gamma before the second move.

Support/Resistance Trades

In this scenario the trader implements a long gamma strategy at a key support or resistance level. The thought process in this situation is that the support or resistance price will act as a repellent since the market will usually either penetrate the key level and accelerate, or fail and retreat. Note that rarely does the underlying stick to these levels! The trader will seek to capture the volatility around these levels with a long gamma position.

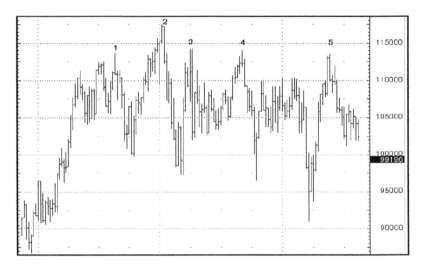

Figure 4

The thought process: The trader has recognized that every time the upper level resistance is challenged, a sharp reaction occurs. Given that this area is one of strong resistance, the trader thinks it unlikely the market would ever stay very long in this area, it will either pull sharply back, or explode through.

The trade: The trader must buy volatility, and therefore has to buy options. The trader wishes to have maximum gamma power so he purchases straddles with the strike price as near the resistance level as possible.

The position: The trader purchases 25 of the XYZ 11500 straddles every time the market approaches this level.

The adjustment method: In this case, the trader is not looking for a mega-move (unless the market breaks out); he is merely looking for a sharp reaction away from resistance. He will sell options against his position to take profits. On a move down, he will scale-sell his puts, possibly holding the calls for the trip back up. (Another strategy is to launch the calls as soon as one is relatively sure of a sell off, and then scale sell the puts).

428

The result: The trader was able to milk this strategy several times. One will often notice points in various markets that seem to be repellent points, meaning that the market doesn't stay there very long. These points are excellent places to plant straddles for a reaction away from the point.

Consolidation Trades

In this scenario the market has entered into a consolidation pattern that indicates a breakout may be imminent. An example of this might be a symmetrical triangle, ascending or descending wedges or triangles, or the handle portion of a "cup and handle" formation and many others. The trader looking forward to a possible breakout in the near future can use the "corkscrewing" movement of the consolidation phase to build his position at superior prices for the impending breakout.

Figure 5

The thought process: The market, while trending lower, has stalled out and is consolidating into a symmetrical triangle. The trader believes that the market will move sharply out of the consolidation pattern.

The trade: The trader is going to purchase volatility, but will build his position using the market movement in the consolidation pattern. He will place a "seed" position of long straddles, and as the market corkscrews within the triangle, he will use the gamma to add to his position at superior prices. When the market moves up he will adjust his delta by buying puts, when the market moves down he will adjust his delta by buying calls.

The position: The trader purchases 20 of the XYZ 10750 straddles and begins adding on market movement. By the time the market breaks out of the triangle he is long 40 straddles.

The adjustment method: This is up to the trader. It depends on market view and expectations. The important part of this strategy came before the breakout.

The result: The market broke out of the triangle and resumed its downtrend.

The Mean Reversion Trade

A brief introduction to this strategy is in order. As we know volatility is "mean-reverting" and regardless of short-term fluctuations, always reverts to the long-term mean. In a nutshell, the system monitors short-term historical volatility (6- to 10-day historical volatility) and compares it to 100-day historical volatility (used as a proxy for the long-term mean).

This comparison can help to identify markets that have breakout potential. Long gamma positions, such as strangles, are placed at key trigger points where market acceleration is likely to occur. When the short-dated volatility drops to less than 50% of the long dated volatility, it is reasonable to expect movement in the underlying to accelerate in order for volatility to revert to the mean.

Naturally, accelerating movement is what the long gamma trader desires, and using these mean reversion strategies can help one locate excellent long gamma situations. Below is an example of a "Mean Reversion Trade":

Figure 6

The thought process: The stock is consolidating with an extremely low short-dated historical volatility reading relative to the long-term mean. The trader believes a breakdown is imminent and that this breakdown will take short-term volatility back to the long-term mean.

The trade: The trader is bearish and therefore purchases puts. Naturally, if he were bullish, he would purchase calls, and if unsure purchase straddles or strangles.

The position: The trader purchases 100 of the OCT 110 puts on the breakdown.

The adjustment method: This is up to the trader, depending on the traders' expectation of velocity, duration and magnitude. He may choose an adjustment method that either maintains, adds to, or subtracts from the position (see adjustment methods above).

The result: The market broke out of the consolidation and spiked downward as short-term volatility reverted to the long-term mean.

The If/Then Explosion Trade

Example: The If/Then Explosion Trade

Figure 7

The thought process: The stock is consolidating with an extremely low short-dated historical volatility reading. The trader believes the July spike down might indicate future trouble and that there is a possibility that there could be a massive sell off, especially since October is approaching.

The trade: The trader is bearish and therefore places a put backspread. A backspread, also known as a volatility spread, is a strategy whereby one sells a near or at the money option, and purchases two or more away from the money options with the proceeds. If the underlying stock moves through the long strike, the gamma kicks in and the position explodes, if not, it is a very benign position.

The position: The trader sells 10 of the 130 puts and uses the proceeds to purchase 20 of the 120 puts

The adjustment method: Since the trader is playing a "lottery ticket" long shot, if he gets lucky and the unexpected happens, he can expect a wild ride. It would be best to hedge with spreads and "roll" the position to maintain maximum exposure to the market for the maximum length of time.

Result: The market broke down and the trader executed several successive "rolls" to stay with the market.

Remember when you are looking back at these case studies, that these examples are just that, examples. Every situation is different. These are meant to be examples of how things could be done.

Every trader needs to examine his style, his risk tolerance, and his psychological make up in order to determine what, if any, strategic gamma scalping strategies are appropriate for him.

INDEX

standard deviations, 92, 127, 138–39, 142, 176, 419; annualized, 129, 131–32, 339
static volatility input, 75
stock, 21–22, 24–25, 35, 141–44, 200–202, 205–8, 213–14, 216–22, 225–28, 232–35, 241–43, 259–60, 262–64, 266–68, 351–56; common, 225; company's, 232; fictitious, 224; lower priced, 243; low-priced high-tech, 243; naked, 353; owning, 21; performing, 206; synthetic, 16, 21–22, 32, 34; tech, 243
stock adjustments, 272
stock bounce, 417
stock convictions, best, 207
stockholder, 219
stock investment, original, 222
stock move, downward, 220–21
stock position, 224, 353, 422; long, 212, 228, 230; real, 421; simulated, 422; synthetic, 30
stock positions, actual, 421–22
stock price, 21–23, 32, 34, 176, 231–32, 241–42, 324, 366; combined, 34; last, 142; static, 352
stock price approaches, 381
stock price fluctuation, 408
stock selloff, 417
stock spike, 365
stock trades, 263, 272
stop-loss orders, 245

straddle, 5, 173–74, 247, 249–52, 254–55, 258–64, 266, 268–73, 290, 359, 370, 427–28, 430; purchases, 424, 428; synthetic, 35
straddle delta, 250
straddle gamma, 252
straddle position, 35, 272
straddle vega, 254
strangle, 5, 173, 247–51, 254, 271, 290, 359, 370, 391, 415, 417–18, 425, 430–31
strategic gamma management, 419
strategy, 147, 195–96, 205–7, 227, 229–32, 243–44, 247, 249, 299–300, 329, 331–32, 345–46, 352–53, 423–24, 428–30; adjustment, 270, 414, 425; arbitrage, 31, 33; bearish, 297; directional, 301; directionless, 372; escape, 349, 356; first, 195, 268, 408; non-directional, 247, 370; profitable, 247; repair, 349, 352
strike price, 22, 34, 133, 140, 315–17
strikes theta, outer, 396
strike theta, 120, 397
substitution, 409–10
supply, 76, 95, 168, 172, 182, 186, 234
support, 14, 415, 418, 423–24, 427
suppositions, 128
synthetic calls, 24, 263

449

202, 249, 291, 320, 322, 325; raw, 74; short, 77, 82, 249, 336, 339, 399–400; subtract, 80; zero, 73

vega risk, 73, 82, 290

velocity, 4, 147, 150, 153, 155, 159, 161, 328, 432

vertical spreads, 27, 35, 275, 283, 295–96, 302

volatile price movement, 317

volatility, 43, 45–46, 71–73, 91–92, 127–32, 134–38, 140–41, 166–67, 176–77, 188–90, 249, 293–95, 325, 339–42, 359–61; 30-day, 341; 90-day, 341; actual, 133, 138, 173, 346; annual, 139; annualized, 419–20; asset return, 75; calculating, 138; changes in, 43, 50–51, 73, 77–78, 271, 294, 384; changing, 177; collapsing, 153, 155; corresponding, 171; current, 75, 133, 140; daily, 138, 140, 420; expected, 132, 341; falling, 135, 186; high, 136, 169, 205; higher, 129, 167, 360; identical, 172; increased, 79, 294; large, 349; long, 189, 362, 378; long dated, 430; longer-term, 339; low, 64, 136, 423, 425; lower, 48, 52, 167, 360; measures of, 132, 165; near-term, 136; option's, 169; realized, 71, 132–33, 138, 140, 339;

rising, 135, 184; selling, 128; short, 83, 130, 204, 362, 378, 390; short-dated, 430; short-term, 431–32; static, 75; surrounding month's, 190; term, 131; varying, 177

volatility cone, 340

volatility curve, 82; implied, 121, 181

volatility environments, 62, 147; high implied, 49; lower implied, 62; normal, 66

volatility environments, rising implied, 46, 48

volatility exposure, 6, 359; implied, 295

volatility fluctuations, 129; implied, 230, 239, 243

volatility levels, 90, 130, 185, 339; high, 185; higher implied, 46–48, 60, 63–64, 113, 115, 166, 229, 236, 240, 362, 365, 398; high implied, 203; low, 185; lower implied, 52; relative implied, 253; relatively high implied, 113; stock's, 130

volatility value, 132–33, 135, 166; expected, 132; long-term historical, 134

vomma, 98, 107

W

wings, 370–71, 373–74, 396, 398, 400

wingspreads, 8, 10

worthless option, 258

CPSIA information can be obtained
at www.ICGtesting.com
Printed in the USA
LVOW13*0043160117

521067LV00022B/779/P

9 780997 577808